IRAN AND Eurasia

Edited by

Ali Mohammadi AND Anoushiravan Ehteshami

Durham Middle East Monographs Series

IRAN AND EURASIA

Ithaca Press is an imprint of Garnet Publishing Limited

Published by
Garnet Publishing Limited
8 Southern Court
South Street
Reading
RG1 4QS
UK

First Edition

ISBN 0 86372 271 7

British Library Cataloguing-in-Publication Data
A catalogue record for this book is available from the British Library

Jacket design by Garnet Publishing
Typeset by Samantha Barden

Printed in Lebanon

Contents

Introduction

This book is about Iran and its relations with the new international environment following the collapse of the Soviet Union, where the threat of Soviet invasion and interference that haunted Iran for much of the twentieth century, has been replaced by geopolitical and security-related dilemmas arising directly from the collapse of the Soviet empire and the broader changes in the international system brought about by such pervasive forces as globalisation and regionalisation.

The contributors to this book therefore try to follow the path that Iran has been charting for itself in this brave new post-Cold War world. At the global level, Iran has to contend with the political and military power of the United States and its Western allies, as well as with the overwhelming economic forces which are shaping the international economic system on a daily basis. Islamic Iran both fears the international footloose capital that is now scouring the world, and needs it at the same time for the country's growth and economic development. Iran, therefore, fears the very enemy that it will have to befriend in order to find a way out of its post-revolutionary economic and technological crisis.

As several chapters in this book show, many of the problems and dilemmas that Iran is facing are not unique to the Islamic Republic, nor are the strategies that it has adopted. Every developing country has had to make judgements on the impact of globalisation on its economy and polity. Perhaps more specific to Iran are the diversity and types of issues which have arisen since the end of the Cold War to affect its regional environment. The contributors to this book provide detailed studies of how these have been influencing Iran's national security concerns and calculations.

Regionally, too, many issues have surfaced to leave their mark on Iranian thinking. As already implied, Iran's geopolitical envelope changed dramatically after the end of the Cold War. But this change was also accompanied by other challenges, namely the collapse of central authority in Afghanistan, a protracted politico-military crisis in Iraq, and the establishment of a US naval presence in the Persian Gulf. The collapse of the Soviet Union provided Tehran with the certainty that the country would not be attacked by its superpower neighbour. At the same time, however, the Soviet disintegration cleared the ground for the emergence of a number of new and potentially fragile states on Iran's northern borders. As if this were not enough of a problem, Tehran also had to contend with Russia, which had been reconstituted as a powerful regional player with its nuclear capability still intact. Although Iranian–Russian relations had been close before the Soviet collapse, after 1991 Iran had to adjust its own strategy towards its large neighbour to take account of Moscow's new role as a dominant regional power with vital interests in its newly defined 'near abroad'. Overnight, therefore, Iran had to cope with a new group of weak neighbours on its doorstep, as well as the presence of a number of regional players (Russia, Turkey, Israel, Greece, Pakistan, India, etc.) with active interests in Central Asia, the Caucasus and the surrounding areas.

The 1990s, of course, saw the rapid evolution of the international system, which in west Asia led to the creation of a new geopolitical environment stretching from the heart of continental Asia to the western borders of the Black Sea. This vast geographic area, with its unique regional and sub-regional characteristics, is referred to as Eurasia in this volume. This vast territory is dynamic and fluid, and is likely to play a decisive role in the fate of the Asian regional system in the next century. For this reason, as much as for the desire to exploit the resources of these new Asian republics, no regional power – Iran included – is likely to play a passive role in the west Asian power games of tomorrow.

Thus, the primary focus of this book is the interplay between Iran and Eurasia's complex geopolitical environment. Eurasia's importance, moreover, as a new geopolitical entity was reinforced by a range of economic, cultural and political assets found there. From what we have seen over the last few years, we can surmise that regional and international players will be exploring every opportunity to extend their reach and influence into the hitherto out-of-bounds arena of Central Asia. As will be examined in several chapters of this book, one of the most important aspects of this struggle has been the scramble for the hydrocarbon riches of the Caspian basin, in relation to both their exploration and their transportation to the consumer.

We have sought to realise two related objectives in this book, and only the reader can judge whether we have succeeded in doing so. One aim was to provide a clear analysis of contemporary Iran and the forces which have shaped its post-revolutionary destiny. Several of our contributors were charged with this task. The other aim was to look at Iran internationally; to provide an understanding of Iran's place in the international system, its foreign policy priorities and its relations with its Eurasian neighbours.

Part I of this book contains five chapters. In Chapter 1 Ali Mohammadi shows that, while there may have been some continuity with its imperial past in Iran's foreign relations, the Islamic Republic's foreign policy has been evolving ever since the early days of the revolution itself. He demonstrates that the reform of Iran's foreign relations and Tehran's adoption of a more moderate line in its relations with the regional powers accelerated under president Rafsanjani and Khatami.

Chapter 2 by Fred Halliday provides an analysis of Iran's complex relations with the international system. His coinage of 'akhundism' mordantly refers to a group of clerics seizing power in Iran in the name of religion to assert their domination over the country's social and political life. The old democratic forces opposed to the absolute rule of the Shah were swept aside to make way for an illiberal regime, but some twenty years on a new age of moderation and tolerance, the 'post-akhundism' age, is now apparently taking root under Iran's new president, Hojjatoleslam Mohammad Khatami.

In Chapter 3 Alireza Ansari attempts to show that, since the election of Khatami in May 1997, Iran has moved energetically forward to improve and expand its foreign relations, not only with its neighbours but also with its traditional antagonists, namely the Western powers in Europe and the United States.

In the following chapter, Chapter 4, Mohammad R. Saidabadi takes up the theme of Iran's foreign relations, concentrating on those with Europe since the elevation of Hojjatoleslam Rafsanjani to the presidency in 1989. The author discusses the significance of international events of the late 1980s and early 1990s in shaping the policy framework within which Iran approaches the member states of the European Union today.

In a wider context, Lubna Abid Ali describes in Chapter 5 how the Islamic Republic is becoming increasingly aware of the need to harmonise the ideological statements made for its domestic legitimation with the pragmatic goal of preserving the integrity of the Iranian state in a rapidly changing global system.

Part II of the book, comprising six chapters, addresses more closely Iran's relations with its Eurasian neighbours. The opening chapter by Anoushiravan Ehteshami, explores the strategic implications of the emergence of new oil states around the Caspian Sea. In a new geopolitical environment in west Asia, he argues, hydrocarbons are emerging as a catalyst for the creation of a new 'energy zone' (Caspian and Persian Gulf), in which Iran provides the only natural bridge between the two oil-rich areas.

In Chapter 7 Mohammad Farhad Atai draws attention to Iran's recent recognition of the need to forge relations with the independent states of Central Asia. He charts recent developments in the hyrocarbon-rich republics of the Caspian and examines the impact of economic, political and cultural crises on the problems of nation building. Just as these countries were not prepared for their suddenly acquired independence following the disintegration of the Soviet Union, Iran was similarly ill-prepared to deal with three new neighbours on its northern border.

Shifting the focus to Iran's eastern border, Alam Payind discusses in Chapter 8 the development of civil war in Afghanistan and explores the future direction of Kabul's policy towards its neighbours, particularly Iran, Pakistan and the Central Asian republics. Since the assassination of nine Iranian diplomats and the mass killing of the Shia minority in Taleban-controlled areas in 1998, Iran has been on the brink of war with the Taleban.

Ali A. Jalali in Chapter 9 provides a detailed account of the problems between Iran and Afghanistan, focusing on the tense border relations between the two countries and the strained relations between Islamic Iran and Taleban-dominated Afghanistan, which also claims to be a true Islamic state.

Going further afield, Gholam-Reza Sabri-Tabrizi examines in Chapter 10 various aspects of the historical tensions between the Chechen people and the Russian empire in its various forms (Tsarist, communist and post-Soviet), and brings into focus the recent independence movement of Chechnya. In this context, the author describes the role of Iran in the religious and cultural movements in the Asian republics of the former Soviet Union.

In the final chapter, Chapter 11, George A. Petrochilos argues that Greece, with its long association with the peoples of Eurasia, the Middle East and Iran, is well placed to serve as a bridge between these turbulent regions and the European Union. For some twenty years Iran has been portrayed in the West as a terrorist state, but since the election of Mohammad Khatami there has been a trend towards reconciliation. It is in this new climate that the Greek link for dialogue with Islamic Iran is assessed.

For reasons that will become clear in the course of this book, the prospects for Iran and Eurasia in the twenty-first century are closely interwined. Change in one, no matter in what direction, will invariably create incentives for change in the other. Thus what follows in this book is a detailed narrative on contemporary Iran, its domestic setting and regional relations, as well as a commentary on the changing nature of the socio-political tapestry we have called Eurasia. The backdrop for our discussion in this volume, then, will be the Eurasian sphere; the foreground, Iran's place and role in the contemporary international system.

Part I

Iran's National Interest and Foreign Policy

1

Iran since the Shah: An Overview

Ali Mohammadi

This chapter begins with an overview of Iran's international relations from a year before the demise of the Pahlavi regime and briefly argues the cause and effect of the foreign policy turmoil. The second section focuses on the task of Iran's foreign policy regarding the uncertain future of Central Asia and the new region, so-called Eurasia.

An overview of international relations

Since the revolution of 1979, Iran's international relations have been in a state of flux as a consequence of revolutionary turmoil. The rhetoric of the revolution and the nature of the populist Islamic movement in Iran brought the previous course of Iranian international relations into sharp perspective. But it should be noted that even before the final demise of the Pahlavi dynasty new perspectives on Iran's international role were being introduced.

The Shah's last governments, in a desperate bid to appease the revolutionary forces, had begun the process of decoupling Iran from close association with the West, and in particular with the United States. To this end, Prime Minister Sharif-Emami's government (25 August to 5 November 1978) promised a range of domestic and foreign-policy-linked reforms, and Prime Minister Bakhtiar (January to February 1979) vowed that Iran would no longer act as America's policeman in the Persian Gulf.

Therefore, when the dust finally settled on the remnants of the Pahlavi regime, and a new government had emerged to rule over the Islamic Republic, much had already changed in Iran.

The country's foreign relations, which had been placed in suspended animation for much of 1978 by an elite preoccupied with survival, had gradually begun to break away from the foundations of the monarchical regime.

However, by the autumn of 1978 the revolutionary coalition had already started to outline its future position on Iran's foreign policy principles and priorities, which were to take these modest changes much further. Largely influenced by the nationalist camp, the revolutionary coalition's ideas on Iran's foreign relations were radical, Third Worldist and decidedly Mosaddeqist in approach. For instance, they attacked the Shah's Western alliances and Iran's close ties with conservative and pro-Western states in the Arab world, most notably Saudi Arabia, Egypt and Jordan.[1] 'Positive neutralism', 'negative equilibrium', and 'non-alignment' became the revolutionary coalition's buzzwords.

Thus, even before the final victory of the revolution in February 1979, new foreign policy priorities were being introduced onto the agenda. It became increasingly evident that, partly as a consequence of the revolution itself and partly out of historical necessity, Iran's view of the world around it was changing; Iran was no longer the obedient ally feted by the West. The new Iran wanted to be noticed, it wanted to retain its regional influence, but, above all else, it wanted to be 'independent and free'. This is evident in the major slogan of the revolution, *Esteqlal va Azadi*, meaning 'national liberation and independence'.

So, not surprisingly, as soon as it took power the new leadership began the process of reorienting Iran's approach to the international system. By September 1979, it had officially joined the Non-Aligned Movement, taking part in the Movement's sixth summit in Havana, having already withdrawn in March from the Central Treaty Organisation (CENTO) which it regarded as a pro-Western regional body .

Within months of the revolution's victory Iran's foreign relations were showing decidedly radical tendencies encouraged by Ayatollah Khomeini and largely supported by a wide range of radical leftist and Islamist groups on the fringes of Iran's new power circles. Although it could be argued that Iran's relations with the PLO – which were established as early as 17 February 1979, barely a week after the fall of the monarchy – provided the first concrete sign of radical changes in Iran's foreign policy, the central characteristics of the new regime's foreign policy were not to appear until well into the Bazargan premiership (February to November 1979). Indeed, it was not until November 1979, when Islamist revolutionaries stormed the American Embassy compound in Tehran and took its American personnel hostage, that the new republic's more unorthodox foreign policy priorities began to take form and international sympathy towards the Iranian national liberation movement gradually began to fade away. By then there was no mistaking the high degree of religious fervour which had crept into Tehran's international relations as reflected by the reporting of the hostage saga throughout the world by international media.

Moreover, before too long, the Islamic Republic displayed a more confrontational side of its foreign policy with its stated intent to export the Islamic revolution. By the beginning of the 1980s Iran had already begun to articulate a foreign policy based on Islam, and on an almost total separation from both superpowers, which were now being portrayed as anti-Islamic and neo-colonial – so-called 'Satanic powers'. Tehran's new policy of distancing itself from the major powers was encapsulated in the vague concept, 'neither East, nor West', which was invented by Iran's Islamist revolutionaries. In its early days, the use of this slogan appeared simply to indicate a shift away from Iran's traditional orientation of active engagement in the Middle East and towards a more isolationist position. In practice, however, the policy came to mean little more than a short-hand for the distancing of Iran from the United States. As has been clear to anyone examining the issues since the early 1980s, Iran's 'neither East, nor West' policy was not designed to sever relations with the rest of the Western world, nor indeed was it designed to create a diplomatic and economic rift with the Soviet bloc.[2] Despite various political and diplomatic tensions since the revolution, the West's position as Iran's main trading partner was never really challenged, and today Iran is again busy pursuing closer economic and diplomatic relations with the United States' Western and regional allies, as well as with Russia and China.

But in its early days, the revolutionary regime's obsession with its neighbours and its declared desire to export its Islamic revolution to the rest of the Middle East had set off alarm bells right across the region. Iran's political attacks on the advocates of so-called 'American Islam', a thinly disguised criticism of Saudi Arabia and the smaller Gulf Arab sheikhdoms, raised the temperature in the Gulf, in whose stability and security the United States and its allies had declared a clear interest. Not surprisingly, therefore, Tehran's aggressive posture and intimidating proclamations brought upon it much hostility from the other regional actors, the most violent expression of which was Iraq's invasion of Iranian territory in September 1980. The Iran–Iraq war that ensued became the longest inter-state conflict of the twentieth century. It not only changed dramatically the balance of power in the region, but also shaped Iran's international relations for the rest of the decade. As far as relations with the major international and regional powers were concerned, Iran remained out in the cold for much of the 1980s.

After eight years of warfare and tension with Iraq, however, signs of change in Iran's international posture surfaced. But, ironically, by the time Tehran was ready to display a more friendly face to the outside world, it was the world around Iran which was in a state of confusion. By the time the Berlin Wall came down in 1989 the international system had entered a period of flux, characterised by uncertainty at the global leadership level and turmoil at the regional level.

No sooner had the Cold War ended than Iraq precipitated a major international crisis by invading Kuwait. This event would have been cause enough for concern in all the regional capitals, what with creating new tensions in the Persian Gulf and obstacles to wider regional stability, had it not been followed by an even greater shock to the international system: the implosion of the Soviet superpower in 1991. Iran had a particular interest in both these dramatic events, as they occurred on its borders, its geography making it unique in this respect.

By the start of the 1990s, then, not only was the world too busy to take much note of Iran's more pragmatic and moderate foreign policy line, but Iran itself was too preoccupied with assessing the impact of the collapse of the Soviet Union to follow up its positive signals with concrete action. Furthermore, it did not seem particularly fitting for Iran to be flagging a more moderate line at a time when the world was grappling with the consequences of the collapse of the Soviet state. Nor was it deemed appropriate for Iran to be seen to be tempering its revolutionary zeal when its long-time enemy and neighbour, Iraq, had just suffered a crushing defeat at the hands of a US-led military alliance after daring to take on the 'Great Satan' in battle. At this stage, moderation was to be pursued prudently and selectively, and not systematically, even by the more pragmatic post-Khomeini Iranian leadership.

Iran and Eurasia

Meanwhile, a new geopolitical environment was born on Iran's doorstep, one that we have chosen to call Eurasia. Stretching from Russia's western borders to its eastern frontiers via the Caucasus and Central Asia, this new geopolitical sphere rose from the ashes of the Soviet empire. During the 1990s, Eurasia's importance as a new geopolitical environment has been reinforced by a range of economic, cultural and political realities and opportunities, one of the most important of which has been the scramble for the hydrocarbon riches of the Caspian basin – their exploration on the one hand and their transportation to the consumer on the other.

The concept of Eurasia has a long history, but it was first introduced in its contemporary form by geopolitical strategists writing about European power structures at the turn of the century, and the changing position of Russia in Asia from the middle of the nineteenth century.[3] Indeed, Soviet scholars used the term much more readily and frequently than their Western counterparts. Security priorities in the region have changed with the end of the Cold War and the collapse of the Soviet Union. By the beginning of the 1990s the concept of Eurasia had entered the discourse of international relations. Commentators began looking at Russia and its surroundings in these terms.[4]

Today Eurasia is a term used loosely and frequently by scholars and policy-makers alike, often meaning the geographical, political, economic, cultural, and social space between the former Warsaw Pact countries of Europe and the eastern edge of the Asian continent.[5] Arguably, insofar as NATO continues to symbolise an Atlantic bias in Western Europe, the concept of Eurasia does not encompass territories west of the Czech Republic. So in strategic terms as well, Eurasia would seem to define the territories on the western edge of Asia and the eastern edge of Europe.

Into this brave new world entered the 'reformed' Islamic Republic, with its emphasis now very much on the national interest and on policies which would realise Iran's regional role, its historic destiny, as defined by the nationalists. Thus from 1990 the leadership was, albeit hesitantly, pinning its colours to a more 'Iran-centric' mast and slowly abandoning the old 'Islam-centric' alternative of the 1980s.

In Iran, as in so many other cases in recent history, reform tends to beget reform. As such the reforms which were set in motion in the early 1990s by Hojjatoleslam Rafsanjani as Iran's first executive president have been continued by his successor. Since winning an overwhelming mandate from the electorate in the May 1997 presidential ballot, President Rafsanjani's successor, Hojjatoleslam Mohammad Khatami, who is a known reformist cleric and a former cabinet minister, has extended the reforms of his predecessor. Rule of law, respect for a humane and active civil society, justice and accountability are just some of the concepts which have come to dominate Iranian political discourse since May 1997. In foreign policy terms too, Khatami's reforms are clearly designed to strengthen the moderate line introduced by Rafsanjani. With an eye on the Eurasian dimension of Iran's international relations, it can be expected that Khatami will push open the doors on which Rafsanjani had been knocking.

At the start of the third millennium the coming crises in the Persian Gulf on one hand, and the uncertain future of Central Asia on the other, will make the study of Iran's international relations in the context of Eurasia more interesting, particularly with regard to the direction that Iran is likely to take beyond the year 2000.

Since the 1970s the Gulf has been the centre of media attention and a place of extreme, volatile politics exemplified by the recent change of ruler in Qatar, the sudden death of Bahrain's sheikh and the uncertain future of Iraq as well as the evidence of economic crises in Iran and Saudi Arabia due to fluctuating oil prices.

After the demise of the Soviet Union and the rapid emergence of several countries on the northern border of Iran, the so-called Caspian Sea basin, has been the focal point of intensive negotiations on such matters as access to free waterways via Iran and ways to enter into the world of free trade. This process, as well as the emerging competing forces in the region, makes the task of formulating Iran's foreign policy complex and problematic. As a result of these rapid and extensive changes in the last decade of the twentieth century, most of the emerging nations had visions about how best to enter the twenty-first century. Not so in Iran. Apart from the 'civilisation' debate initiated by President Khatami, the ruling clergy developed no vision about the country's national interest and the prosperity of its people in the new millennium. It was somewhat ironic that as the host of the Islamic conference for the first time Iran has raised tremendous expections among the Muslim nations particularly within the Central Asian region.

In Central Asia the scenario is quite different: the existing tensions stem from two revolutions, those of 1917 and 1991. The question of Islam and nationalism, and the impact of Russian colonisation on the region are now emerging. In the communist revolution of 1917, the people of Central Asia were discovering nationalism and gradually showed a desire for pan-Turkism and the Persian language as symbols of independence from Russian domination. But Stalin consolidated his power in the region; he crushed all nationalist movements and imposed communism on them which they were not prepared for. Then in 1991, after the demise of Soviet imperialism, the question of national identity and self-determination once again became a very important issue. By December 1992, a year after gaining independence, all Central Asian republics were facing common problems. The most pressing one was the economic crisis: how to build a future independent of Russian domination.

Thus the question of Islamic cultural identity subsequently arose in Chechnya (see Chapter 10 for a full discussion of this issue) and again in 1999 Daghestan, which is part of the Russian Federation, called for independence as a result of an emerging Islamic cultural identity. It is quite clear this issue of cultural unity which has been repressed in the region for many years will not settle easily and the future of the five newly established Central Asian republics is uncertain because they had not created their own guerrilla forces or liberation armies against any encroachments by their neighbours. Kazakhstan became a de-facto nuclear power. Tajikistan became the centre of a bloody civil war. Uzbekistan became part of a military force which is borrowed from Russia. Since the end of the cold war, nationalism has shown two faces across the world: a reactionary face looking backwards to past glories, racism and fascism, and a modernising face that looks to the future in the building of a wider ethnic community. Now in Central Asia the communist parties have tried to turn themselves into nationalist parties and this has created strange political creatures making the task of Iranian foreign policy so much more complex. There is also a high degree of intolerance, violence and ugly undemocratic rule, but also a rush to embrace democracy, capitalism, Western culture, Islam, foreign languages and the concept of a family of Central Asian peoples. Many of its new neighbours are looking for help from Iran whilst the future of the whole region is uncertain. The rise of the Islamic movement in Daghestan, the war in Afghanistan, the tension between Azerbaijan and Armenistan and furthermore the existing national war in Tajikstan together make the Islamic Republic's foreign policy like a jigsaw puzzle whose pieces must fit together in order to keep a friendly relation with Russia. As Ahmed Rashid's study of Islam and nationalism in the area shows,[6] neither the post-1917 nor the pre-1991 system worked, but managed to wipe out the economic and political traditions of the Central Asian peoples. The new generation were suddenly faced with the task of building a future without the benefit of an inherited foundation. Nationalism and a crisis of identity have inexorably led to an extraordinary revival of Islam and a firm rejection of the Soviet system. The struggle in Daghestan is a case in point.[7]

The northern neighbours of Iran will continue to be jostled by competing international interests, both economically and politically. Whilst Russia and the West are trying to entice Central Asia away from the Islamic world, it will also continue to be pulled in different directions until Iran is able to resolve its differences with the Arab world. The issue of Islamic cultural unity remains unresolved for the time being. Today with the first official visit of President Khatami to Saudi Arabia and improving diplomatic relations with Egypt, the future cooperation among the Islamic countries is positive despite the conflict of interest between Turkey and Iran and some unresolved issues of the dispute between Iran and Iraq. As a result of further close cooperation between Iran and Saudi Arabia, the Central Asian countries are likely to move closer to the Islamic countries, and Iran's role in this respect can be more significant.

NOTES

1 David Menashri, *Iran: A Decade of War and Revolution* (New York: Holmes and Meier, 1990).

2 For a fuller picture, see Nikki R. Keddie and Mark J. Gasiorowski (eds.), *Neither East nor West: Iran, the Soviet Union, and the United States* (New Haven: Yale University Press, 1990); Miron Rezun (ed.), *Iran at the Crossroads: Global Relations in a Turbulent Decade* (Boulder: Westview Press, 1990); John L.Esposito (ed.), *The Iranian Revolution: Its Global Aftermath* (Miami, Fla.: Florida International University Press, 1990); Anoushiravan Ehteshami and Mansour Varasreh (eds.), *Iran and the International Community* (London: Routlege, 1991).

3 Milan L.Hauner, 'The disintegration of the Soviet Eurasian Empire' in Mohiaddin Mesbahi (ed.), *Central Asia and the Caucasus after the Soviet Union* (Gainesville, Fla.: University Press of Florida, 1994).

4 Michael Mandelbaum (ed.), *Central Asia and the World* (New York: Council on Foreign Relations, 1994).

5 Anoushiravan Ehteshami, *The Changing Balance of Power in Asia* (Abu Dhabi: The Emirates Center for Strategic Studies and Research, 1998).
6 Ahmed Rashid, *The Resurgence of Central Asia: Islam or Nationalism?* (London: Zed Books, 1994).
7 Ali Mohammadi, 'Central Asia uncertainties', *Third World Quarterly*, vol. 15, no. 4 (1994).

2

Post-akhundism: Some Tentative Notes on the Future of Iran*

Fred Halliday

This chapter posits a gradual change in the Islamic Republic and demonstrates the transition in the existing regime towards sound government. As today is the age of post-modernism, post-feminism et al., it is appropriate, Halliday argues, to use the term post-akhundism for clarifying the current direction of the present regime in Iran.

Halliday provides an analysis of Iran's complex relations with the international system. Akhundism is a sarcastic term referring to the particular social group of clerics which seized power, using religion as an instrument to consolidate their domination of Iran and to eliminate the other well-known forces which for many decades struggled against the Shah to achieve democracy.

The background

Some years ago, BBC television included, as one of a series of discussions on issues in contemporary culture, a programme on the 'post-modern' age. In it participated several speakers, one being the French philosopher Alain Finkelkraut, another the Jamaican sociologist Stuart Hall, another the well-known Indian writer, whose works were once much valued in Iran and whom I suspect will one day be so valued again, Salman Rushdie. During the course of this discussion Rushdie remarked, in reference to the title of the programme, that we lived in 'a very post age' – not only do we have post-modernism but we have post-industrial society, post-communism, post-feminism, post-colonialism, and no doubt more. It is in the light of that remark that I would like here to offer another

---

* A shortened version of this article was published in *Index on Censorship*, vol. 26 no. 4 (1997).

item on the list of the 'posty', namely 'post-akhundism'. Although much interested in theory, I am not much myself given to coining new theoretical terms: but I do offer this one, and claim it as my own, as a means of grappling with some ideas about the future of Iran, where that great and beautiful country is going, where its long-suffering people may be headed, and how the great richness of its culture and land may be deployed, for better or worse, in the years to come.[1]

All of us who have known and appreciated Iran over the years, in my case more than three decades, are concerned about this issue, about the terrible price paid by the Iranian people for the policies of their tormentors, home-grown and foreign, over recent decades. We must, for reasons of general intellectual prudence as much as out of awareness of our own mistaken expectations in the past, be cautious about predicting the future. We must, equally, hold onto the belief that it is possible to discuss the future in some broad, speculative spirit, and indeed that it is the moral responsibility of all, Iranian and not, who are concerned about Iran to discuss these questions, without false abstention or dogma. The sixty and more million people of Iran, not least the majority aged under twenty who have their lives ahead of them, are certainly concerned with it. Others outside, including the CIA, the US Congress who voted aid for anti-regime activities, and the ever-malevolent Iraq, are also seeking to influence the course of events.[2] It would, therefore, be a form of intellectual bankruptcy and moral cowardice not to participate in this debate either. There could be no more important topic to raise and discuss at a conference devoted to analysing Iran's relationship with the international system.

To define what I mean by 'post-akhundism' it is, first, necessary to define what it is counterposed to, namely 'akhundism' itself. The term 'akhund' occurs in common Persian usage to denote a clergyman, less respectful than *mullah* or *ruhani* or *alim*, but certainly a term which a believing Muslim could happily use.[3] 'Post-akhundism' means, in one sentence, a society and political system in which this social group ceases to dominate. It is not to be confused, although it certainly will be, with 'post-Islamism' – something that is as remote and undesirable as would be the decay or disappearance of any great religion. The term 'akhund' is also, however, part of the vocabulary of modern Iranian politics, having been used both at the time of the Constitutional Revolution and in the Mossadeq period to denote a conservative, politically and socially intrusive member of the clergy, with the further implication of ignorance, hostility to modern ideas and bigotry. Ayatollah Kashani was, in the early 1950s, the archetypal akhund. The term 'akhundism' came into political usage at the time of the revolution itself, and was used to denote an unwelcome, unwarranted and authoritarian intervention of the clergy in the political process. It was, so far as I can gather, a term used by a variety of different writers, writing from different standpoints: thus secular journalists used it; as did Bani Sadr; as did, from their own militant position, the *Forgan* group who assassinated Ayatollah Mutahhari. *Forgan* in turn based its hostility to politically active clergy on the thinking of Ali Shariati.[4]

Others will be able, in the future, to provide a proper history of the term. I would only want to stress here two points: first, like so many other terms used in political parlance, 'akhundism' is part of, indeed a product of, the modern political history of Iran; second, that it came above all to denote the kind of regime and society created by the revolution of 1978–9. The central claim of the regime has been that it is an Islamic Republic: but there are many interpretations of Islam, and many ways of applying its precepts to politics. This is a point which no amount of official rhetoric since 1979 has been able to obliterate, not least within the clergy itself. What Iran has had since 1979 could more accurately be characterised not as *jumhuri-i islami* but as *jumhuriy-i akhundi*, i.e not an Islamic republic but an akhundi republic. It is the crisis, and possible demise, of that republic which I want to consider here.

Jumhuriy-i akhundi

One may define 'akhundism' by reference to four components. First and most obviously it denotes the retention, through monopoly or predominance, of political power by the clergy, most evidently in the position of the *velayat-i faqih*, the position of supreme religious jurisconsult or authority, occupied first by Khomeini and then by Khamene'i, but also in the presence of clergy in the top political positions of state – president, cabinet, speaker of parliament, etc. – and throughout the state apparatus, down to local level.

Iran, alone of modern revolutions, has not had a ruling party and indeed abolished the Islamic Republican Party, the candidate to be so described, but the reason for this apparent anomaly is that, in effect, the network of mosque committees and the clerical apparatus controlling them has functioned as a ruling party: through it, the clergy have ruled. Those in Iran whose slogan now is *marq bar-zid-i velayat-i faqih*, 'Death to the Opponents of Velayat-i Faqih', have in their own way understood this point very well. It may be that a non-clergyman will become president, or that lay experts, the *mugallidin*, literally 'followers', are brought into the cabinet, but they would be the equivalent of civilian ministers, technocrats or whatever in a military regime or non-party elements in an old communist regime: in the final instance, and on important matters, they would know who was the boss.

Secondly, one can understand by akhundism the continued and central role of religious bodies, the mosque and the madrasa, in political and social life – be this as a source of public and political opinion, an authoritative source of educational and social values, or as a means of controlling the distribution of goods and welfare. Unlike other revolutionary regimes the Islamic Republic of Iran has not sought to control the economy, leaving this to the private sector, and dismissing economics as in Khomeini's words *mal-i khar*, the business of donkeys, but it has taken care to ensure that its base support is minimally provided for.

Thirdly, by akhundism one may understand a particular interpretation of Islamic and Iranian tradition; a specific, authoritative rendering of what is 'true' Islam, 'correct' Islamic practice, 'appropriate' cultural values and the rest. All nationalist and revolutionary movements and states have sought to present, out of the diversity of meanings and currents in their own past, and by importing without acknowledgement ideas from abroad, a particular dogma about what is, and is not, appropriate to their community. The Islamic revolution has been no exception: thus much that is part of Iranian culture, and of Islamic history, is excluded in the name of a new, coercively imposed orthodoxy. This is as true for the whole theory of 'Islamic government', *hokumat-i islami*, and its correlative *velayat-i faqih* – ideas that would have struck many people in previous epochs as rather odd, if not heretical – as it is for the bans on alcohol, on women singing and much else in the Iranian tradition that the Khomeini regime has sought to uproot. One of the most unpleasant, and indicative, moments in the history of the akhundi regime was the cultural revolution, *inqilab-i farhangi*, of 1980.[5]

This grotesque event, like that of Mao in China, was designed as much to root out and suppress elements of culture indigenous to the

Persian tradition, to impose one bigoted definition of that tradition and of Islam, as it was to confront the supposed source of corruption, the imperialist, western, cultural corruption. Again we see this now in the frenzy of those in Iran now so concerned to keep out the cultural influence of the West, to stop consumerism, satellite TV and the rest, the so-called *bombardiman-i tablighati*, and the *tahajum-i farhangi*, literally cultural bombardment and cultural aggression, against which militants are now campaigning.

Finally, under akhundism we have to include something more unpleasant, more dangerous, more costly than all of these, namely a culture and a politics of coercion, and at time terror, by those in power, such that dissent outside certain limits laid down by the regime is cruelly and remorselessly punished. The Islamic Republic of Iran has not, by the standards of twentieth-century revolutionary regimes, been amongst the most repressive, or murderous. The pluralism which it has allowed within its own camp, and the range of debate it now allows within society, mark it off, to its credit, from the totalitarian experiments of at least two of its neighbours, and from that of most other post-revolutionary regimes. But this relative degree of what one may term conventional repression contrasts with the particular gender-based harassment of women, a petty-minded vindictiveness and intrusiveness of a truly odious kind, that has become its hallmark. Moreover this remains a regime which has committed, and continues to commit, terrible crimes against its own people, to murder, assassinate, torture, imprison, silence, drive into exile, or just plain old beat up those it suspects of opposition and of independent thought. Most of those killed by this regime have, moreover, been people who fought for and supported this revolution: I have dedicated my most recent book to four of them, democrats and friends killed by the akhund.[6]

Life under such a regime permits of three options: cooptation, silent opposition from within, exile. Nothing that has happened since 1979, and nothing that is now happening inside Iran, would lead anyone to believe that this form of coercion has significantly, or permanently, altered. There is great discontent within the country, and there is a debate about where the country could, and should, be going. There are those who, occasionally and with great courage, voice their criticisms of the regime, be it in foreign or domestic policy. Some suggest a more or less secular line of advance; others are seeking new solutions and policies within Islam. It is good that such voices are emerging, and no one who knows the richness of culture and intellect, and the enduring personal courage, of many in the Iranian political and intellectual class can doubt that there are many who share such concerns. The fact remains that while some are allowed to speak there are no guarantees, let alone anything remotely corresponding to the rule of law: critics are thrown out of their jobs, magazines are closed, writers are beaten up, others are held in jail, to rot or die there, and a much larger number are, of course, forced to remain in exile. In one word, this remains a regime that cannot be trusted. Such is the price, the very expression, of akhundism.

Post-akhundism can, therefore, be defined in contradistinction to this model. In brief, following the four points made already, it would comprise the following: (i) a departure by the clergy from dominant political positions in the country, including the ending of the authority of the *velayat-i faqih*; (ii) the restriction of the role of the mosque to the religious functions hitherto occupied by it and the restriction of its influence on law, education, clothing and the like; (iii) the opening of a debate on the diversity of cultural and religious options within the country and the recognition that all countries, and not least Iran, exhibit a diversity of religious, ethnic and cultural voices; (iv) the growth of a culture of tolerance, and genuine pluralism, leading to democracy in the full sense of the word. It would not mean that all those responsible for the terrible crimes of the Islamist regime would be brought to justice: it would, however, require that, as in other former dictatorships, the truth be investigated and known, that the fate of those killed be established, and the names of those responsible placed on public record.

Such a process would, of course, involve a broader shift of the very role of religion in the political life of Iran, a shift towards secularism. It would also involve an acceptance that the kind of dogmatic, akhundi regime imposed in 1979 was neither wanted by the majority of the Iranian people nor consonant with its traditions and culture nor compatible with its needs at the end of the twentieth century. Far from such a process being 'anti-Islamic' or designed to weaken the religious beliefs of the Iranian people it would allow Islam, of a more free and creative kind, to flourish. The Iranian people, in their great majority, have long been and will remain Muslims, but, as in other countries afflicted with fundamentalism, they know the truth of the old saying that there are two kinds of Muslim, those who have Allah in their hearts, and those who go around shouting 'Allahu Akbar' in the streets. The imposition of the Islamic Republic may indeed, as many wise people have pointed out, have itself contributed to the discrediting of Islam by identifying the religion and its culture with one particular form of regime and society and in so doing have provoked a backlash that sweeps more than the regime away with it.[7]

Much is made by fundamentalists of the dangers of secularism, as if this was equivalent to atheism or anarchy: but no society is entirely secular, and secularism can, therefore, be seen more as a relative separation of religion and public life, rather than as a complete rupture. What form the separation takes, how far it goes, depends on each society. That such a separation is desirable, and indeed a necessary part of modern life, is indisputable.

Sources of alternatives

So far I have suggested that we can think of a form of society and politics after the akhundi experiment of the post-revolutionary years, and few not blinded by their own dogma can doubt that sooner or later this experiment will be gone, consigned to the *zabalidan-i tarikh*, the 'rubbish-bin of history' (a favourite phrase of Khomeini's) as much as the Pahlavis or the communist regimes of the post-1917 period were. The signs of this are everywhere: an economy that has declined steadily since the revolution, unemployment, inflation, massive corruption, growing dissaffection among the urban population and youth, a foreign policy that has missed almost every opportunity presented to it and which is mortgaged to unrealistic, confrontational goals, a leadership trapped by its own illusions and the need to keep its immediate following in order. In a broader sense the whole project of the Islamic revolution has, in a remarkably short space of time, run out of steam. No-one believes it can produce a better society, in Iran itself or elsewhere. It offers no future. This is not to say that it will fall tomorrow: many people have made fools of themselves with that prediction. You all know the joke of the man who comes to Tehran in two hundred years' time from Mars. Everyone is smiling and holding up three fingers. When he asks what this means someone whispers to him: 'In three months the mollahs will be gone' (*se mah diqe–mirand*). This is a regime which retains the support of a section of the population; which has built up a set of military and security institutions designed to protect it from challenge; whose leaders, with perhaps twenty years of political life ahead of them, remain determined to stay in power; and who, by no means least, are prepared to imprison and kill to remain in power. Abroad, the Iranian revolution may be discredited, but the rise of Islamist fundamentalism in a range of countries suggests that for many years to come there will be those who can claim that the great world-wide revolt of the *mostazafin*, Khomeini's term for the oppressed, hailed by Khomeini, is continuing.

In a rough comparison, one can say that the Islamic Republic is today where Soviet communism was in the 1960s or early 1970s – in evident decline, bereft of inspiration or original ideas, but able to last for a considerable time yet, in the absence of unexpected cataclysm from within or without. Indeed like communism in the 1970s it may show the greatest activity internationally at the moment when it is burning out at home. Where, then, does this leave 'post-akhundism'?

While there is little point in speculating on how or when the Islamic Republic may fall, it may be valuable to pose the question of where alternative ideas, and influences, could shape the future of Iran and draw on the energies of its peoples. The fate of the communist regimes, different in some respects from the Iranian case, and while instilling caution about our ability to predict, may nonetheless offer us some help in this respect. In broad terms, one can identify three such sources of alternative, three directions from which the future of a post-akhundist Iran may be influenced. Each merits attention not least because, far from giving us answers, each suggests a large element of uncertainty. These sources of alternative are: firstly, political and social currents within Iran, including in this the exiled communities; secondly, international pressures; thirdly, Iranian history and traditions.

Iranian politics and society

As far as the regime is concerned there *is* no alternative within Iran other than those offered by its controlled political process. Such alternatives are not negligible, as the recent parliamentary elections showed: between the conservatives, the radicals and the Islamic modernisers there are important differences, which might become greater in the future or at a time of crisis. They are however all limited both by the need to play the game of the Islamic Republic and by the political and cultural constraints imposed by the revolutionary consensus: few can believe that any offer an answer to Iran's problems, or are even willing honestly to confront them. The majority of Iran's population remains outside this licensed political game and, most importantly, the majority of them are young. We can only guess at what they think, or know, but on one thing we can be reasonably sure: they are not fooled by the rhetoric of their leaders. They almost certainly do not want a return of the monarchy; they may remain suspicious of the West; they do not want to see Islamic values insulted; but they may well want economic development, greater access to consumer goods, freedom of expression and of movement. They probably also want peace. They are the people on whom the future of the Iranian political system rests.

In between the regime and the population lies another source, that of the underground or semi-legal political groups. Many of these remain in one way or another active and each offers itself as the alternative to the regime. Each has, it should be noted, a right to put their views before the Iranian people and have their popularity tested in a democratic way. The refusal of the regime even to allow the Freedom Movement of Iran of the late Mehdi Bazargan to operate freely and contest elections shows just how fearful it remains of the opposition. And beyond the FMI lie many others – monarchists, liberals, left-wing groups, Islamic groups and the Mojahidin. Perhaps some of these will play a role in the future, but one cannot assume they will: the fate of other post-dictatorship regimes is that often such groups command less support than they might think. It must also be said that, on the basis of their actions and programmes abroad, the opposition, *as a whole*, does not impress. Many remain imprisoned by the ideas and quarrels of the past. The monarchists and their ilk dream of rolling the clock back, even if they pretend otherwise. The left has not taken in the consequences of the failure of Soviet communism and too much of it still thinks and talks in the stilted language of the dogmatic left. The Mujahedin, who have usurped the democratic right of the Iranian people by proclaiming their own president and who subsist on the generosity of Saddam Hussein, the man who has killed more Iranians than anyone since Hulagu, have become a sect, defiant in their opposition, suicidal in their political choices, corrupted by a grotesque cult of the personality. They too can, and should, be allowed to present themselves before the Iranian people in a democratic choice: the least one can say is that one should not assume that they too represent the people, or much of it. Those who, in the West, have been cajoled into endorsing their claim to be the legitimate representatives of the Iranian people should think again.

The greatest problem with the exiled and underground political groupings is, however, somewhere else, and that is in the absence of a coherent, credible, democratic force capable of taking its distance from the regime and its fossilised opponents and offering a modern, open future to the Iranian people, at home and abroad. There are some groups which do so, focusing on human rights and on democracy, the latter taken not as just another dogmatic slogan but as something real and creative. But too many, on the left and in the regime, still take fright at what is, disparagingly and quite wrongly, referred to as 'liberalism'. There were those who defended liberal values, whether in secular Mosaddeqist form, in the National Democratic Front or in the Islamic form of the Freedom Movement of Iran.

Here I must say that a particular source of regret to me, and one that has, in my view, cost the Iranian people very dear, is that both of these currents abandoned their independence, and betrayed the combative liberal legacy they had once defended, by capitulation to other, authoritarian factions. It is not a question of such a radical democratic force having an effective capacity now, or of being in the forefront of the opposition: rather it is a matter of such a group having preserved its identity and traditions, the better to be able, when an opportunity arises, to command the respect of the politically active, at home and abroad, in a word, keeping the torch alight.

On the secular side, the initial courageous stand of the National Democratic Front, who were in the forefront of initial defence of human rights and the rule of law, ended in tragedy: the great Shokrallah Paknejad, long imprisoned by the Shah, was rearrested and murdered in jail; Hedayat Matin-Daftari, the surviving leader and grandson of Mosaddeq, the man as much as any other who could and should have preserved the integrity of the liberal left, entered into a misguided embrace of the Mojahidin that has, in effect, silenced that tradition.

Others, who rejected the term 'liberalism', might nonetheless have offered some element of resistance. Bazargan and his group became, before their fall in November 1979, accomplices of the imposition of the clerical dictatorship: I well remember a heated argument with Ibrahim

Yazdi, then foreign minister, on the issue of press freedom. Seated in some ornate room of the foreign ministry, underneath a chandelier, he accused *Ayandegan* of being part of a counter-revolutionary conspiracy. I also recall arguments with Bani Sadr, then editor of *Inqilab-i Islami*.[8] The record of other Islamist intellectuals – including Sadegh Qotbzadeh, who spearheaded the Islamisation of the media – needs no extended discussion here. Mostafa Chamran, another of this group, was one of those mainly responsible for the chauvinistic assault on the Kurds in 1979 and 1980 – likening them, in a wholly misguided analogy with their earlier experience in the Arab world, to the Israeli-backed forces in southern Lebanon.

The issue of liberalism takes us to the heart of this story. Perhaps the greatest crime of the Stalinist left in Iran was to give the term 'liberal' as a term of abuse to the fundamentalists. I remember standing on the streets of central Tehran in the summer of 1979 as the fundamentalist mob demonstrated against the newspaper *Ayandegan*, and shouted the slogan *marg bar liberalizm* – 'death to liberalism'. I had been in the offices of *Ayandegan* when the *Pasdars* came to close it: they told me they had come 'to defend the revolution'. *In ruzname qoh ast*, one of them said. 'This newspaper is shit'. When I pointed out that two million people read it they were quick to reply: *In do million nafar ham goh* and 'these two million people are shit too'. *Ayandeqan's* crime had been to print the truth and to criticise the regime, not least over the issue of 'akhundism'. Yet this term, a grotesque simplification at best, is used because it suits precisely the agenda of akhundism, since all critical or independent ideas are cast as some form of alien conspiracy, and all defence of democracy or the rule of law is cast as hostile to the Iranian people.

There is in Iran, it hardly needs emphasising, a strong and enduring current of suspicion towards foreign, not least western, ideas and for good reason. We hear a lot these days about Iran as a threat to international peace, but this is, in any regional evaluation, misleading. The main source of instability in the Persian Gulf is Iraq, in the Caspian Sea Russia, in Afghanistan Pakistan, in the Levant Syria and Israel. Historical proportion is also a corrective: on any balance sheet of the past century Iran has had far more wrong done to it than it has done to others – invaded in two wars, its elected government overthrown, its resources long extracted at unjust prices. Yet this should not mean that all alien ideas are to be rejected, any more than it means that all supposedly indigenous ones are to be defended. Iran needs more, not less, liberalism in this sense: that, if anything, is the lesson of the years since 1979.

In any survey of trends internal to Iranian society and politics mention must be made, and is increasingly being made, of alternative conceptions of Islam itself, i.e. of political and social models that are framed within an Islamic tradition but which are critical of this regime and which may, to a greater or lesser extent, seek to reconcile Islamic ideas and Iranian reality with what are broadly seen as western or international norms of democracy, development, law or whatever. This is sometimes generically termed *andishe-yi digar*, 'alternative thinking'. There is a long tradition in the Middle East and in Iran, of what is, in general terms, referred to as modernist Islamic thinking, from al-Afghani and Abduh through Rashid Rida in Egypt, or indeed someone like Mehdi Bazargan in Iran.[9] Such currents were present in the revolutionary period itself, but in recent years a number of names have begun to be mentioned in the Iranian case; I shall not embarrass them by mentioning them here, but we all know who they are. Such voices are welcome, and the originality and courage of their authors must be saluted. There is little doubt that if a gradual transition is to be possible, and if a new political system consonant with the discourses and traditions of Iran is to be found, then such thinking has an important role.

However, the experience of other Islamist states and, by analogy, of communist states suggests some caution about such thinkers, about those who, in broad terms, seek to propose reforms from within. The first is that, quite simply, the issue is not one of interpreting tradition, or texts, or culture at all: it is political power. You are not going to persuade a dictatorial clergyman to give up power by offering a new *tafsir* (an interpretation of religious text), any more than you would persuade a dictatorial *apparatchik* or Politburo member by quoting bits of Lenin or Bukharin. Indeed once the clergyman, or politburo member, sees a challenge, especially one he cannot dismiss easily as ideologically impure, he will resort to other means of silencing you, of which we have seen some in Iran quite recently. The other, more complex, reason for this caution is intellectual: to use regime ideology or theology in an instrumental way, i.e. to defend a concept such as democracy or human rights or the equality of men and women with useful quotes from a religious tradition is perfectly feasible and in some cases necessary. To argue and believe, on the other hand, that all these things are indeed to be found in a religious tradition, and that all the resources for conceiving of a modern political or social order are to be found within a particular religion, is a delusion, just as it was to think they could be found in the Bible or the Talmud, or in the writings of Marx or Lenin.

To get caught up in the system of religious thought is to become a victim of it. Much, therefore, as the new trend in modernist Islamic thinking in Iran is to be welcomed, there are serious reasons for doubting whether it can provide the intellectual, let alone political, basis for a challenge to the akhundi system. It also leaves out of the question something which only history itself can answer, namely whether the Iranian people do, at the end of it all, want another version of Islamic politics.[10]

International factors

The fate of communism suggests that the second dimension of influence, that of the international and external, will also play a significant role in the future of Iranian politics, however much the regime seeks to insulate Iran from it. In one sense the whole project of shutting out the outside world is a hopeless one, as other revolutionary regimes – the USSR, China, Cuba – have found. The very ferocity of the current concern with cultural influence from abroad reflects the realisation that this cannot be kept out. Moreover, the pressures of the international system mean that the more Iran, partly for domestic reasons, seeks to play up its confrontation with the West, especially the USA, the more the external will have its impact, through undermining of economic confidence, trade embargoes, blocks on credit etc. There is no way out of this and no amount of circumvention of such pressure, through developing ties with China or the Arab world, or seeking to play the Europeans off against the USA, will make things much better. What this means for the Islamic Republic is that, as with other revolutionary regimes, it will over time be worn down by the pressure of the international system, whether that pressure comes through direct state-initiated policies such as the USA's 'dual containment' or through more diffuse pressures of the international market or the globalised culture of consumerism, pop music and the rest. The title of an article published some years ago by a British journalist sums it up: 'Nintendo versus the Mollahs'. It is not a good choice, but in the end we may suspect Nintendo will put up a good fight.

All of this will, of course, come as no surprise to the regime itself which will see in it confirmation of the many threats posed by imperialism. Indeed not only fundamentalists but also much of the left has for decades set itself against external influence – cultural, economic and political – as if all such influence is some form of external pressure. But this is, and was always, a simplistic view. Throughout history, and not least Iranian history, societies have been influenced by transnational flows – of people, ideas, culture, goods, ideologies. In the colonial/imperial period the same thing occurred and with the usual contradictory effects: if imperialism brought external domination and exploitation of oil reserves, it also brought science, economic development, and a potentially emancipatory, modernist politics. The irony is that the Islamic regime that spends so much time denouncing external ideas has itself benefited from, and used, many of these – independence, revolution, republic, development and sovereignty being cases in point. The question that is posed for Iran today is whether a similar, creative borrowing can occur, not least with regard to the two forms of external model most relevant to Iran, economic development and political democracy. These ideas are not, whatever chauvinists or relativists may say, peculiar to the West but are aspirations shared, in the modern world, by all peoples and ones to which the Iranian people are as entitled as anyone else. We have seen how, in regard to the dictatorships both of Latin American and of communist Europe, external pressure has contributed to bringing the peoples of these countries nearer to the attainment of such goals, and the same could, potentially, be the case for Iran.

Reinterpreting the Iranian past

Whether such a change is possible in the Iranian case, and how far it accords with the sensibilities and aspirations of the Iranian people, depends, however, on the third form of influence mentioned above, namely Iranian history and traditions – I say 'traditions' in the plural because the greatest distortion, perpetrated by Pahlavi monarchs and Imams alike – has been to argue that there is only *one* tradition in Iran. An essential part of the move to post-akhundism lies in breaking the hold which the regime now has on the definition of the Iranian past. The Islamic Republic presents by no means the only, and almost certainly not the wisest, model of political leadership and administration in Iran, not only because of its economic failures and its violations of human rights, but also because it denies the very ethnic and regional diversity of a country in which, we should never forget, the Persians are at best half the population. The most impressive, and wisest, of all the political leaders whom I had the occasion to meet from the revolutionary period was the Kurdish leader Abdul Rahman-Qassemlu, a man who recognised that the ethnic diversity of Iran should form part of, not be counterposed to, the consolidation of democracy and independence for Iran. The use of a chauvinist, centralist, Islam to crush the aspirations of Kurds and others is one of the most singular disasters of this regime.

One can expect too that the traditions of a vibrant critical press and of public discussion associated with it will also be recovered. In a broader, cultural perspective the hedonistic, doubting, wine-loving *ghazal* of Hafiz and Sa'adi will have as much place as the sermons of the mollahs from Qom; the philosophy of al-Ghazali will be as central as the dogma of Ayatollahs; the music, literature, humour and, yes, alcohol of the Iranian people will be recognised as just as much theirs as the one-dimensional definitions of the cultural revolution. Not least the Iranian people will be able to recapture perhaps their greatest cultural inheritance, their mordant sense of humour: the first person to edit and publish the Joke Book of the Islamic Republic, *kitab-i shukhi-yi jumhuri-i islami* will surely have produced a best seller, and a repository of much popular, and yes, traditional, wisdom. The future of Iran involves a re-appropriation of the past; above all it involves taking the definition of that past away from those who have done it so much violence with their simplistic, and in many cases ignorant, codifications.

Conclusion

Iran stands today at a decisive, difficult point in its history, one in which the apparent certainties of the revolutionary period have crumbled, but in which the shape of an alternative future, and of the forces that could shape that future, remain as yet obscure. The idea that this regime can in the longer run survive, or meet the aspirations of its people, is one that no serious observer can accept, not least because the pressures on it, from without and within, are mounting, and the leadership of the Islamic republic is so manifestly lacking in the will, or policy, to resolve them. What form the alternative takes is for history, and the Iranian people, to decide and there are many possibilities, some more attractive than others. The idea of post-akhundism is offered as a contribution to the discussion of these futures and as a tentative survey of from where alternative ideas may emerge. Actually the result of the May 1997 election and the foreign policy intiatives of President Khatami reinforce the post-akhundism scenario, which is inevitable particularly if the trend for the rule of law and establishment of civil society continue based on rational discourse and peaceful means; akhundism has no place in Iranian politics beyond the year 2000.

NOTES

1 Many of the themes touched on in this paper have parallels in the article of Dr Asef Bayat, 'The coming of a post-Islamic society', *Critique*, Fall (1996), p. 45. Bayat writes: 'By "post-Islamism" I mean a condition where, following a phase of experimentation, the appeal, energy, symbols and sources of legitimacy of Islamism get exhausted, even among its once-ardent supporters. As such, post-Islamism is not anti-Islamic, but rather reflects a tendency to resecularise Islam'.
2 'CIA's open secret attack on Ayatollahs', *The Guardian*, 27 January 1996
3 The origins of the word are obscure, some suggesting it may be a corruption of 'agha khahad' – 'Mister/My Lord wishes'.
4 Shahrough Akhavi, *Religion and Politics in Contemporary Iran* (Albany: State University of New York Press, 1980), pp. 177–8.
5 The cultural revolution began following a statement by the Revolution Council on 19 April 1980 which called for a 'fundamental change' in the university system. Echoing a statement by Khomeini on the occasion of the Persian New Year, it asserted 'that there must be changes and transitions in culture and education; and that the colonial culture and non-Islamic educational system alien to our nation must be smashed' (BBC Summary of World Broadcasts ME/6400/A/7, 21 April 1980).
6 Fred Halliday, *Islam and the Myth of Confrontation* (London: I. B. Tauris, 1996).
7 E.g. Roy Mottahedeh, *The Mantle of the Prophet* (London: Chatto and Windus, 1986), p. 390, citing the example of the hostility to clerical power that arose at the end of the Safavi period.
8 Bani-Sadr in his message to the nation of 22 April 1980, endorsed the call 'for fundamental changes in the education system' (BBC Summary of World Broadcasts ME/6402/A/7, 23 April 1980). On 22 April he led a crowd of supporters into Tehran University, an action that resulted in clashes with opposition groups based there.
9 Hamid Enayat, *Modern Islamic Political Thought* (London: Macmillan, 1982).
10 I have argued this, with regard to the concept of human rights, at length in Chapter 5 of *Islam and the Myth of Confrontation*.

3

Iranian Foreign Policy under Khatami: Reform and Reintegration

Alireza Ansari

This chapter explores the various influences that have helped determine Iranian foreign policy since the inauguration of President Mohammad Khatami in August 1997, looking in particular at the role of the president himself in the determination and shaping of that policy. Ansari argues that, contrary to common assessments and perceptions, President Khatami not only plays a key role in formulating policy, but he also accords it a high priority such that it is arguably central to his vision of a reconstructed and reformed Iran, reintegrated within the global economic and political system. Far from seeing foreign policy as a secondary sphere of activity determined by domestic considerations – in some ways an extension of domestic politics – President Khatami, it is argued, sees foreign policy as integral to domestic development, with both enjoying a reciprocal relationship whose consequences may have a beneficial effect on local attitudes and the direction of socio-political development within the country.

The background

Since the election of Seyyid Mohammad Khatami to the presidency of the Islamic Republic in May 1997, Iran has moved energetically to consolidate and expand its foreign relations, not only with its regional neighbours but also further afield with its more traditional antagonists in Europe and North America. Concrete steps have been taken to consolidate relations with Iran's Arab neighbours and to reiterate Iran's stance that it poses no threat to the stability and security of the region. In particular relations have been solidified with Saudi Arabia, invoking memories of an earlier regional axis which saw the two OPEC giants seek to cooperate and if possible coordinate policy on both economic and political issues. While obvious differences remain the tenor of the relationship is markedly different. Crown Prince Abdullah attended the Organisation of Islamic Conference meeting in Tehran in December 1997, the highest ranking Saudi visitor to Iran for almost two decades, while the chairman of the Expediency Council, former President Rafsanjani, spent almost two weeks in the kingdom in early 1998. Since then senior ministerial visits between the two Gulf powers have been regular and the language has moved from one of suspicion and confrontation to one of support and constructive dialogue. Relations have similarly warmed with Egypt, another Arab state consistently vilified by the revolutionary regime in its heyday. While not condoning Egypt's peace treaty with Israel, Iran now appears to be a willing to re-establish diplomatic relations. As if to prove a point, Iran has also taken concrete steps to build bridges with Iraq, although in this case, while pilgrimages may be seen as a stage in the road map to better relations, it would be fair to point out that the road map is a long and twisted one. A key indicator of Arab–Iranian relations, the Abu Musa dispute has also taken something of a back seat in the past year, reflecting perhaps its status as a consequence rather than a cause of Arab–Iranian mistrust.

However, by far the most interesting developments have been in Iran's relationship with its key protagonist, the West, and particularly the United States. In the 18 months since Khatami's election, there has been a dramatic transformation in attitudes encouraged not only by constructive statements by leaders on both sides, but also by the orchestration of 'events' intended to facilitate a 'crack in the wall of mistrust'. These have included sporting events, in particular wrestling, and a fortuitous meeting at the World Cup in France, but have also been extended to conversations and meetings between former hostages and hostage takers finally leading, during the anniversary of the US Embassy takeover in November 1998, to an invitation by hostage takers to their former captives to visit Iran. That radicals in the establishment have dismissed the idea and a newly discovered *Fedayeen-e Islam* have sworn to assassinate any returning hostages may serve to remind us not to get carried away with the rhetoric of *rapprochement*, but neither should it deflect from the fact that a wide range of individuals generally considered *persona non grata* by hardliners have already visited Iran, including Anthony Cordesman, Geoffrey Kemp, and most peculiarly, Rupert Murdoch. While critics may protest that in practical terms there has been little progress on US–Iranian relations, and that sanctions indeed remain in place, it would be erroneous to suggest that developments have been insignificant and superficial. On the contrary, a change of tone and methodical deconstruction of the distrust is an essential prerequisite to the construction of better relations in the future, if these relations are to be built on firm foundations, above and beyond the immediacy of short-term economic interest or political expediency.

Indeed I will argue here that President Khatami, and the political establishment supporting and encouraging him, employ a conception of political development of which foreign policy occupies an integral and pivotal aspect – one that operates within a strategic perspective and depends upon the construction of a legitimate basis from which to conduct and implement policy. This chapter seeks to show this by first exploring some of the key determinants of President Khatami's foreign policy articulation, and then investigating the strategy by which he seeks to pursue and impose his agenda.

The dynamics of determination

Any foreign policy is determined by a variety of different influences and events, many of which have been comprehensively elucidated by other authors.[1] It is clear for instance that, since the inauguration of the 'era of reconstruction' in the aftermath of the war and during the presidency of Hashemi Rafsanjani, one of the key influences on the increasingly constructive and pragmatic foreign policy being pursued was the need for economic reconstruction and development. Broadly speaking, policy-makers in Iran, recognising the urgent need for economic development, argued that foreign policy should serve those needs more constructively than they had done in the past. More stable political relations, particularly within the region, were seen not only as a way of encouraging investment, but also providing Iran with a local market to sell its goods. Europe was also courted as Iran's main trading partner, and in the import boom which characterised the first Rafsanjani administration, European companies were only too eager to reciprocate. There were of course critics within Iran, and while the development of foreign policy relied in part on forging a consensus within the political establishment, more extreme critics were by and large dismissed as ignorant of the realities of international relations.[2] However, Iranian foreign policy-makers soon came to appreciate the flaw in their analysis of the international situation and in particular of attitudes towards the Islamic Republic.

The flaw was basically that, although countries both within the region and further afield were willing and often eager to pursue economic relations, in particular trade with Iran, and on occasions were willing to cooperate on political matters, the underlying strategic political environment remained negative. The level of distrust of Iran's intentions was so great by the turn of the 1990s that even the blatant aggression of Iraq against Kuwait could not be decisively exploited by Iranian diplomats. To policy-makers within Iran, emerging from the relative isolation of the Iran–Iraq war, and with President Rafsanjani at the helm, the realisation that they had lost the initiative during the first decade of the revolution and that the international environment was in effect ideologically reconstructed against them was a bitter pill to swallow. In the first place, the image of the Islamic Republic in the outside world, firmly established during the traumas of the early revolution, and not countered by anyone within the regime (indeed in some cases encouraged), was at odds with the image many policy-makers held within the country. A self-consciousness developed and, nurtured within the ideological cocoon of the early revolution, found itself confronting an image of itself it could not easily comprehend. Thus the surprise expressed by many officials when their apparent 'goodwill' in ensuring the release of the hostages in the Lebanon was not immediately reciprocated, or when Iran stood aside during the Kuwait War in 1991, and stuck resolutely to sanctions. Indeed, arguably, the Iranian reaction reflected a somewhat naive assumption in the certainty of a realistic conception of international relations. For them, the goalposts were constantly being moved, confirming perhaps the perfidy of the West and the fickleness of the Arabs.

But for others, some of whom had increasingly served in diplomatic missions in the West, other lessons were being drawn. One catalyst for this re-articulation of foreign policy may have been the resurrection of the Abu Musa and Tumbs dispute with the United Arab Emirates. Iranians found that, far from being able to reap the rewards of their prudent policy during the liberation of Kuwait, they were now being subjected to accusations of military occupation, and the speed with which the international media seized upon the issue came as something of a shock. As Deputy Foreign Minister Abbas Maleki said at the time, 'The volume of press coverage on Abu Musa is bigger than the island itself.'[3] Immediately the Iranian government found itself defending the foreign policy of the Shah, as it sought to argue that the 1971 occupation of the islands was in fact legitimate; and for the first time Iranian academics and policy-makers, while noting that the Shah had made mistakes domestically, publicly conceded that this did not at all reflect on his foreign policy, which had been on the whole well conducted.[4]

While such an admission was anathema to the radicals and hard-liners, it did signal a return to strategic depth in foreign policy analysis and development. This cannot but have been helped by the existence of numerous 'retired' members of the imperial diplomatic corps within Iranian think-tanks and universities who were able to contribute to the radical rethink.[5] A number of key historical lessons had to be learnt, and these, it is argued, while not unchallenged, have helped determine Iranian foreign policy to this day. Indeed, while such an outlook had proponents, it has only really come to fruition following the inauguration of President Khatami, whose election success not only provided a window of opportunity for an ideological re-assessment and readjustment, but also provided a man with the credible conviction to pursue this shift energetically.

The logic of defending the Shah's foreign policy led inexorably to an analysis of why it could be considered a success. One of the first reasons recognised was the Shah's ability to integrate Iranian political and economic development and historical purpose into an essentially Western narrative framework. Thus it was recognised that the relationship between the Shah and the United States was not simply one of disinterested patron–client, but incorporated an essential ideological dimension which ensured that, whatever eccentricities were exhibited by the Shah, his allies always 'understood' him. It was this 'understanding' that allowed the Shah to seize the islands and to dominate the Persian Gulf with Western acquiescence and encouragement, and while the Shah might berate the West for laziness (for some a tactical blunder), such an understanding remained a strategic pinprick. Indeed, so intimate was this 'understanding' that the departure of the Shah radically inverted the relationship.

There can be little doubt that the revolutionary regime, eager to distance itself from its predecessor, sought to encourage the new 'mis-understanding', and it was only, as noted above, during the Rafsanjani administration that the extent of the chasm became apparent. The immediate response was unsurprisingly somewhat crude as analysts sought to imagine how this situation could be reversed. Noting that the Shah used the threat of the Soviet Union to integrate himself and Iran within a burgeoning US Cold War narrative, Iranian policy-makers now sought a way in which the West could once again depend on Iran as a bulwark against Russia. This attempted re-creation of the past was however confounded by the new relationship between post-glasnost USSR/Russia and the United States, and the fact that the geopolitics of the region was irreversibly altered by the collapse of the Soviet Union. There was simply no 'red threat' anymore. The increasing volatility and instability of the FSU however did allow another resurrected policy to emerge – the presentation of Iran as a centre of stability. While some countries would remain sceptical, it was a theme that was to be emphasised with increasing success in the 1990s, as the international environment became correspondingly less stable and commercial pressures began to make themselves felt in the form of oil companies seeking viable routes for exporting Caspian oil. One key aspect of this ideological dimension to foreign policy was a growing appreciation of the role of the international – in particular Western – media organisations, and the role they could play in the manipulation of public opinion. Again, while some argued vociferously for a more coherent strategy towards the Western media, the learning curve was a steep one and it has only been since the election of President Khatami that the government can be said to have enjoyed some measure of success.

Historical determinants

In sum, during the first decade of the revolution, foreign policy always came a poor second after domestic considerations and in many ways was simply an extension of domestic rivalries. As such there was rarely enough attention given to the development of a coherent foreign policy, and criticisms from abroad were ignored, if not in actual fact considered a virtue. During the second decade, the period of the 'second republic',[6] there was an increasing awareness that this could only be rectified through the development of a more coherent strategy, independent of though not separate from domestic considerations. Indeed in some circles the sphere of foreign relations was seen not only as serving domestic needs and as such reactive to them, but as an aspect of political activity which could be expanded, explored and utilised in such a manner that positive results could be brought to bear on domestic developments. As such the value of foreign policy as an aspect of government was raised as the relationship between domestic and foreign policy was increasingly reciprocal and potentially mutually beneficial. As this view gained prominence the traditional revolutionary dogmas of isolationism retreated, but throughout much of the second decade tensions existed, stemming from those who wanted to maintain revolutionary purity through isolation, but also from the prevarications of those who supported economic relations in order to service domestic needs but were ambivalent about taking the next step. Indeed vacillation and ambiguity may be said to have been the hallmark of the Rafsanjani administration, increasingly aware of the need for a more professional focus but hesitant and awkward about the practical steps required to achieve it.

This revision in attitudes towards foreign policy determination reflected the political and philosophical debates which had permeated much of domestic Iranian intellectual and political discourse for the better part of a decade,[7] and mirrored the emergence and pre-eminence of supporters of what may best be characterised as the moderate or progressive wing of the Islamic revolutionary movement. Any political movement carries with it a broad range of opinions reflecting varied historical experiences and socio-economic backgrounds, but within the limitation of ambiguity some broad ideological characteristics can be discerned. Most members of this movement share a particular interpretation of recent Iranian history and of the course of the Islamic revolution itself, along with an integrative approach to relations with the outside world, in particular the West. In short, the revolution of 1979 is the latest and greatest of Iranian popular movements this century aimed at securing freedom, independence and security for the people and state. As such it is a worthy successor to both the Constitutional Revolution of 1906 and the National Movement of 1951–3 led by Dr Mosaddeq.

Reflecting on the failure of both these movements to achieve their aims, there is less inclination to blame foreign powers, but instead greater introspection and concern that the social and political framework had not been sufficiently prepared and that consequently anarchy became an all too convenient stepping stone for renewed autocracy. In order to avoid this happening again there must be sufficient social and political preparation; in other words, a concerted effort to re-align the political culture and mentality of Iranians away from a fatalistic submission to autocracy. In analysing the failure of the Shah, many commentators in Iran similarly argue that the Pahlavi experiment failed because sustainable economic development must be founded on a platform of political legitimacy – something which the Shah quite clearly failed to achieve.

It is quite apparent from this brief sketch that their interpretation of the cause and aims of the Islamic revolution differs quite markedly from many of the revolutionaries, who either from a belief in structural determinism or from religious conviction do not see political and economic pluralism as a possible or indeed desirable consequence of the revolution. The moderates on the other hand are emphatic that the aims of the revolution were to promote economic and political plurality, and in support of their vision have added to the familiar totems of 'freedom' and 'rule of law' the concept of 'civil society'. As such they have inclined to the argument that the revolution was diverted from its true course – a reality most obviously revealed by the stark contrast between political realities and the covenant between state and people expressed in the Constitution of the Islamic Republic of Iran – although the reasons for this diversion vary from problems caused by the war with Iraq to the regrettable consequences of internal rivalries. The revolution is therefore a continuing dynamic and as a political project awaiting completion is *hegemonic* in its conception.[8]

An appreciation of this domestic dynamic, that is the historical interpretation and philosophical outlook it encapsulates, facilitates an understanding of the gradual transformation of foreign policy determination outlined above. The concept of hegemonic competition derived from historical experience was relatively easily transferred to the sphere of foreign policy. But the 'moderates' brought with them further distinctive ideas. While most revolutionaries found little difficulty in the application of a hegemonic contest – indeed the concept of the 'Great Satan' or preoccupation with the threat of a 'cultural onslaught' revolved around it – the moderates refused to countenance a purely antagonistic relationship. For them, the competition was not a one-dimensional confrontation, Manichean in its crude categorisation, but a multifaceted dialectic in which a dynamic synthesis was the key to a progressive integrative development. One of the clearest indications of this integrative approach is reflected in the continuing work of Abdolkarim Soroush, who has argued that a rejection of the West is too short-sighted and that Iranians must count among their intellectual inheritance the legacy of the West, as well as pre-Islamic and Islamic Iran.[9] Thus while most would agree that the international system was 'unjust' and favoured the economic and political interests of the Great Powers,[10] the moderates provided a distinctly different solution which increasingly came to be seen as more compatible with Iran's position in the international order. While many influential hardliners rejected this approach, as they rejected the domestic agenda, the election of Seyyid Mohammad Khatami on 23 May 1997 with an overwhelming majority was a significant victory for the moderate movement.

Khatami and the strategy of legitimation

Khatami's inauguration was a significant turning point heralding the increasing ascendancy of the moderate conception of political development and the role of foreign policy in that development. It would be erroneous to believe, however, that the victory was total. On the contrary, Khatami's election, while significant in the hegemonic contest and indicative of a trend with deep social roots, reflects a continuing dynamic: as such, foreign policy is still determined through negotiation and consensus with other parties and factions in the Iranian political arena. It would however be equally erroneous to suggest, as some have attempted to do, that foreign policy determination is beyond the control or influence of President Khatami and his allies, or that the Leader, Ayatollah Khamene'i, represents an ideological pole inflexibly at odds with the moderates. Such a confrontational model of Iranian politics, often extended to encompass foreign relations as well, is just as crudely Manichean as the hardline philosophical world view outlined above. As the following will show, the reality is considerably more complex, and as President Khatami and his allies seek to pursue and implement their political agenda they have frequently resorted to negotiation and compromise with their domestic enemies in order that the strategic goals can ultimately be achieved.

President Khatami believes in the Islamic revolution, but is also aware that it has fallen short of its lofty ideals. For him, history, in a Hegelian sense, is the progress of consciousness of freedom,[11] and it is precisely in this area that the revolution in particular, and modern Islamic interpretations in general, have failed to deliver. Indeed, for him, Islam without freedom is not Islam at all.[12] Elected on a platform of civil society, freedom and the rule of law, President Khatami has been consistent in his reiteration of a desire to see a more pluralistic economic and political environment within the country. Like his predecessor, Khatami is faced with an ailing, 'sick' economy which urgently needs an injection of capital, preferably foreign. However, unlike President Rafsanjani, Khatami is more acutely aware of the complementary nature of the economic, political and ideological aspects of this process and arguably better placed to exploit it. Thus while there is a need for foreign capital, President Khatami not only recognises the need for a stable political and regional environment to secure this investment, but crucially also recognises the potential of the benefits of positive foreign relations on domestic political development. The logic of pluralism at home is greater plurality abroad and the relationship is reciprocal. And just as the domestic agenda must be constructed on firm foundations, so must the reintegration of Iran into the international order. Thus dialogue and reintegration are the hallmarks of Khatami's foreign policy, while his strategy is one of communication and co-option targeted towards the three main vehicles of communication and ideological dissemination: expatriate Iranians, the international media and the foreign intelligentsia.

An excellent example of the reciprocal effects of foreign policy on the Iranian domestic agenda and a key influence in the attempted realignment of Iran within the international order was the rise of the Taleban in Afghanistan. Ever since the withdrawal of the Soviet Union from Afghanistan, Iran had been competing with other regional powers, in particular Pakistan, to ensure a favourable resolution to factional fighting and the establishment of a sympathetic government in Kabul. The emergence of the Taleban was a significant reversal as this radical Sunni organisation increasingly imposed an extreme form of Shariah law in Afghanistan, thus promoting rather than reducing the flow of refugees, but also adopted a vehemently anti-Shia and, by extension, anti-Iranian disposition. While the cautious welcome afforded to the emergent Taleban by the US State Department on the occasion of their conquest of Kabul was viewed with some embarrassment in US academic circles, and may indeed have prompted serious reflection as to how far US policy would go to 'punish' Iran,[13] the impact of the Taleban on the direction of domestic political development was far more significant. Its significance was recognised by the moderates and singularly misunderstood by their opponents, as was to become apparent in the election campaign which brought Khatami to power. For Iranians, the rise of the Taleban and their extreme brand of Islam provided them with a barometer and reference point with which they could measure and assess their own Islamic government. What they saw not only horrified them, but also caused them to draw comparisons with the social and cultural zealots within Iran.

In successfully encouraging the view that Ali Akbar Nateq Nouri represented the vanguard of a Taleban style of Islamic government, and in identifying their fear with his person, Khatami's supporters inflicted the coup de grâce to the campaign of Nateq Nouri, who only recognised the potential damage of this unfortunate association extremely late in the day. It would not be too far to argue that it represented a political stroke of genius.[14] In protesting his innocence Nateq Nouri simply confirmed his guilt in the eyes of the electorate and effectively condemned himself to electoral oblivion.[15]

At the same time, Seyyid Mohammad Khatami was portrayed as the antithesis of the Taleban, epitomising in his person the qualities of rationality, moderation and intellectual rigour. He was in effect the model of progressive Islam, modest in both demeanour and wealth, while dignified and respected; intellectually vital and knowledgeable not only in Islamic philosophy but also in Western philosophy, a key ingredient in his appeal to the intelligentsia. This domestic distinction was not lost upon an increasingly inquisitive international audience, for whom Khatami's electoral triumph was similarly unexpected. The importance of the Taleban and the image they represented for the intelligentsia is convincingly shown by the attitude they took during the growing confrontation in the summer of 1998, when contrary to expectations it was the moderate intelligentsia who advocated a full scale assault on the Taleban against the advice of most army and Revolutionary Guard commanders. Despite the obvious practical reasons against such an intervention, it would seem that they had themselves fallen victim to their own myth.

So convincing has this identification of President Khatami been that his domestic opponents have been consistently frustrated in their attempts to blame Khatami for the economic difficulties which continue to mount during his first term in office.[16] Khatami for his part, it is argued, is acutely aware of the impact favourable international events may have on his consolidation of power within Iran. That is not to say, of course, that the emergence of the Taleban has not caused President

Khatami distinctive problems – an unstable eastern frontier goes counter to Khatami's desire for a stable and secure environment for economic development and investment – but it shows how their presence has been used to good effect in the development of the Khatami myth both within and outside Iran.

On the whole, President Khatami has been fortunate in that international events have provided him with opportunities to promote his agenda and encourage a gradual shift in international attitudes towards Iran. Persistent problems with both Afghanistan and Iraq, personified in the American psyche by Osama bin Laden and Saddam Hussein, have allowed Iran to push with greater success than previously its identification as an island of stability, while the detonation of nuclear weapons in India and Pakistan has deflated US accusations of Iranian pursuit of weapons of mass destruction. More importantly within a regional environment was the continued intransigence of the Netanyahu government in Israel over the peace process and the disaffection this caused among America's Arab allies. Indeed, Israeli intransigence was by default making Iran's stated position about the injustice of the peace process seem realistic, if not true. The international environment has thus been favourable to a realignment, but the opportunities presented had to be seized.

The first major opportunity presented itself within the first few months of the new administration. While the next Organisation of the Islamic Conference (OIC) meeting was scheduled to be held in Tehran in December 1997, there was considerable anxiety among Iranian officials about the level of attendance and an eagerness to use the event as a showcase in which to market the new Iran. Great efforts were therefore made to ensure that senior representatives from each country would attend, and to complete the conference facilities in time for their arrival. Success however was assured by Arab frustration with the Netanyahu government, which meant not only that the previous Mena (Middle East and North Africa) meeting at Doha was poorly attended, if not boycotted, but conversely that the OIC meeting in Tehran was well attended. The contrast was a stark one. For Iran the arrival of dignitaries such as Crown Prince Abdullah of Saudi Arabia, referred to earlier, symbolised the return of their country to international recognition and respectability, while for the United States it was a clear reminder that Iran was not isolated. However, the meeting also allowed President Khatami to make his mark on the international stage, although his immediate audience was a regional one. Thus, while Ayatollah Khamene'i opened the conference with a speech many considered harsh, vitriolic and antagonistic to the West,[17] President Khatami rather pointedly opened his talk with these words, 'I do not know if I should begin my speech with the bitter issues that are, or the joyous issues that should be.'[18] Recognising that his audience was composed in part of representatives from 'moderate' Arab states, Khatami then proceeded to deliver a much less confrontational speech with a good deal of reflection on self-inflicted wounds in the Islamic community. In both its tone and nature it was characteristic of the moderate intellectual movement that had propelled him to power. In place of Khamene'i's, 'The materialistic Western civilisation encourages everyone to become materialistic', Khatami urged a better understanding of the West:

> We should know that between the Islamic civilisation – or more correctly the civilisation of the Muslims – and our lives today, there stands a phenomenon known as Western civilisation whose positive achievements are not few, and its negative effects are also manifold, especially for non-Westerners. Our age is one of domination of Western civilisation and culture. Understanding it is necessary. An effective understanding goes beyond the frills of that civilisation and reaches the roots and foundations of its values and principles.[19]

Indeed the speech is quite significant in highlighting a number of themes which were to become the hallmarks of Khatami's hegemonic project. Moving on from a reassessment of the past, and the failures of an Islamic civilisation to retain its cultural and scientific dominance, Khatami argued that in order to recreate such a vitality, a careful study of past strengths, stripped of anachronistic weaknesses which may have been relevant to a specific historical period, but were no longer valid, had to be pursued. This historical reassessment, and the replacement of dogma with vitality, was a quintessentially 'ideological' project, and the creation of a 'modern' Islamic civilisation required the 'materialisation of an Islamic civil society'.

Clearly with his audience in mind, President Khatami then drew on the conceptual imagery of Medina, arguing that just as 'Western civil society was primarily inspired by the Greek city states . . . the historical and theoretical essence of the civil society that we have in mind is rooted in the esteemed Prophet's Medina'.[20] Furthermore, the changing of the name of Yathrib to Medina was 'not merely a change of titles'. The change signified that 'a spiritual, historical and geographical entity was created in the world that was essentially the harbinger of the dissemination and spread of a particular type of culture, world view and ethos . . .' The international dimension is revealed when it is argued that real peace and security can be achieved when one has a deep understanding of the culture and thoughts of others, for which a dialogue is necessary. But this dialogue cannot achieve anything if one is insecure in his own identity.

> True dialogue will only be possible when the two sides are genuinely aware of their roots and identity, otherwise, the dialogue of an imitator who has no identity with others is meaningless and is not in his interest.[21]

The relationship is therefore ideally dialectic, in which each gains from interaction with the other, and development in one sphere must proceed and sustain development in the other. The centrality of 'thinkers and scholars' to the project is stressed, indeed they are described as 'the pivot and axis of this movement'. At the conclusion of his philosophical framework he alluded to the discourse on the clash of civilisations and described it as arising from 'hegemony-seeking relations' which had to be countered through 'dialogue'. On the sidelines of the Conference he suggested that he might initiate this dialogue by submitting a message to the great American people. He did not say when, nor suggest what he might actually say, but it was sufficient to whet some appetites.

In due course he was to agree to submit his message and begin his dialogue with the American people in an interview with CNN on the 7 January 1998. President Rafsanjani had conducted interviews with US television companies before, but what made this exercise different, it is argued, was President Khatami's acute recognition of the power and influence of international media organisations (in particular television) and their potency as a vehicle for ideological communication and dissemination.[22] In 1995, as the head of the National Library of Iran, Khatami delivered a paper at a conference on information science, entitled, 'Observations on the Information World'.[23] His comments are revealing.

> In its contemporary, complex forms, information technology represents one of the highest achievements of modern culture which uses its control over information to solidify its domination of the

> world. Thus, inquiry into the nature of the information world is inseparable from uncovering the nature of modern civilisation itself. And until we address this important question we will not be able to muster the confidence and wisdom to understand our relationship to modern civilisation. Otherwise, we will live in a world whose rules have been set by others, at the mercy of circumstance, not as masters of our fate . . . The flood of information in our age saturates the senses of humanity so extensively that the ability to assess and choose is impaired even among Westerners who are producers of information, let alone us who have a peripheral role in the information world. Electronic information is the brainchild of modern civilisation. Thus, the power of today's information-based mass culture is tied to the legitimacy of the values of Western civilisation for which the information revolution counts as the most prominent achievement.

There can be little doubt therefore that President Khatami was fully aware of the opportunity afforded to him by CNN, and it is significant that he opened the interview with a prepared statement which revealed both his understanding of Western civilisation and his strategy for reintegrative legitimation. In other words, not only did he indicate his knowledge of American history, and indeed his respect for the 'great American people', but he also suggested an ideological symbiosis through which Iranian political development was associated and integrated, and thus legitimated in the eyes of Western observers. At one level, the Iranian president impressed his audience with his comments on the Pilgrim Fathers and Plymouth Rock, and importantly, his 'regret' for the US Embassy take-over in 1979. He also expressed disapproval of the burning of US flags, and noted revealingly that anti-US slogans were not intended as insults against the American people or to undermine the American government, but that, 'these slogans symbolise a desire to terminate a mode of relationship between Iran and America.'[24]

These concessionary comments were the ones most readily picked up by the pundits in the United States, along with his now famous urging that 'there must be a crack in this wall of mistrust in order to prepare for a change', but they were not, it is argued, the most significant aspects of the speech. These were reserved, in the main, for the American intelligentsia, and it is worth noting that the initial reaction scarcely commented on them. In the first place he reminded his audience of the shared history between the United States and Iran and the regrettable consequences of that relationship when viewed in a deeper historical context.

> There is a bulky wall of mistrust between us and American administrations, a mistrust rooted in improper behaviour by the American governments. As an example of this type of behaviour, I should refer to admitted involvement of the American government in the 1953 *coup d'état* which toppled Mosaddeq's national government, immediately followed by a $45m loan to strengthen the *coup* government. I should also refer to the capitulation law imposed by the American government on Iran.[25]

In emphasising these incidents, well known by most Western students of Iran, and regretted by a few, Khatami sought to redraw the historical map and include events which would make what happened subsequently more understandable. His statement also reiterated the importance of these events within Iranian political culture, which was finally recognised by Secretary of State Albright in a speech to the Asian Society in New York several months later, a not insignificant concession in itself. But more important than all this was President Khatami's assessment of American democracy and his reference to de Tocqueville's 'Democracy in America', which he noted, with no little irony, most Americans had obviously read. This was a clear signal to the Western intelligentsia that there existed a common language and interactive space. In his analysis of de Tocqueville the parallel he wished to draw with the Iranian experience was clear.

> In his view [de Tocqueville], the significance of this civilisation [American] is the fact that liberty found religion as a cradle for its growth, and religion found the protection of liberty as its divine calling. Therefore in America, liberty and faith never clashed, and as we see, even today most Americans are religious people. There is less war against religion in America. Therefore, the approach to religion, which was the foundation of Anglo-American civilisation, relies on the principle that religion and liberty are consistent and compatible . . . We feel that what we seek is what the founders of American civilisation were also pursuing four centuries ago. This is why we sense an intellectual affinity with the essence of American civilisation.[26]

In combining the myths of the founding fathers with the rational intellectual analysis of de Tocqueville, and associating it with developments within Iran, President Khatami sought to integrate the Iranian historical experience with that of the West and to weave a complex integrative narrative into a single text. Rather than a hegemonic clash, the case was being made for a hegemonic synthesis. The tools of this synthesis were not governments, but 'thinkers and intellectuals', the most obvious immediate vehicles being the employees of CNN itself. Indeed while US government officials debated the importance of the interview and generally expressed disappointment at the limited initiatives on offer, there was little room for doubt at CNN headquarters, where an 'historical conjuncture' was already being manufactured.[27]

Combined with a generally sympathetic response from US academics eager to make use of new opportunities for renewed contact, the US government was forced within a week to reverse its initial caution, and in fact welcome the opportunity for exchanges. Arguably, President Khatami, through CNN, had out-manoeuvred the inertia of the US foreign policy establishment and forced the pace. In the information age, the big battalions were on the airwaves, and if anything, President Khatami underestimated the ideological punch of the modern mass media in the West.

Over the next six months the trickle of exchanges, beyond the high profile sports encounters, which saw not only the Stars and Stripes hang in Tehran but the singing of the US national anthem, grew, as more journalists and academics flew to Tehran to 'rediscover' Iran. Far from simply being the 'Cleric who charmed Iranians', it was increasingly apparent that Khatami had succeeded in charming key sections of the Western intelligentsia as well.[28] The accelerated change in the tone of the relationship between Iran and the West and the implications this would have on policy, in particular the many vested interests on both sides which had thrived on the 'double demonisation',[29] became an increasing cause for concern.

The gathering momentum of the foreign policy sphere appeared to be losing touch with domestic political realities and as a consequence invoking a reaction which would be counter-productive to the process President Khatami wished to initiate. Whatever the excitement among the media therefore, both sides sought to put on the brakes. President Khatami found his administration under attack from a number of fronts and in the summer of 1998 he lost both his trusted ally, the Mayor of Tehran, and his lieutenant, the Interior Minister Abdullah

Nouri. While these developments caused some unease and could have forced a retrenchment, the consensus seems to have been that the broad direction of policy had to be maintained and pursued, though with less haste.

Several conclusions could be deduced from this decision. First, it was clear that the administration and some members of the political establishment did not feel that the new foreign policy initiatives were unsustainable in the domestic environment and its continuing dynamic. Furthermore, this dynamic, with its occasional reverses, could indeed be harnessed and managed in such a way as to benefit itself; and this could be achieved precisely because the tectonic shift in attitudes towards the Islamic Republic of Iran was already providing foreign commentators with an ideological cushion with which to explain and understand, if not ignore altogether, the vagaries of domestic politics in Iran.[30] Iran was once again a potential 'island of stability' in an otherwise unstable region and there can have been few who did not recognise the coincidence of interests in both Iraq and Afghanistan, especially in the aftermath of the US missile strike against the Taleban.

Efforts to provide a common ideological framework within which to locate these interests continued with President Khatami's visit to the United Nations General Assembly in September 1998. During his brief trip he had the opportunity not only to address the General Assembly, but more importantly to talk to expatriate Iranians in the United States and also to discuss his ideas with foreign reporters, two groups who arguably have formed the vanguard of the ideological project. In his address to the expatriate Iranians, President Khatami showed his mastery of political discourse and his ability to tailor his talks to his audience in an effort to co-opt them,[31] but also revealed the depth of his theoretical literacy in the importance of both ideologies and myths. As such, his focus on Ferdowsi's *Shahnameh* and the 'spirit of Iranians' showed his ability to communicate with ordinary Iranians, while his attention to the mythic foundations of the nation was quite clearly addressed to the intelligentsia both within and outside the hall, declaring in no uncertain terms that he spoke *their* language. Thus, he said,

> mythology is a highly vast and complicated subject, which has received much respect, analysis and research in our time. Mythology describes the spirit of various nations. And there is no nation or

> people whose history is free of myth. Of course, in conformity with the weight of civilisation and the history of a nation, the myth of a nation is deeper and more complicated. And civilised nations usually have myths. The ethical myth and the myth epic indicate the spirit of the Iranians.[32]

Arguably, President Khatami's emphasis on the philosophical foundations of his political thought and his desire to explore these with a wider audience, while generally considered impressive, was also creating an impression of detachment. There was certainly some concern in Iran that this 'philosophical' approach was missing the target, as when, at the end of a press conference in New York, President Khatami decided on an impromptu elucidation of the problem of justice in human history and Plato's analysis of it.[33] There can be little doubt that much of the audience were somewhat bewildered by the digression. Indeed his presentation to the General Assembly, while more circumspect and cautious, was not averse to a brief digression on his philosophy of history, which as 'the glorious history of truth and the realisation of justice' was effectively Hegelian in its conception. At the same time during the press conference he revealed the historical influences on his determination of the importance of ideology in Iran. When asked by a Western journalist whether political parties would soon be part of the Iranian political landscape, Khatami answered emphatically that parties could be established, 'right now'. He then explained:

> Unfortunately, it is not up to the government to establish parties; the people must do this themselves. The experience of civil society is a new one for us. Although we embarked on this one hundred years ago [the Constitutional Revolution of 1906], we did not succeed in practice. The constitutional system was a system that could have formed the basis of an acceptable civil society for our culture and nation. Unfortunately, internal disputes and intervention by foreigners meant that an oppressive dictatorship emerged from the heart of our constitutional system [ie Reza Shah]. After World War II . . . again there was a good opportunity for freedom. In view of the lack of maturity of our domestic forces, we turned on each other with such ferocity that we failed to institutionalise this freedom in the country. With the *coup d'état* of the 28th Mordad [against Dr Mosaddeq], that period also came to an end.[34]

Such comments serve to remind us that his philosophical and ideological outlook do relate to a historical reality and that President Khatami recognises the dialectic which exists, in the same way as he recognises the relationship between foreign and domestic policy and, he would argue, the relationship of the West with the East. Arguably, he conceptualises both relationally and dynamically[35] and the momentum of the dynamic must be maintained and indeed sustained, through initiatives both ideological and practical.

Faced with mounting pressures at home, President Khatami, in agreement with the main members of the political establishment, decided to deliver another ideological *coup de grâce* – this time directed at foreign critics – and solve the Salman Rushdie issue, which had plagued Iranian–EU relations for nearly a decade. It was a bold stroke and a skilful exercise in diplomatic crisis management by both the main governments involved, with both effectively selling it as a triumph to critics at home. While criticism mounted in Iran, it has remained marginal and the restoration of diplomatic relations has not been stalled. In publicly confirming once again that the Iranian government would not send assassins to kill Salman Rushdie and disassociating themselves from the bounty offered by the 15th Khordad Foundation, the Iranian government could justifiably argue that the honour and dignity of the nation had been maintained. In return Britain recognised the religious inviolability of the fatwa and its permanence, as well as the insult caused to Muslims, thus maintaining its credibility among its Arab and Muslim constituents. In other words, Iran had confronted Great Britain (the great bogeyman of modern Iranian history) and had emerged unscathed, pride intact, if not a little enhanced. Henceforth Iran could treat Britain on equal terms and as such a new Anglo-Iranian relationships could be constructed on firm and legitimate foundations, free from either fascination or hatred.[36]

There was a heavy price to pay for this move, however, as concessions had to be made to domestic opponents. Neither was the legitimation complete, but it was a significant step, and overnight President Khatami removed the one serious obstacle to the intellectual rehabilitation and reintegration of Iran. While differences would remain, it was the condemnation of a writer which had prolonged the antagonism of much of the Western intelligentsia. Seemingly oblivious to the reality of the compromise solution in the days and weeks after the resolution, media coverage of Iran became overwhelmingly sympathetic and above all 'understanding'. All this despite a concurrent crackdown on the press within Iran. The resolution of the Rushdie affair, however, represented an excellent example of the multifaceted continuing dynamic at work, with progress in foreign policy complementing and occasionally compensating for developments at home. In this case, it may be conjectured, the long-term rewards abroad far outweighed the immediate losses at home, and arguably would in time help reverse those losses.

Conclusion

President Khatami's success in presenting himself, both at home and abroad, as a champion of progress, justice and democratic plurality continues unabated and represents one of the most rapid and dramatic shifts in ideological perception and interpretation in recent years. The image of the turbaned mullah, fanatic and dogmatic, which permeated Western perceptions has been transformed in the space of a year. Arguably President Rafsanjani sowed the seed and President Khatami has reaped the harvest, and there is undoubted truth in the fact that the rapidity of this transformation was in part due to a receptive political will nurtured over the previous decade.

But it is worth remembering that under President Rafsanjani positive movements were being consistently undermined by an overwhelmingly negative undercurrent, which made constructive relations between Iran and her neighbours, to say nothing of the West, erratic and tenuous at best. Interest might remain in economic cooperation but could only be institutionalised through ideological integration and a recognition of an integral commonality. While President Rafsanjani appealed to Iranians abroad not to relinquish their identity, Khatami went further and explored the nature of that identity. In adding further dimensions to the discourse he facilitated entry by groups that previously remained suspicious or excluded. Thus he targeted the foreign intelligentsia as well as the media and made it clear that he 'understood' their language, even if at times it appeared he knew it better than they did.

Antagonistic isolation, while useful for the reconstruction of Iranian identity and confidence, had now to be replaced by dialogue and synthetic integration. Ironically, the strategy is in many ways similar to that pursued by Mohammad Reza Shah when he sought to integrate Iran within a burgeoning Cold War myth and make Iran indispensable to the

Western project – a truly strategic partner. The critical difference was that, while the Shah consolidated and indeed expanded his foreign relations, he did so from a domestic foundation of illegitimacy, and as his attempts to legitimise his rule at home foundered he increasingly compensated abroad, further alienating himself from realities at home. The Shah's strengths began abroad and remained abroad. Khatami's election has provided him with an altogether different basis for legitimacy, founded within the domestic political environment and which must now be expanded abroad. In so doing, he must retain a balance in this development and remember that foreign policy can complement and occasionally compensate, but must always be rooted in the firm foundations of domestic political legitimacy.

NOTES

1 See for example A. Ehteshami and R. Hinnebusch, *Syria and Iran: Middle Powers in a Penetrated System* (London: Routledge, 1997), Chapter 3, pp. 27–57.
2 See Larijani's comments reported by IRNA dated 2 May 1997; BBC SWB ME/2910 MED/13 dated 5 May 1997. There has been continuing tension between those who believe contact is both useful and necessary and others who insist it can only pollute the Islamic revolution. One of the more notorious cases was that of Larijani, whose visit to London in 1996 and discussion with the then head of the Middle East section of the Foreign Office effectively destroyed his political career.
3 Deputy Foreign Minister Abbas Maleki, 11 October in *Iran Focus*, November 1992.
4 'This is not the Shah's policy, it is Iran's national interest and a matter of Iranian sovereignty. Whether it is a monarchy or republican or any other type of regime is irrelevant. The Shah did not come from Mars, he was an Iranian.' Farhang Rajaee of Tehran University, responding to criticism that the Islamic Republic is defending the Shah's policy; quoted in *Iran Focus,* November 1992.
5 Views were also garnered from exiled officials.
6 A. Ehteshami, *After Khomeini: The Iranian Second Republic* (London: Routledge, 1995).
7 See for example M. Boroujerdi, 'The encounter of post-revolutionary thought in Iran with Hegel, Heidegger, and Popper' in S. Mardin (ed.), *Cultural Transitions in the Middle East* (Leiden: E.J. Brill, 1994), pp. 236–59; also A. Matin-Asgari, 'Abdolkarim Sorush and the secularisation of Islamic thought in Iran', *Iranian Studies*, 30:1/2 (Winter/Spring 1997), pp. 95–115.
8 'Hegemony, relations of force, historical bloc' in D. Forgacs (ed.), *A Gramsci Reader* (London: Lawrence & Wishart, 1988), Part 2, Chapter VI, pp. 189–222.

9 Boroujerdi, 'The encounter', p. 243. The roots of this thinking can be found in the conception of the Iranian revolution as a worthy successor to the French and Russian revolutions, thus conveniently integrating Iranian and European histories, despite the apparent rejection of the latter.

10 Iranian attitudes are possibly best summed up in the note by Karl von Clausewitz: 'The aggressor is always peace-loving . . . he would prefer to take over our country unopposed.' See his *On War* in Paret & Howard (eds.), p. 370. Hence the dictum, 'The conqueror always loves peace.' In this understanding, the world system is engineered to support the West, which of course promotes peace in order to maintain the status quo. As a consequence this must be opposed.

11 See for example, President Khatami's speech to the United Nations General Assembly, New York, 21 September 1998: '. . . one can discern the trajectory of history towards liberty. The history of humankind is the history of liberty.'

12 See President Khatami's inaugural address at the Majlis on 4 August 1997. Also BBC SWB ME/3346 MED/9 dated 1 October 1998: 'President Khatami addresses Tehran students at the beginning of the academic year', dated 29 September 1998. For a discussion of the concept of freedom, see M. Khatami, *Fears and Hopes*, trans. A. Mafinezam in *Hope and Challenge: The Iranian President Speaks* (Binghamton University, Institute of Global Cultural Studies, 1997), pp. 35–7.

13 In appearing to support the Taleban the US administration effectively sent the message that radical Islamic ideology was not the problem; being Iranian was. Such logic proved distinctly unpalatable to many US intellectuals on moral grounds let alone the consequence of inevitable confrontation it implied. While the characteristics of Islamism may change, Iranian identity could not.

14 G.W.F. Hegel, 'The German Constitution' (1802) in *Hegel's Political Writings*, trans. T. M. Knox (Oxford University Press, 1964), p. 216.

15 Nateq Nouri's loss of the political initiative is indicated by his campaign speeches in May 1997, the first of which dealt with his revolutionary qualifications. Increasingly aware of electoral disaffection, he then hastily sought to deal with more concrete issues such as women and the prospect for multi-party politics, both issues Khatami had made his own. See BBC SWB ME/2917 MED/3-11 dated 13 May 1997; ME/2920 MED/7 dated 16 May 1997; and ME/2926 MED/7 dated 23 May 1997.

16 Much to the consternation of the hardliners, Khatami's popularity has been consistently high after a year in office.

17 SWB ME/3099 S1/1 dated 11 December 1997; Khamene'i's speech to the OIC conference dated 9 December 1997: 'The materialistic Western civilisation encourages everyone to become materialistic. Money, gluttony and lust have become recognised as great efforts, and in vast parts of this world purity, honesty and the spirit of sacrifice have been replaced by deceit, conspiracy, greed, jealousy and other ugly characteristics.'

18 SWB ME/3099 S1/4 dated 11 December 1997: Khatami's speech to the OIC conference dated 9 December 1997.

19 Ibid., S1/5.

20 Ibid., S1/5.

21 Ibid., S1/6. See also BBC SWB ME/3339 MED/2 dated 23 September 1998: 'President Khatami addresses Iranian expatriates in the USA', dated 20 September

1998: 'The first rule of dialogue . . . is to know yourself and identity. The second rule is to know the civilisation with which you want to maintain a dialogue.'

22 See J. Thompson, *Ideology and Modern Culture: Critical Social Theory in the Era of Mass Communication* (Oxford: Polity Press, 1990), pp. 163–272; see also A. Gramsci, *Selection from Cultural Writings,* ed. D. Forgacs (London: Lawrence Wishart, 1985), pp. 386–427.

23 See Khatami, 'Observations on the Information World' in *Fears and Hopes*, pp. 61–71.

24 BBC SWB ME/3120 MED/4 dated 9 January 1998: CNN interview dated 8 January 1998.

25 Ibid., MED/5.

26 Ibid., MED/2. President Khatami also drew parallels with America's fight for 'independence' much as Dr Mosaddeq had done 46 years earlier. (It is worth noting that de Tocqueville's discussion of the role of religion in American democracy is absent from many modern abridged editions.)

27 The reasons for this are of course multifaceted and while they may include genuine interest in dialogue, they surely also reflected the network's desire to fully exploit its 'exclusive'.

28 E. Sciolino, 'The cleric who charmed Iranians', *New York Times*, 1 February 1998; see also 'On the virtues of the West by Mohammad Khatami' in *Time* magazine, 19 January 1998.

29 W. Beeman, 'Double demons: cultural impedance in US–Iranian understanding', *Iranian Journal of International Affairs* (Summer/Fall 1990), pp. 314–19.

30 Khatami's success is well indicated by the attempt by Iranian hardliners to utilise the Western media in their favour by purchasing advertising space in *The Times* in which to publish a speech by Ayatollah Khamene'i on the occasion of the Hajj. It was a very crude attempt at media manipulation and showed a clear misunderstanding of the nature of the Western media. However, as far as Khatami's strategy was concerned there could be no better example of imitation being the sincerest form of flattery.

31 Unusually, this encounter was broadcast on CNN.

32 BBC SWB ME/3339 MED/1 dated 23 September 1998: 'President Khatami addresses Iranian expatriates in the USA', dated 20 September 1998.

33 BBC SWB ME/3344 MED/11–16 dated 29 September 1998: 'President Khatami's press conference at the UN', dated 22 September 1998.

34 Ibid., MED/13–14.

35 K. Mannheim, *Ideology and Utopia* (London: Routledge & Kegan Paul, 1960), p. 135.

36 BBC SWB ME/3339 MED/2 dated 23 September 1998: 'President Khatami addresses Iranian expatriates in the USA', dated 20 September 1998.

4

Iran's European Relations since 1979

Mohammad R. Saidabadi

This chapter concentrates mainly on Iran's relations with the European Union (EU) member countries after the inauguration of President Rafsanjani in 1989. But it begins with a broad analysis of Iran's foreign policy since the Islamic revolution of 1979. The major factors which affected Iran's relations with Western European countries during the first ten years after the revolution are highlighted. Saidabadi discusses how significant and interrelated international factors and events of the late 1980s and early 1990s shaped the policy framework within which Iran approached the EU states. Iran's recent strategy of dealing separately with each individual EU member has succeeded in encouraging each European country to improve its relations with Iran. As a result, Iran's economic and political relations with the EU countries have improved markedly in the 1990s. The chapter concludes with an overview of major obstacles to closer ties between Iran and Europe in the future.

Iran's foreign policy 1979–89

Iran's foreign policy in the first decade of revolution was characterised by three different phases which coincided with '1: revolutions and 2: political upheaval'.[1] In the first revolution, which toppled the Shah's regime, from the appointment of Mehdi Bazargan as Prime Minister of the provisional government in February 1979 until the seizure of the US embassy in November 1979, the main principle of Iran's foreign policy was equilibrium. This period, which formed the first phase of Iran's foreign policy, was directed and guided by the nationalists who were regarded as liberals by the Islamists. 'Under the equilibrium principle, the Iranian government took the international system for granted and tried to protect and promote Iran's national interests by maintaining a balance of power and influence in relation to other states.'[2] While the provisional government accepted the reality and dominance of the world by the superpowers, Bazargan advocated 'the interests of Iran by means of Islam' whereas Ayatollah Khomeini believed in promoting 'the interests of Islam by means of Iran.'[3]

The short-lived political ascendancy of the nationalists ended with the seizure of the US embassy on 4 November 1979 (the so-called Second Revolution) because it was then that the Iranian revolution began to lose international sympathy. The events reflected political upheaval rather than revolutionary enterprise. Bazargan's resignation from the premiership two days after Ayatollah Khomeini's followers seized the US embassy and took the embassy staff hostage is regarded as the beginning of the second phase of Iran's foreign policy. This coincided with the introduction of two new principles that replaced the notion of equilibrium. These two new principles were 'neither East nor West but the Islamic Republic' and the 'export of revolution'. These principles were incorporated into the Constitution of the Islamic Republic of Iran which was ratified in December 1979. During this second phase the dominance of Islamists, supported by Ayatollah Khomeini, had a considerable influence on Iran's foreign policy. By this time, Iran's foreign policy makers 'questioned the very legitimacy of the existing international system; they sought to protect and promote Iran's Islamic interests by rejecting the dominance of both superpowers in the international system and by exporting the Islamic revolution throughout the world.'[4]

Abolhasan Banisadr's fall from the presidency in June 1981 marked the third political upheaval and coincided with the third phase in Iran's post-1979 revolutionary foreign policy. The third phase was initiated by the exclusion of 'the liberals' from power, and resulted in a complete dominance by Islamists over Iran's political system.[5] From this time onwards, the two tenets of the second phase became the backbone of Iranian foreign policy.

Regarding the first principle of Iran's foreign policy, 'neither East nor West but the Islamic Republic', Ayatollah Khomeini stated: 'A nation that cries in unison that it wants the Islamic Republic, wants neither East nor West but only an Islamic Republic'.[6] In his speech to a group of members of the Lebanese militia, Amal, on a visit in 1981, Ayatollah Khomeini said: 'We will not compromise with any superpower.

We will not go under either American dominance nor that of the Soviet Union. We are Muslim and we want to be free and independent.'[7] On another occasion, he stated: 'Because Islam is not the path of either East or West, but it is the straight path and the Islamic Republic is based on Islam and is not following either Eastern or Western camp, both camps disagree with it.'[8] From his point of view 'neither East nor West but the Islamic Republic' was a notion of independence from the West and the Eastern bloc, one which signalled the creation of a new political system in Iran according to Islamic rules.

The second principle, 'the export of revolution', was derived from Ayatollah Khomeini's perception that Islam is not limited to one country or even to Muslim countries, but exists for the happiness of all human beings. He believed that as the Islamic Republic of Iran was a vanguard of an Islamic revolutionary movement, it had a special duty to help not only Muslim countries but all oppressed nations throughout the world. He said: 'We should endeavour to export our revolution to the world. We should set aside the thought that we do not export our revolution, because Islam does not regard the various Islamic countries differently but is the supporter of all the oppressed peoples of the world.'[9] On many occasions, he emphasised that Iran was trying to expand Islam's influence throughout the world and stand against the arrogant domination of the world by any power, that the Islamic Republic was fighting to uproot the corrupt roots of Zionism, capitalism and communism and destroy the regimes founded on these principles. He also stated that Iran's revolution was not confined to Iran, but was the starting point for the Great Revolution in the Muslim world and that it was the duty of Iran to share its experiences with all Muslim, oppressed and exploited peoples of the world.[10] However, he emphasised on several occasions that these ideas would not be exported by force, stating at least once: 'When we say we want to export our revolution, we do not want to do it with swords.'[11]

Implementation of these two principles in the third phase of Iran's foreign policy was subject to two different interpretations. While in the third phase Islamists were prevalent in Iran's political leadership, they were divided into two schools of thought. Although both were revolutionary and both believed that Islam was the fundamental element of revolution and politics, they differed in some respects. The first school, labelled the 'idealists', hoped to establish the 'Islamic World Order' immediately, without regard to the problems that might be created in Iran's relations with other states. The second school, known as the 'pragmatists', also believed in the establishment of the 'Islamic World Order', but did not reject the realities of the existing international system. The former believed that the focus of Iran's foreign policy should be trained on 'the world's people rather than on its governments', whereas the latter took conventional relations between states for granted.[12] Another significant difference between the two schools of thought in relation to implementation of Iran's foreign policy was the means of, and strategies for, exporting the revolution. While the idealists' focus pointed outwards, laying greater emphasis on actions outside Iran, the pragmatists' pointed inwards, stressing the need to consolidate the base for Iran's future ability to export the revolution.

Iran's relations with Western Europe 1979–89

In the initial phase of the revolution, revolutionary sentiments and public opinion favoured the idealists. The external environment surrounding the newly born Islamic Republic of Iran helped the idealists to dominate Iran's political hierarchy and to guide Iran's foreign policy. Following the establishment of an anti-American Islamic government in Iran and the hostage crisis of 1979, US activities in the Persian Gulf increased. Iranian perceptions of these activities as actions intended to contain and ultimately destroy the revolutionary regime intensified Iran's anti-US policy. To this was added sanctions by Western states against Iran during the hostage crisis followed by the outbreak of the Iran–Iraq War in 1980, a war Iranians saw as imposed by the United States and its Western allies. In other words, 'the would-be "source of all threats" felt itself threatened.'[13] This feeling hardened Iran's foreign policy towards Western European countries and the United States.

Iran's relations with Western European countries in the first decade of revolution were dominated by a European fear of the destabilising effects of the Iranian revolution on Middle Eastern states generally and the Arab states of the Gulf region in particular. In addition, the Iran-Iraq War worsened Iran's relations with Western Europe.[14] This coincided with the dissemination of revolutionary Islamic ideas in the Gulf region. Both were regarded by the Arab states as sources of instability in the region and as threats to their governments. This assumption, which intensified with Iraqi attempts to manipulate the Arab world by claiming to be defending Arab unity and integrity, resulted in the provision of facilities and assistance to the Iraqi regime by the Arab countries of the Gulf in the form of financial and political support. It marked the beginning of a period of mistrust between these states and Iran. In this context, the Gulf Cooperation Council (GCC) was formed in 1981 in order to create a joint defence against any aggression, but particularly aggression from Iran. As Hooglund remarked, 'one primary objective [of the GCC] was to counter the export of Iran's revolution to the Arab side of the Gulf.'[15] In fact, Iran's refusal to accept UN Security Council Resolution 598 resulted in a deterioration of its relations with the Arab Gulf states to the lowest ever level. Western European countries, anxious to maintain the status quo in the region, did not want to jeopardise their good economic relations with the Arab states of the Gulf by improving their relations with Iran. The arms embargo on Iran by the US and Western European countries and their official position of neutrality, or, in many instances, their military and political assistance of Iraq, occurred in this context.

The second factor was the confrontation between Iran and the US, which had a negative impact on Iran's relations with many Western European countries, most of which followed a policy similar, in one form or another, to that of the United States. As Fred Halliday has argued, 'Given their [the United States and Western European countries] shared interests in the Middle East, and given their membership in NATO under US direction, the European countries could not, even if they were minded to, act in a manner radically at odds with the United States.'[16] The shooting down of the Iranair Airbus by a US warship in July 1988 was a further disaster for US–Iranian relations. This generated a confrontational mood in Iran towards the West, especially the United States, and led to yet further deterioration in relations between Iran and Western European countries.

The third factor influencing Iran's relations with Western Europe was Iran's attempt to counterbalance pressure from the Western European countries by making the most of its relatively good relations with the Soviet Union and Eastern European countries. One notable example was Iran's decision to acquire arms from Eastern European countries following the West's arms embargo during the war. So while Iran's relations with most Eastern European countries improved, the Western bloc was even more reluctant to promote its ties with Iran.

The fourth factor which aggravated Iran's relations with Western European countries was the Salman Rushdie affair. In February 1989 Ayatollah Khomeini called on Muslims to kill the Indian-born British author, Salman Rushdie, charging him with blasphemy in his novel, *The Satanic Verses.* The shaky relations between Iran and most Western European countries now reached their lowest point and in some cases, such as Britain, this led to breaking off diplomatic relations in 1989.

However, it is worth noting that, during the early 1980s, there had been a temporary improvement in relations between Western Europe and Iran as a result of trade and other economic factors. For instance, in May 1983, a trade mission from Britain visited Tehran, where optimism was expressed about the trade potential for British firms. Britain has subsequently come fourth in the list of Iran's trading partners.[17] Meanwhile, West Germany, concerned with maintaining economic ties which had made it Iran's leading trading partner, adopted what practically amounted to a neutral stance on the Iran–Iraq War, thus maintaining normal relations with Iran. The maintenance of economic relations between Iran and Western Europe caused what may now been seen as a temporary improvement in general Iran–Western Europe relations in the 1980s.[18]

A new policy framework for Iran–EU relations since 1989

From the late 1980s onwards, several factors inside and outside Iran created a situation in which Iran's relations with Europe evolved, becoming relatively constructive and benefiting from greater mutual understanding. The end of the Iran–Iraq War in 1988 ushered in a new era in the Persian Gulf. It reduced the fear of the Arab states in the region and of Western European countries that the Islamic Republic of Iran was attempting to export its revolution to the Persian Gulf and was threatening their interests through war with Iraq. At the end of the war Tehran contributed to this new perception by energetically pursuing a policy of normalising its strained relations with its Persian Gulf neighbours.

Iraq's invasion of Kuwait in August 1990 and President Rafsanjani's policy following the Kuwait War were conducive to the process of normalising Iran's relations with the Arab states of the region. 'The strong condemnation of Iraq [by Iran], and the subsequent endorsement of the United Nations resolutions concerning the Kuwait crisis, were noted with satisfaction and gratitude by the Persian Gulf states.'[19] After the invasion of Kuwait the regional Arab states regarded Iraq rather than Iran as a source of danger and instability in the area, and began to perceive Iran as the victim of Iraqi aggression.

Both these phenomena, the end of the Iran–Iraq War and the Kuwait War, brought Iran's relations with individual neighbours in the Gulf, and with the Arab states of the region as a whole, to their highest point in ten years. From the early 1990s onwards, bilateral relations expanded through official talks and the exchange of delegations with various states in the region. Following the Gulf Cooperation Council summit meeting in Qatar in December 1990, the GCC members declared that they would welcome better ties with Iran, and that Iran should be included in any future regional security system.[20] On 25 December 1991 the GCC declared its readiness 'to lend momentum to bilateral relations', as Ramazani expresses it, with Iran in a bid to encourage the pursuit of common interests.[21]

Iran's policy of peaceful coexistence in the region and the process of normalising relations with its Arab neighbours opened a new era in Iran's relations with the Western European countries without jeopardising the relations of those countries with their regional Arab friends. The end of the Iran–Iraq War and the Kuwait War undermined the Western European states' perception of Iran as a source of regional destabilisation. This change of view was a fundamental and necessary step for further improvement in Iran's relations with Western Europe.

The collapse of the Berlin Wall and disintegration of the Soviet Union between 1989 and 1991, bringing an end to the Cold War, made the Iranian leadership consider the role which might be played by a united Europe. However, the end of the Cold War also reduced Iran's ability to manoeuvre profitably between East and West.[22] While in the past Iran viewed the Soviet Union and the Eastern bloc as a counterbalance to the West as a whole, it was now deemed necessary to put more emphasis on the EU as a counterweight to the United States. Iran expected European countries to pursue a more independent policy towards itself and to distance themselves more from the US line; therefore Iranian policy-makers attempted to improve and promote relations with Europe. In other words, since the early 1990s, Iran has tried to open up an independent avenue in its foreign policy towards the European Union, conceiving it as quite separate from the United States and superpower politics.

The impact of economic reconstruction on Iran–EU relations

The death of Ayatollah Khomeini in 1989 resulted in the inauguration of Ali Akbar Hashemi Rafsanjani as President in August 1989. This event marked the beginning of a new era in which the balance of power turned to the relative dominance of pragmatists in the political arena of Iran. The main task of Rafsanjani and his technocrat administration was to restructure Iran's economic system and to alleviate Iran's political isolation.

An important aspect of President Rafsanjani's foreign policy for the Persian Gulf has been the principle that Iran should not be humiliated or intimidated by its neighbours, nor should if make them feel insecure. He added: 'We should all cooperate to build our region. The Persian Gulf area should become like an area around a home, like a common farmland.'[23] Regarding the orientation of Iran's foreign policy, in a message in 1993 to John Major, the British Prime Minister and then President of the European Community, Rafsanjani stated: 'The Islamic Republic of Iran is committed to international law, opposes interference in the internal affairs of other states, recognises the observance of domestic laws as a democratic move and denounces the use of force in international relations.'[24] Furthermore, in a message on the occasion of the Iranian New Year on 21 March 1993, he stated: 'We will introduce our revolution without interfering in the affairs of others and strongly oppose terrorism, forceful impositions and hegemonic ambitions.'[25]

From the beginning of Rafsanjani's presidency, Iran's foreign policy, as Rafsanjani described it, was based on loyalty to the goals of the revolution, Iran's independence and the negation of foreign domination.[26] He explained that in the contemporary world 'we do not always have the power to choose. I believe our principles are obeyed, but in some cases, we may be limited and we may have to forego some of these principles.'[27] In fact, since the end of the Iran–Iraq War, Iran's foreign policy has been guided by coexistence, but not necessarily reconciliation, with other states. The re-establishment of Iran's diplomatic relations, in one form or another, with countries such as Jordan, Tunisia, and Egypt, and the improvement in its relations with Western European countries such as Britain and France, manifest Iran's new approach in its foreign policy. This trend towards improvement in Iran's relations with Western Europe was reflected in Iran's attempt to show goodwill by using its influence in Lebanon to secure the release of Western hostages.

Since the acceptance of the UN Resolution 598, and particularly after the establishment of the Rafsanjani administration, Iran's first priority has been the consolidation of the Islamic revolution at home. During the 1990s, the requirements of the state's Islamic orientation, as well as national survival and economic reconstruction, have created an inward-looking mood in Iran. During a news conference in June 1994, Rafsanjani said: 'We have said that we would elucidate our ideology and those interested could accept it. We will employ all our potential for the development of our country.'[28] In the 1990s this new orientation was complemented by a renewed emphasis on Iran's national interests. The new policy was set in motion during the Kuwait crisis, when Iran cooperated with the United Nations and rejected Iraq's proposal to link the Palestinian question to its withdrawal from Kuwait, a position that reflected Iran's national security interests, as Iran characterised the conflict as one between two evil forces.[29]

The eight-year Iran–Iraq War had inflicted enormous damage upon Iran. In the aftermath of the war, Iran's economic difficulties included widespread unemployment, the growing gap between rich and poor, high inflation and reduced industrial productivity – all of which underlined the significance and necessity of postwar reconstruction. Realising the extent of Iran's problems, Rafsanjani tackled the arduous task of economic and political restructuring. In this context, the means of implementing the major principle of Iran's foreign policy, 'the export of revolution', found a new framework and definition. In the 1990s, exporting the revolution meant presenting Iran to the world as the Islamic example of 'an economically prosperous, and politically progressive' country, and creating an acceptable type of society – that is to say, acceptable both to its inhabitants and to the wider world.[30] President Rafsanjani acknowledged this, stating: 'If the meaning of exporting revolution is to bring a message to people's ears, then I must say that our aims are not yet sufficiently clear in the minds of the people of the world.'[31] Adhering to the notion of exporting the revolution, Rafsanjani believes that it has been misunderstood throughout the world.

> We wanted to export our revolution by invading other countries, through war and military action. If under the present [postwar] conditions we manage to create an acceptable type of society and set up a suitable model of development, progress, evolution, and

correct Islamic morals for the world, then we will achieve what the world has feared; that is, the export of the Islamic revolution.[32]

In a recent speech to a group of ulama, Rafsanjani, addressing Iran's achievements in the postwar reconstruction era, said: 'By demonstrating its independence to the world, and as a dignified model, Iran can be effective in introducing Islam.'[33] It can be concluded that, from Rafsanjani's point of view, the export of revolution together with the presentation and the spread of Islam throughout the world should be achieved through the creation of a model society.[34]

The imperatives of Iran's postwar economic and political reconstruction, and changes in styles and methods for the export of the revolution, opened up a new era in Iran's relations with the international community. Despite its deep ideological mistrust of current international organisations, the requirements of international life have led Iran to maintain its ties with them and even participate actively in their meetings.[35] In the 1980s, the idealists assumed that rejection of international organisations expressed through the absence of Iranian delegations would advertise Iran's revolutionary message and enable the export of revolution to other nations, particularly in the Third World. In contrast to the 1980s, the pragmatists in the 1990s chose another way to deliver Iran's revolutionary message. The pragmatists have concluded that, in order to help reform international organisations which are part of the 'unjust international order' and dominated by 'arrogant powers', and to export the revolution, it is vital to know how to work within the present international system.[36] Thus, the requirements of Iran's economic and political reconstruction, and the availability of international organisations such as the United Nations as international arenas in which Iran can spread its message, led the Islamic Republic to be represented actively in these organisations.

While the export of revolution in the first decade following 1979 took the form of the dissemination of the revolutionary message and action in theatres of conflict such as the Gulf region, the Lebanon, and during the Iran–Iraq War, in the second decade Iran has attempted to implement the export of revolution by presenting itself as an Islamic example of an economically prosperous and politically progressive country. While the imperatives of the security of the Islamic Republic under turbulent international circumstances, especially during the Iran–Iraq War in the 1980s, were the main characteristics of Iran's export of revolution, the requirements for the political and economic reconstruction of postwar Iran in a peaceful environment are the main features of the export of revolution in the 1990s.

The imperatives of Iran's postwar economic and political reconstruction were laid out in Iran's First Five-Year Economic and Political Plan prepared by the Rafsanjani administration in 1989. In essence it represented the government's manifesto for resuscitating the national economy. It covered the period from 1989 to 1993, and provided an important framework within which the government could embark on a programme of economic reform. The strategy for reform included policy initiatives such as: privatisation of a large number of industries and mines, the revival of the Tehran stock exchange, the abolition of the multiple exchange rate mechanism and its replacement by a single free market floating rate, the founding of a number of free trade zones, encouragement of direct foreign investment, and easing of foreign investment regulations.[37] Skilled Iranians residing abroad have been encouraged to return to their country in order to develop export industries with a high-tech content.

In sum, the objective of these measures and of the First Five-Year Plan generally was to create appropriate conditions to stabilise and normalise the war economy in the hope of leading Iran towards a path of growth.[38] The First Five-Year Plan abolished limits on foreign investment and ownership, smoothed the way for the privatisation of industry, and allowed the government to secure foreign credits. Foreign investors could now own up to 100 per cent of a business and repatriate profits without hindrance.[39] In joint ventures they were allowed to take a share of up to 49 per cent – 'higher than the 35 per cent under the Shah'.[40] The establishment of free trade zones in Iran was another step in strengthening Iran's trade links with foreign countries and attracting more foreign investment. In the free trade zones set up, each with separate social and legal codes, the government offered terms to foreign companies that were not otherwise available. 'Some of the terms offered are 15-year tax breaks, no currency restrictions and 100 per cent ownership of any exploration finds.'[41] The Second Five-Year Plan which began in March 1995 provided for continued economic reform.

Improvement in Iran's relations with the EU countries

In the light of these factors, Iran–EU relations in the 1990s have improved. This improvement can be seen in two different areas. These areas are: first, the EU policy of 'critical dialogue' with Iran, rather than simply following the US policy of sanctions and the isolation of the Iranian government; and second, the improvement of Iran's economic ties with most EU countries. Recent American sanctions against Iran sought to decrease the resources available to Iran and increase the isolation of the Iranian government. The Clinton administration, accusing Iran of building up nuclear weapons capabilities and of supporting terrorism, declared a trade embargo on Iran in April 1995 and demanded that its European allies do likewise. But the Europeans declined to follow suit and instead pursued the policy of 'critical dialogue' with Iran and maintained their relations. While Britain was under pressure from the US to join the American embargo, a British Foreign Office spokesman said that London did not view total sanctions as being applicable in the case of Iran.[42] Criticising Washington in an interview, the German Economic Minister Guenter Rexrodt said: 'We do not believe that a trade embargo is the appropriate instrument for influencing opinion in Iran and bringing about changes there that are in our interests.'[43] Grasping the opportunity to replace American firms with French companies such as Total in oil projects in Iran, France criticised the damaging US policy of sanctions and boycott and boosted its own economic relations with Iran. Overall, economic competitors of the US in Europe did not respond positively to its demands and many even attempted to take the opportunity to fill America's place in trade with and investment in Iran.

The European refusal to follow American policy, and consequent US failure to execute comprehensive and all-embracing sanctions against Iran, led the US Congress to pass a bill by which a 'secondary boycott' would be imposed on those European companies investing $40 million or more every year to help develop oil and gas resources in Iran. Clinton's signature on 5 August 1996 changed the bill into an act. Accordingly, the US 'would penalise non-US companies trading with Iran by denying them loans and prohibit their imports to the US and exclude them from US government contracts'.[44]

The bill provoked strong protests from the European Union and individual governments in Europe. They argued that such a 'secondary boycott' against companies doing business with Iran violated international law. For example, President Jacques Chirac's spokeswoman, Catherine Colonna, said: 'The bill contains unacceptable measures of extra-territorial jurisdiction which violates international law.'[45] The German Foreign Minister Klaus Kinkel announced that the US sanctions law was not acceptable. He stated: 'We will not be dictated to about whom we do business with. If the US continues [on this course], we will have to consider appropriate steps in Europe.'[46] On another occasion Kinkel elaborated that on the issue of how to treat Iran – with or without talks – the Germans and the Americans have different opinions.[47] Fearing a full blown transatlantic row, the British government attempted in vain to dissuade the US government from passing the bill. Meanwhile, a Foreign and Commonwealth Office spokesman said: 'We cannot accept US pressure on its allies to impose sanctions under the threat of mandatory penalties on our companies carrying out trade with these countries in the oil and gas sectors.'[48] Statements from other EU member countries criticised the US bill.[49] A statement issued by Ireland on behalf of the EU said: 'The Union reaffirms its determination to act in the appropriate international fora, including the World Trade Organisation, in defence of . . . the interests of member state companies if these are affected by the legislation.'[50]

The European policy of 'critical dialogue' towards Iran generally, and European Union refusal to follow America's treatment of Iran in particular, resulted in Iranian officials making statements which raised the EU's hopes on the Salman Rushdie issue. On the eve of one of the regular EU–Iran meetings held in June 1995 in Paris, the Iranian Foreign Minister Ali Akbar Velayati announced: 'Our government is not going to dispatch anybody, any commandos, to kill anybody in Europe.' He added: 'It is our determination to expand our relations with Europe.'[51] While the Iranian Parliamentary Speaker, Ali Akbar Nateq Nouri, stated that the edict was an 'irrevocable edict', he added: 'We as the government of the Islamic Republic of Iran will not send commandos to kill Salman Rushdie.'[52] The Vice-Chairman of Iran's Parliamentary Foreign Affairs Committee and a member of the National Security Council, Mohammad Javad Larijani, said: 'There is a better understanding from both sides of the issue involved. The world is a better place if we try to act a little bit more rationally.' He then said: 'Salman Rushdie should feel safe about any Iranian government involvement in any plot to harm him in any way.'[53] During his visit to London in October 1995 Larijani drew a clear distinction between the edict on Salman Rushdie as an Islamic ruling and the Iranian government's respect for international law.[54] This trend of dialogue between Iran and the European Union, in which Iran assured the EU of the safety of Rushdie from attack backed by the Iranian government, and the EU's relative downplaying of the divisive potential of the Rushdie issue also continued under the Spanish and then the Italian presidency of the European Union. The EU's Italian president, in a statement in February 1996, rejected calls for firmer action against Iran, preferring instead to continue its previous policy of 'critical dialogue' towards Iran.[55] While this policy angered Salman Rushdie who attacked the West for not doing enough to resolve the case,[56] it was welcomed by the Iranian daily, the *Tehran Times*, which suggested that 'the EU should be given a pat on the back for not submitting to pressures from circles determined to disturb Iran–Europe relations.'[57] Although Iran has maintained the Fatwa, the Iranian government attempted to explain that the edict is a purely religious matter unrelated to itself, and indeed has sought to depoliticise the Fatwa. Recent remarks by Iranian officials and the constructive attitude of the EU have created an atmosphere which is leading to further improvement in Iran's relations with the EU.

On the whole, political relations between Europe and Iran have improved in the past few years, a trend that seems to be continuing. Business ties are growing rapidly, and offer some grounds for further optimism in the political sphere as well. In the wake of Iran's postwar reconstruction, and in the light of the new economic reform measures introduced by President Rafsanjani in the 1990s, European states are keener than in the past to improve their relations with Iran. While UN sanctions against Iraq have forced British companies to look for new business opportunities elsewhere, and even though the British Department of Trade's Export Credits Guarantee section, which insures exporters against non-payment, offered only short-term cover for Iran in 1991, British exports to Iran in January–April 1991 were 90 per cent higher than in the same period in 1990.[58] In 1995, Britain exported £332 million worth of goods to Iran, compared with £289 million the year before.[59] The spokesman for the Committee for Middle East Trade (COMET), a Department of Trade - sponsored body which encourages trade with the region, stated: 'A joint chamber of commerce would certainly be a great advantage to British businessmen, and would help boost the already encouraging trade figures.'[60] As British businessmen are conscious of the need to avoid being overtaken by Germany and Japan in the race to secure Iranian contracts and export deals, they have tried to re-establish the Iranian–British Chamber of Commerce which had ceased functioning in the aftermath of Iran's revolution. This desire has been corroborated by some British businessmen who work as regional advisors in COMET and also by Roger Barber, Director of Trade Relations of COMET.[61] However, on the Iranian side there has not been a serious effort to set up the Iranian–British Chamber of Commerce. It seems that the negative response from the Iranians is due to the fact that they do not regard London–Tehran political relations as desirable as relations with certain other European countries such as Germany. Still, Ali Naqi Khamushi, head of the Iranian Chamber of Commerce, said that 'the Iranian–British Chamber would be reopened as soon as the Iranian Foreign Ministry gave its approval.'[62] Thus it can be argued that Iran is not willing at the moment to give more opportunities to Britain in the area of trade and commerce than are already present and that it tries to use better trade relations with Britain as a political lever.

The absence of the British–Iranian Chamber of Commerce notwithstanding, one of the joint venture projects between Iran's Mines and Metals Ministry and the Dubai-based International Development Corporation was the construction of a £1.4bn aluminium smelter at Bandar Abbas, for which Britain's Lloyds Bank acted as financial adviser.[63] Iran's efforts to broaden and consolidate its international trading links were evident at the Tehran Trade Fair in October 1992, which was attended by 54 countries and 200 foreign companies. Germany, Japan and Italy – Iran's three leading trade partners – as well as Britain, had the highest profiles at the fair. While Iran bought goods and services valued at $920m from Britain in 1991 and more than 100 British companies attended the Tehran Trade Fair in 1992, an Iranian foreign ministry official, Gholamreza Ansari, said that prospects for future cooperation are improving mainly in the fields of industry and technology transfer.[64]

At the 21st Tehran International Trade Fair of October 1995 with 53 participating countries, British companies featured, including Shell International, British Airways, Lloyds Bank, and Leyland Trucks, spread across 37 stands. According to the director of the British organisers, Andrew Maclean, Britain expected to be the second largest foreign group at the fair.[65] Furthermore, Iran's non-oil exports to Britain rose by 27 per cent in the first eight months of 1995. The trade figures also indicate some signs of improvement in UK exports to Iran, which rose overall between January and August to £228m against £218m in 1994.[66] At the 22nd Tehran International Fair of October 1996, some 1500 foreign companies from 54 countries took part. The number of companies from Germany, France, Italy and England had increased by 30 per cent in comparison with the previous year.[67]

A recent major improvement in British–Iranian relations was an agreement on settling the pre-revolution debt. The British government's Export Credit Guarantee Department (ECGD) confirmed that an agreement in principle had been made to settle Iran's pre-revolution debt, and talks on more recent debts could start in the near future. Clearing all outstanding amounts between the two countries might pave the way for a resumption of medium-term credit cover.[68]

France has also boosted its relations with Iran through investment and involvement in infrastructure projects in Iran. A French company, EPTM, has started to rebuild the Kharg oil export terminal at a cost of $220m. Another leading French firm, Technip, is managing the rehabilitation and completion of the war-damaged Bandar-i Khomeini petrochemical complex. Technip is also building a petrochemical complex at Tabriz and a refinery at Arak.[69] In July 1995 the French firm Total signed a $600m deal with Iran to develop the two offshore Sirri oil and gas fields, a contract which had earlier been awarded to the US firm, Conoco. Recently French Transport Minister Bernard Pons travelled to Tehran, seeking primarily to promote exports of French technology and goods. As an outcome of this visit, cooperation in building airport and rail facilities was boosted as well as a sharing of land and sea facilities, including Iran's southern ports for the transit of French goods to Central Asia.[70] Iran has signed an economic protocol with France in order to export goods through France to other European countries.[71]

Germany, which has been a leading trade partner of Iran for a long time, exported 26 bn marks worth of goods to Iran during the First Five-Year development plan which started in 1989.[72] Germany's oil imports from Iran during the first seven months of 1995 amounted to 1.152 million tonnes. This showed an increase of five per cent compared to the same period in 1994.[73] Contributing 14.4 per cent of Iran's imports in 1994, Germany ranked first among the leading suppliers of goods, before Japan, Italy, and the UK.[74] Trade between Norway and Iran has doubled in 1995. While in 1994 Norway bought 46.3 million Norwegian

Kroner worth of goods from Iran, in 1995, the value went up to 96.2 million.[75] Italy's imports of Iranian oil during the first nine months of 1995 amounted to 7.33 million tonnes, an increase of four and a half times compared with the same period in the previous year. This made Iran the third largest exporter of crude oil to Italy, after Libya and Saudi Arabia.[76] Also Italy provided Iran with $561m loans for the development of Iran's steel industry. Four Italian banks, along with banks from Germany, Japan, the Netherlands, France and Britain, funded the loan.[77] The most recent figures, for 1994, show EU countries exporting just over £3bn worth of goods to Iran and importing more than £3.8bn worth.[78]

Six months after the introduction of US sanctions on Iran in early 1995, more than 120 foreign firms, including European businesses, were in Tehran to learn about Iran's various projects to develop the oil and gas fields. The projects on offer had a combined value of $7bn. Iranian oil minister Gholamreza Aghazadeh, addressing participating representatives of foreign companies including Shell, Total, Italy's Agip SPA, and Finland's Neste Oy, assured the listeners that those bids which were accepted would be guaranteed against any political or economic risk.[79]

Conclusion

Iran's determination to develop political and economic relations with the EU – particularly in order to counterbalance US policy towards Tehran – has created substantial room for the Rafsanjani administration to manoeuvre and has also provided more flexibility in its foreign policy towards the EU. In response to criticism that his administration had gone too far in pursuit of closer relations with Europe, Rafsanjani said: 'Our relations with Europe are still not enough and we should have better relations with Europe. In comparison with the United States, Europe is better, but still our relations with Europeans leave much to be desired.'[80] Due to the EU policy of engaging Iran in 'critical dialogue', Tehran was well-disposed towards the EU's active role in the Middle East and appreciated the EU's, and particularly France's, willingness to act independently of the US in Middle Eastern affairs.[81] The policy of 'critical dialogue' has resulted in a situation where Iran has announced that there would be no threat to Salman Rushdie from its government. Consequently, the Rushdie affair, which has been for some time the major obstacle to better relations between Iran and the EU, is no longer in the forefront. Iran's role in negotiating a ceasefire between Israel and the Lebanese Hezbollah guerrillas in April 1996, in the exchange of prisoners and bodies between Israel and Hezbollah brokered in cooperation with Germany, can be regarded – to borrow from the French Foreign Ministry spokesman Yves Doutriauxit – as the recent positive result of the EU's critical dialogue with Tehran.[82]

However, several obstacles to better Iran–EU relations remain. The unresolved Rushdie affair, Iran's opposition to the Middle East peace process, and the Iran–US confrontation are the major obstacles to further improvement in Iran's relations with the EU. The Rushdie affair, which may resurface at any time, could aggravate Iran–EU relations. Iran's opposition to the peace process between Israel and the Arab states has left Iran almost alone in the opposition camp. Although President Rafsanjani in his statement on 29 November 1996 said that Iran was 'ready to cooperate with peace-loving governments and international organisations in establishing real peace in Palestine', he added: 'the present peace is not a real peace, but is a compromise and is far from justice.'[83] In this context, the United States and its European allies are currently attempting to bring Syria into the process. This has forced Europe to put pressure on Iran to revoke its opposition, which subsequently has left Iran to choose between better relations with Europe or maintaining its opposition to the peace process. The long-standing Iran–US confrontation will inevitably have an important impact on Iranian–European relations. Yet, if the current EU policy of maintaining a dialogue with Iran is not impaired by the hostile attitude of Washington towards Tehran, then it is possible to be optimistic about future relations between Iran and the European Union countries.

In May 1997, after the landslide victory of President Khatami over the traditionalist candidacy of the Speaker of the Majlis, Nateq Nouri, the liberal President continued the same policy even more vigorously to improve relations with the European Union in a manner similar to his predecessor. By mid-1998 both France and Italy had established full diplomatic relations, and the British government, by getting assurance from the Iranian President that no assassination squad would be sent to attack Salman Rushdie, was in the course of establishing full diplomatic relations. Also the German government, in order to secure a profitable contract, has compromised on the Myconos affair, thus improving its relationship with Iran. All the same, Iran needs to improve its image further in order to be more active on the international scene.

NOTES

1 This is the terminology of Ayatollah Khomeini.
2 R.K. Ramazani, 'Iran's export of the revolution: politics, ends, and means' in John L. Esposito (ed.), *The Iranian Revolution: Its Global Impact* (Miami, Fla.: International University Press, 1990), p. 44.
3 Mehdi Bazargan, *Enghelab-e Iran dar dou harkat* [The Iranian revolution in two phases], (Tehran: Chap-e Cevom, 1983), pp. 110–11, quoted in R.K. Ramazani, 'Iran's foreign policy: contending orientations', *The Middle East Journal,* 43:2 (Spring 1989), p. 205.
4 Ramazani, 'Iran's export of the revolution', p. 44.
5 Anoushiravan Ehteshami, *After Khomeini: The Iranian Second Republic* (London: Routledge, 1995), p. 144.
6 Foreign Broadcast Information Service (FBIS), *Daily Reports, Middle East and North Africa* (MEA), 10 December 1979, p. 29.
7 *Dar jostojooy-e rah az kalam-e Imam: enghelab-e Islami; byanat va ealamyahay-e Imam Khomeini 1962-1982* [In search of the path from Imam's statements: Islamic Revolution; Imam's statements and speeches 1962–1982] (Tehran: Institute of Amir Kabir Publications), vol. 10, pp. 250–1.
8 Ibid., p. 251.
9 Imam Khomeini's message on the occasion of the new year, 1980, *Sahifay-e- Noor* [Collection of Imam Khomeini's guidelines] (Tehran: Sazman-e Madarek-e Farhangi Enghelab-e Islami, 1982), vol. 12, p. 19.
10 For more information on Ayatollah Khomeini's view on the export of revolution, see, *Sahifay-e Noor*, vol. 3.
11 See, *A'iin-e enghelab-e Islami; gozidayi az andishaha va a'ra-e Imam Khomeini* [Blueprint of the Islamic Revolution; selection of Imam Khomeini's thoughts and views], pp. 415–19.
12 Shireen T. Hunter, *Iran and the World: Continuity in a Revolutionary Decade* (Bloomington & Indianapolis: Indiana University Press, 1990), p. 43.
13 Adam Tarock, 'Iran's foreign policy since the Gulf War', *Australian Journal of International Affairs,* 48:2 (November 1994), p. 267.
14 For more details on Iran's relations with Western European countries in the pre-revolutionary period and during the 1980s, see Anthony Parsons, 'Iran and Western Europe', *The Middle East Journal,* 43:2 (Spring 1989), pp. 218–29.
15 Eric Hooglund, 'Iranian populism and political change in the Gulf', *Middle East Report* (January–February 1992), p. 20.
16 Fred Halliday, 'An elusive normalisation: Western Europe and the Iranian revolution', *The Middle East Journal,* 48:2 (Spring 1994), p. 312.
17 Hunter, *Iran and the world,* p. 146.
18 On trade issue between Iran and Western European countries, see Anoushiravan Ehteshami, 'Iran and the European Community' in Anoushiravan Ehteshami

and Manshour Varasteh (eds.), *Iran and the International Community*, (London and New York: Routledge, 1991), pp. 62–6.

19 Tarock, 'Iran's foreign policy since the Gulf War', p. 268.

20 Ibid., p. 269.

21 R.K. Ramazani, 'Iran's foreign policy: both North and South', *The Middle East Journal*, 46:3 (Summer 1992), pp. 401–2.

22 Fred Halliday, 'Introduction' in Ehteshami and Varasteh (eds.), *Iran and the International Community*, p. 4.

23 FBIS, *Near East & South Asia* (*NES*), 12 March 1991, p. 43.

24 'Foreign policy of the Islamic Republic of Iran: issues and stances', *The Iranian Journal of International Affairs*, 7:364 (Fall/Winter 1993/4), p. 782.

25 Ibid.

26 FBIS, *NES*, 4 October 1988.

27 FBIS, *South Asia* (*SA*), 17 April 1987.

28 *Middle East Insight*, 10:4/5 (May–August 1994), p. 53.

29 Hooshang Amirahmadi, 'The Islamic Republic and the question of Palestine', *Middle East Insight*, 10:4/5 (May–August 1994), p. 52.

30 Ramazani, 'Iran's export of the revolution', p. 57.

31 FBIS, *NES*, 14 February 1989.

32 Ibid., 17 October 1988 and 14 October 1988.

33 'Ulema before a serious test: President', *IRNA News Agency*, 31 December 1996.

34 For the issue of a model society and Iran's view of same, see Farhang Rajaee, 'Iranian ideology and worldview: the cultural export of revolution' in John L. Esposito (ed.), *The Iranian Revolution: Its Global Impact*, (Miami, Fla.: Florida International University Press, 1990), pp. 71–3.

35 Hunter, p. 173.

36 Ibid., pp. 170–1.

37 For a broad analysis of the issues relating to Iran's economic liberalisation strategy under Rafsanjani, see Massoud Karshenas and M. Hashem Pesaran, 'Economic reform and the reconstruction of the Iranian economy', *The Middle East Journal*, 49:1 (Winter 1995), pp. 89–111; also L. Haddad, 'Open door policy and the industrialisation of Iran', *Journal of contemporary Asia*, 24:1 (1994), pp. 81–94.

38 For more information on these issues, see Anoushiravan Ehteshami, *The Politics of Economic Restructuring in Post-Khomeini Iran,* CMEIS Occasional Paper, no. 50 (Durham: University of Durham, July 1995), pp. 10–13; also Hooshang Amirahmadi, 'Iranian economic reconstruction plan and prospects for its success' in Hooshang Amirahmadi and Nader Entessar (eds.), *Reconstruction and Regional Diplomacy in the Persian Gulf* (London and New York: Routledge, 1992), pp. 113–35.

39 Dilip Hiro, 'The Iranian Connection', *The Middle East*, no. 207 (January 1992), p. 21.

40 'Come in, the door is open', *The Middle East*, no. 213 (July 1992), p. 34.

41 'Just doing business', *The Middle East*, no. 241 (January 1995), p. 29.

42 'Britain opposed to Clinton ban against Iran', *IRNA News Agency*, 2 May 1995.

43 *Reuter News Service,* 2 May 1995.

44 Ian Black, 'Britain tries to halt US sanctions bill', *The Guardian*, quoted in *Reuter News Service*, 19 February 1996.

45 'France concerned about US legislation on Iran', *Reuter News Service,* 30 January 1996.
46 'Germany's Kinkel warns US about Iran sanctions law', *Market News Service,* quoted in *Reuter News Service,* 15 August 1996.
47 'Germany defends Europe's policy on Iran', *Reuter News Service,* 6 August 1996.
48 'Foreign and Commonwealth Office – US sanctions legislation against Iran/Libya', *UK Government Press Releases,* quoted in *Reuter News Service,* 5 August 1996.
49 The UK Department of Trade and Industry in its statement said: 'It is for the UK and the EU to decide with whom they will trade.' (Martin Walker, Simon Beavis and Stephen Bates, 'Fury at US law to curb terror', *The Guardian,* quoted in *Reuter News Service,* 6 August 1996). Italian Foreign Minister Lamberto Dini in an interview said: 'This is a bad law that goes against trade regulation. It is discriminatory and does not respect the international principles regarding relations between countries.' See 'Italy urges calm despite "bad" US sanctions law', *Reuter News service,* 6 August 1996.
50 'EU concerned about US moves against Iran, Libya', *Reuter News Service,* 21 August 1996.
51 'Iran set to drop Rushdie death threat', *Reuter News Service,* 5 June 1995.
52 'Rushdie's death would end problem', *Reuter News Service* 1 June 1995.
53 'Iran set to drop Rushdie death threat', *Reuter News Service,* 5 June 1995
54 A well-known Iranian cleric, Mohammad Javad Hojati Kermani, said in his column in an Iranian newspaper: 'Imam Khomeini never intended nor ordered the government of the Islamic Republic to carry out the edict.' Morteza Sarmadi, Iran's foreign spokesman, was quoted as saying that Iran could not lift the Fatwa, but gave 'its commitment to respect international regulations'. From 'Seven years on', *The Times,* quoted in *Reuter News Service,* 14 February 1996.
55 'Seven years on', *The Times,* quoted in *Reuter News Service,* 14 February 1996.
56 David Ljunggern, 'UK author Rushdie attacks West over death threat', *Reuter News service,* 14 February 1996.
57 'Newspaper says Rushdie issue should not hinder closer ties between Iran and EU', *IRNA News Agency,* 14 February 1996.
58 Ibid.
59 Walker, Beavis and Bates, 'Fury at US law to curb terror', *Reuter News Service,* 6 August 1996.
60 'Trade ties', *The Middle East,* no. 202 (August 1991), p. 37.
61 Based on the author's meetings and interviews in COMET, London, April 1996.
62 'Trade ties', p. 37.
63 Scheherazade Daneshku, 'Grappling with a sluggish economy', *The Middle East,* no. 198 (April 1991), p. 35.
64 Peter Feuilherade, 'Everybody's welcome, up to a point', *The Middle East,* no. 206 (December 1991), pp. 36–7.
65 'Britain boosts presence at Tehran Trade Fair', *IRNA News Agency,* 27 September 1995.
66 'Iran's non-oil export to UK up 27 per cent', *IRNA News Agency,* 4 October 1995.
67 *Iran Daily,* 1 and 2 October 1996.
68 'Iran and Britain reach agreement on settling pre-revolution debt', *Reuter News service,* 16 September 1995.

69 Chris Kutschera, 'Doing it our way', *The Middle East*, no. 203 (September 1991), p. 32.
70 'Iran, France to cooperate in airport, rail project', *Reuter News Service*, 27 February 1996.
71 *Kayhan Havai*, 13 November 1996.
72 'Germany celebrates national day at Tehran trade fair', *IRNA News Agency*, 4 October 1995.
73 'Germany's oil imports from Iran up by 5 per cent in 1995', *IRNA News Agency*, 19 September 1995.
74 *Economist Intelligence Unit*, 27 February 1996.
75 'Norway doubles trade with Iran', *Reuter News Service*, 9 February 1996.
76 'Export of crude oil to Italy up in 1995', *Reuter News Service*, 6 January 1996.
77 *Kayhan Havai*, 13 November 1996.
78 Walker, Beavis and Bates, 'Fury at US law to curb terror'.
79 'Iran assures oil investors of stability, security', *IRNA News Agency*, quoted in *Reuter News Service*, 9 November 1995.
80 *Iran Daily*, 5 November 1996.
81 See Ali Akbar Velayati's interview, *Iran Daily*, 24 October 1996.
82 Paul Taylor, 'France warns US against Iran trade sanctions', *Reuter News Service*, 5 August 1996.
83 The statement issued by President Rafsanjani on the International Day of Solidarity with the Palestinian People. See *Iran Daily*, 30 November 1996.

5

Patterns of Continuity in Iran's Foreign Policy

Lubna Abid Ali

This chapter argues that the foreign policy of the Islamic Republic of Iran is clearly moving towards moderation and pragmatism. The Islamic regime is becoming increasingly aware of the need to harmonise the ideological content of statements designed for the domestic legitimation of its actions with the pragmatic goal of preserving the Iranian state in a rapidly changing global system.

Ali discusses how the Islamic regime is gradually adopting a more tolerant policy towards the international community, but argues that despite the modulation, there are clear signs of continuity in its foreign policy.

The background

The foreign policy objectives of the Islamic Republic of Iran are determined by the perceived threats from its neighbours, its geopolitical situation, domestic socio-political conditions and interrelated regional and international developments.[1]

The underlying factors may be listed as follows: (1) the challenge to avoid a gulf between ideology and pragmatism; (2) regional instability due to the collapse of the bipolar world order as well as the outbreak of the Second Gulf War that ended in the massive militarisation of the Gulf region to the virtual exclusion of the predominant regional actor, Iran; (3) concern with economic reconstruction and development related the aftermath of war and the massive earthquake of June 1990;[2] (4) the breakup of the Soviet Union and the emergence of independent states lying to the north-west of Iran; (5) the power struggle and the civil strife in areas of Afghanistan and Tajikistan with which Iran has cultural, ethnic, linguistic and historical affinity; (6) the stringent sanctions imposed on

Iran by the United States in the aftermath of the 1979 Islamic Revolution, which gradually resulted in the international isolation of Iran.

It is the aim of the Islamic regime to re-enter the international community and in this context, cooperation with other states is the key new component of Iranian foreign policy.[3]

There are four major underlying currents basic to Iran's approach to foreign policy. First, the role of Islamic ideology and particularly Khomeini's approach to the concept of *velayat-i-faqih* (the rule of the jurist).[4] The ideological content of Iran's foreign policy is perceived as a threat by the United States and the conservative regimes in the Gulf littoral. This view is the result of a narrow interpretation of Islam by certain scholars and intellectuals in the West. Conversely, it has been argued that the nature of the Islamic ideology emanating from the Islamic Republic of Iran is not fundamentalist, but has its roots in 'reformist Islam'.

Second, the geographical location of Iran indicates, however, that there cannot be any effective security arrangement in the Persian Gulf region without the active participation of Iran. Thus US policy to isolate Iran internationally is bound to fail.[5]

Third, Iran's foreign policy tends to concentrate on regional issues, particularly in relation to those newly independent countries on the southern border of Russia and the Caucasus regions. It attempts to link national interests with the economic restructuring of the Iranian state. Shireen Hunter has remarked on the tendency to accord primacy to national interest even over Islamic ideology.[6] Similarly, Fuller states: 'Basically, national interest, and *raison d'être*, prevailed in determining relations with other states, regardless of their ties with the US.'[7]

Finally, the hallmark of this foreign policy is cooperation. This is not a monolithic ideology, but rather a mixed bag. It has strands of Islamic universalism, Shia particularism, Third Worldism, Persian culturalism and Iranian nationalism. In the new world order, the goals and objectives of the states have also changed.[8] The concept of vital interests has been eroded by a new culture of interdependence, and economic cooperation through bilateral as well as multilateral transactions. In his August 1993 address to the Majlis, President Rafsanjani stated: 'We think and we believe that Islam can spread further and gain more influence in a calm and secure atmosphere rather than in an atmosphere filled with tension and adventurism.'[9] This policy is based on the two important instruments of conflict resolution, compromise and concession. Thus the central argument is that Iran's incorporation into the regional and international political systems would benefit both the US and the Persian Gulf region. Moreover, a stable Iran would be a counterweight to the other extremist groups within Islamic countries. Thus Iran's relations with Russia and the US should be viewed in this context.

Current Islamic ideology in Iran has its roots in reformist Islam and can be traced to the works of Sayyid Jamal al-Din Assadabadi, Mohammad Abduh Rahman al-Kawabi, Allameh Eqbal, Ayatollah Motahari, Ayatollah Mahmoud Taleghani and Dr Ali Shariati. The stress is on accommodation and adaptability, cooperation and tolerance. An essential corollary is the condemnation of *taqlid* (imitation) while practising *ijtehad* (process of reasoning) with the participation of the people. Allameh Mohammad Hussein Tabatabai thus emphasised that the task of the *fuqaha* (jurists) is more demanding than ever. Noorbakhsh has also stated that they must take the Shariah as a base only, heavily concentrating on interpretations which deal with the complicated issues at 'the heart of man and society'.[10]

An underlying rationality in the interpretation of Islamic fundamentals distinguishes reformist Islam from the orthodox school.[11] It thrives on the positive role of religion and religious institutions in the life of people in the Islamic community. Noorbakhsh has further explained this idea: 'Reformist Islam and its ideals, specifically democracy and democratisation, have been ignored to the point that Muslims are assumed to be unable to participate in rational discourse and Islam is deemed to play the role of a traditional faith which opposes modernity.'[12] Accordingly the theorists of modernisation who base their arguments on a dichtomous approach, i.e. traditional versus modern structures, argue against the emergence of democratic institutions in Muslim countries.[13]

Another misconception of Islamic ideology stems from the argument that Islam promotes strong governments and a weak civil society.[14] Iran stands out as an example where an Islamic movement developed in civil society to challenge the authority of the state. This view has the support of several scholars.[15] For instance, according to Hamid Dabbashi, reformist Islam in Iran challenged the dictatorship of the Shah and demanded the freedom to establish a viable political system.[16] President Rafsanjani's support for democracy is manifested through the establishment of a parliament (Majlis) consisting of 270 representatives. Since 1980, the

Islamic Republic has held elections after every four years. By observing the principles of *shura* (consultation) and *ijma* (consensus) drawn from the Quran and the Sunnah, the system to some extent comes close to Robert Dahl's definition of democracy as a unique process of making collective and binding decisions.[17]

The second major current underlying Iran's foreign policy is the geographical location and the geopolitical significance of Iran. It is the predominant power in the Gulf region, possessing a 750 mile shoreline. With a population of 60 million people, twice that of all the other Gulf states combined, it enjoys pre-eminence in the region. Iran's strategic location connects land-locked Central Asia and the Caucasus in the north to the Gulf in the south. Iran is thus the central link between the Caspian Sea and the Persian Gulf. To highlight the strategic significance of the Gulf, since 1987 there have been a series of international conferences on the region held by the Institute of International and Political Studies (IIPS) in Tehran. The foreign policy objective of Iran is to promote regional cooperation among the littoral states of the Gulf. The aftermath of the Second Gulf War has led to a tremendous increase in the physical presence of extra-regional military forces in the area. Iran, having a longer coastline than any other littoral state, has genuine concerns about security in the Gulf region.

Iran's efforts to rebuild its war-torn military capabilities seem modest when compared to the quality and quantity of armaments acquired by the neighbouring states. According to the estimates of James A. Bill, Iran must survive alongside the Gulf Cooperation Council member states with 624 aircraft including such advanced warplanes as F-15s and Mirage 2000s, as well as strike and interceptor Tornadoes. Even after Desert Storm Iraq still has 261 tactical aircraft.[18]

Moreover, Iran's defence spending was far less than that of either Saudi Arabia and Iraq. For instance, Saudi Arabia bought $30.4 bn worth of US weapons between 1990 and 1993. This regional militarisation is particularly threatening since it has been concurrent with the conclusion of a number of military and security pacts which explicitly exclude Iran.[19]

During the Kuwait crisis Iran maintained neutrality. However, the disintegration of Iraq is viewed in Iran as an alarming scenario. But in the context of bilateral relations three factors seem to favour Iran: (1) a change of regime within Iraq could prove a catalyst in bringing the two states closer to each other, as both have experienced the impact of economic sanctions and international isolationism; (2) the presence of Shia clergy in Iraq, in Najaf particularly, sharing a close affinity of outlook with their counterparts in Iran; (3) the Kurdish population in Iran could be used as a destabilising factor in Iraq – historically the Kurdish card has been successfully used by Iran to create instability inside Iraq for the promotion of its national iterest.

Iran's relations with Qatar and Bahrain are improving steadily and commercial activity has increased since the Gulf crisis. Qatar views Saudi intentions, rather than those of Iran, with apprehension. Its desire to promote regional cooperation is visible through a $40m donation of fire-fighting equipment to Kuwait. Iran has a margin of manoeuvrability to exploit favourable opportunities within the framework of such organisations as OPEC, OIC and NAM. It is after all the second largest producer of oil in OPEC, and owns 15 per cent of the world's natural gas reserves. Strategically, it holds a pivotal position for the transshipment of oil, energy, goods and technology from Asia to Europe and the Far East.

Iran's relations with the Arab countries and her links with Hamas and Hezbollah in Lebanon are quoted to identify the Islamic Republic's support of fundamentalist movements in the Muslim world. However, it was pragmatic considerations, regional imperatives and superpower relations in the context of a bipolar world order that brought the policies of Iran and Syria closer together. But with the disintegration of the Soviet Union, the emergence of the US as the single predominant power and the step-by-step implementation of the Middle East peace process, the regional as well as international milieu has changed. The conclusion of a Syrian–Israeli peace agreement may further dilute the closeness of relations between the two countries.

As regards financial contribution to Hamas and Hezbollah, Kuwait and Saudi Arabia have contributed $30m since the Second Gulf War while Iran, a new donor, has given $31m. Iranian endeavours to expand areas of cooperation with its Arab neighbours however discourage an over-reliance on extra-regional powers and a coordination of energy and foreign policies which focus on regional concerns.

The third major undercurrent of the Islamic Republic's foreign policy is linked with its regional initiatives, involving Iran's role within the framework of the Economic Cooperation Organisation (ECO) as well as in Central Asia and the Caucasus. These include joint economic ventures and regional transport networks. For example the 1,500 mile pipeline for the transportation of natural gas from Turkmenistan to Europe runs through Iran. Another joint venture involves Iran and Pakistan building a 1,600 km pipeline which will transport Iran's gas to Pakistan, and the extension of the same would also provide India with Iranian gas. The opening of the 165 km Mashhad–Sarakhs railway which completes the historic rail link dubbed the New Silk Route was inaugurated in May 1996. This would allow China and Central Asia access to the port of Bandar Abbas in the Persian Gulf and to the Mediterranean through Turkey.

Relations between Kazakhstan and Iran are also thriving with 25 agreements signed between the two states. In addition, Iran is a major exporter of agricultural commodities and is assisting in the construction of the port of Akatu. Uzbeks and Tajiks share Iranian Shia Islam and have common ethnic and linguistic ties with Iranians. There are three major features in the Islamic Republic's Central Asian policy: firstly, energy cooperation in Central Asia; secondly, transshipment of oil and gas; thirdly, an ideological appeal to the 300 million Muslims of the region. This set of relationships is not without complications. Among the irritants could be the common ethnic, cultural, religious and linguistic ties which are a source of weakness as well as an asset for Iran. For example, any notion of a greater Azerbaijan could have repercussions on Iran. The war between the two border states of Armenia and Azerbaijan and the civil strife in Tajikistan could also have a destablising impact on the Iranian side of the border.[20] Within the framework of ECO Turkey could prove a tough competitor for Iran. Turkey has close links with the West and could provide Western capital and technology to the Central Asian states. Finally the Iranian objective to receive a continued flow of armaments and arms technology from Ukraine and Russia is made possible only by maintaining a neutral stance in regional conflicts.

Now let us consider Iran's relations with the USA and Russia. The geopolitical significance of Iran and the size of its economy mitigate against the international isolation of Iran. Thus US sanctions against it have prompted Iran to develop friendly relations with some of the G7, as well as Russia, China, India. US policy of isolating Tehran could force Iran to forge even stronger ties with Russia which is at present the principal supplier of arms, ammunition and military technology to Iran.

Article 152 of the constitution of the Islamic Republic of Iran states that the goal of foreign policy is the preservation of an all-embracing independence and the territorial integrity of the country.[21] Related to this is the territorial integrity of the former 'Soviet South'. This common perception is one of the major bases of Russo-Iranian solidarity in the post-Cold War era. In the economic field Iran has proposed the establishment of the Caspian Sea Cooperation Organisation (CASCO). This involves cooperation between the five littoral states of the Caspian Sea and covers areas ranging from fisheries to scientific research.

Much has been written by Western scholars about a possible Iranian–Russian agreement to complete the Bushehr nuclear plant. In addition, there has been speculation about the possiblity of nuclear cooperation between Pakistan, Iran and China.[22] Such a scenario seems unrealistic and exaggerated. Firstly, the pragmatists in Iran are above all interested in the economic rehabilitation of the country in the aftermath of war and natural disaster. Secondly the members of the International Atomic Energy Agency visited Iran in 1992 and 1993, and reported the Islamic Republic's nuclear activities to be entirely consistent with Iran's stated desire for peaceful use of nuclear energy.[23]

On the question of Iran's relations with the United States, there are grievances on both sides. In January 1996 in Iran apprehensions were fuelled by the news of money being allocated by the Clinton administration for covert activities inside the country to destabilise the Islamic regime. On the other hand, Rafsanjani's support for international norms of behaviour based on humanitarian principles received attention from the West. Thus for the sake of peace and stability in the Gulf region in particular, and in the world generally, there is a need for a reassessment of US policy towards Iran. This does not mean a unilateral change but a reciprocal and corresponding tempering of policies on both sides. Both states need each other's cooperation on different issues. For a decade, American businessmen have been anxious to enter the Iranian market.[24] Similarly, the Iranian people need technology and capital and the unfreezing of Iranian assets by the US. The initiation of a constructive dialogue is required, coupled with confidence-building measures.

As for Iran's relations with Pakistan, again these are governed by pragmatism, not ideology.[25] Pakistan was the first country to recognize the Bazargan government after the revolution in 1979. Both Pakistan and Iran formally withdrew from the Central Treaty organisation (Cento) in 1984. Iran–US relations deteriorated while Pakistan remained the cornerstone of US policy in south-west Asia. Pakistani officials believe that relations with Iran are strategically vital, however, despite the fact that current interaction between the two states is complicated and consists of a mixed bag of objectives. The strategic issues related to a conflict of interests are centred on the nature of Pakistan's relations with the US. When Benazir Bhuto assumed the office of Prime Minister of Pakistan, the country was about to be declared a terrorist state by the US. Thus rectifying the international image of Pakistan was at the top of the foreign policy agenda of the Pakistani government. In order to secure the much needed capital and technology for the economic growth of Pakistan the government had to tackle the tough challenge of gaining the confidence of the US administration. Pakistan has been an integral part of the US security system for some time. Conversely, Iran wants to see the US navy off the Gulf, but this clearly has not been Pakistan's objective. India, Pakistan's traditional rival, sympathises with Iran over this matter in accordance with its policy on the Indian Ocean.[26] While in this context India and Iran are in harmony, Iran's foreign policy focuses primarily on the Persian Gulf region.

Still, Pakistan's presence as an independent state is valued in Tehran, since it constitutes a buffer between Iran and India. During the Afghan war, Pakistan received substantial aid for hosting Afghan refugees, whereas Iran, with about two million Afghan refugees, was left without any financial assistance from the West. During President Rabbani's visit to Tehran in March 1996, President Hashemi Rafsanjani specifically mentioned that Afghanistan's territorial integrity and independence was essentially linked to the security of Iran. Iran's fears have been aroused by the ascendancy of the Taleban, a Wahhabi-dominated faction of Pashtu origin in Afghanistan. A situation that might end up in the dismemberment of Afghanistan, or one that might serve America's policy of containing Iran is viewed with apprehension in Tehran.

However, the overall emphasis of Iran's foreign policy lies in exploiting opportunities for cooperation rather than in harbouring animosity over differences in external affairs perspectives.

The Iranian government has so far kept itself aloof from the Shia–Sunni division within Pakistan. Though the leader of TNFJ (Tehrik-i Nifaz-i Fiqqah Jaffariyah), Allameh Arif Husseini, was trained in Najaf and Qum the party as a whole had no links with Iran. Similarly in 1992 when President Rafsanjani visited Pakistan, he made no mention of Sadiq Ganji's murder in Lahore. Consequently, the enduring common interests are: (1) economic cooperation and participation in joint ventures between Iran and China via Pakistan, emphasising particularly the creation of rail and road links between the two countries; (2) border security of Baluchistan in collaboration with Pakistan; (3) efforts to jointly combat narcotics trafficking in the Golden Crescent.

In conclusion, the foreign policy of the Islamic Republic of Iran exhibits patterns of continuity rather than change. Even the factional strife within the clergy does not point towards any abrupt departure from the original ideals of Islam in the forseeable future. In the neighbouring states where the masses are impoverished, the socio-economic imbalances are shocking. The Iranian revolution provides a model and offers a revival of faith in the Muslim community as an ongoing process. This acquires a special significance because the people in Pakistan and Central Asia share the same *Weltanschauung* as their counterparts in the Islamic Republic of Iran.

NOTES

1 Graham E. Fuller, *The Center of the Universe: The Geopolitics of Iran* (Boulder, Colo.: Westview Press, 1991).
2 K.L. Afrasiabi, *After Khomeini: New Directions in Iran's Foreign Policy* (Boulder, Colo.: Westview Press, 1994), pp. 36–41.
3 Abbas Maleki, 'Cooperation: a new component of the Iranian foreign policy', *The Iranian Joural of Foreign Affairs*, 5:1 (Spring 1993), p. 52.
4 Lubna Abid Ali, 'Foreign policy behavior of a post-revolutionary state: a case study of Iran', Ph.D. Dissertation, Quaid-Azam University, Islamabad (1990).
5 Fuller, *The Center*, p. 266.
6 Shireen T. Hunter, *Iran after Khomeini* (Washington DC: Center for Strategic and International Studies, 1992).
7 Fuller, *The Center*, p. 267.
8 J.G. Ruggie, 'Continuity and transformation in the world polity: toward a neorealist synthesis' in R.O. Keohane (ed.), *Neorealism and its Critics* (New York: Columbia University Press, 1986), pp. 131–158.
9 *Iran Times*, 13 August 1993, p. 1.
10 Mehdi Noorbakhsh, 'The Middle East, Islam and the United States: the special case of Iran', *Middle East Policy*, 2:3 (1993), p. 83.
11 Abbas Maleki, 'Into the Year 2000: the vista of Irano-Russian relations, *Central Asia and the Caucasus Review*, 4:12 (Winter 1995/6).
12 Noorbakhsh, 'The Middle East', p. 84.
13 Samuel P. Huntington, 'Will more countries become democratic?', *Political Science Quarterly*, 99:2 (September 1984).

14 Daniel Lerner, *The Passing of Traditional Society: Modernising the Middle East* (New York: Free Press, 1958).
15 Daniel Pipes, *In the Path of God: Sunnah, Islam and Political Power* (New York: Basic Book, 1983), pp. 187–88.
16 Hamid Dabbashi, *Theology of Discontent: The Ideological Foundations of the Iranian Revolution* (New York: New York State University Press, 1993), p. 336.
17 Robert A. Dahl, *Democracy and its Critics* (Yale University Press, 1989), p. 5.
18 James A. Bill, 'The United States and Iran: Mutual Mythologies', *Middle East Policy*, 11:3 (1993), p. 103.
19 Sohrab Shahabi and Farideh Farhi, 'Security considerations and Iranian foreign Policy', *The Iranian Journal of International Affairs*, 7:1 (Spring 1995), p. 94.
20 Ibid.
21 Hossein Mohyeddin, 'Constitution of Islamic Republic of Iran', (Tehran: Islamic Guidance, 1985), p. 83.
22 Nayan Chanda, 'Red rockets glare: China's sale of missiles to Pakistan and alleged shipment of nuclear weapons to Iran', *Far Eastern Economic Review*, 156:36 (September 1993) pp. 10–11.
23 Bill, 'The United States', p. 104.
24 J.P. Murphy, *Pragmatism* (Boulder, Colo.: Westview Press, 1990).
25 Kapur Ashok, 'Relations with Pakistan and India' in Miron Rezun (ed.), *Iran at the Crossroads: Global Realities in a Turbulent Decade* (Boulder, Colo.: Westview Press, 1990), p. 75.
26 Ibid.

Part II

Iran and its Neighbours

6

Geopolitics Beckons: Hydrocarbons and the Politics of the Persian Gulf

Anoushiravan Ehteshami

Ehteshami looks at the tensions between the US and Iraq in the 1990s and the impact of the war on regional stability. He also focuses on geopolitics, the prospects for the oil industry and the new interdependencies emerging between the two oil regions of the Caspian and the Gulf. The evidence suggests that although the Cold War seems to have ended in most other regions of the world, it continues in the Persian Gulf.

The Persian Gulf in the 1990s

It can be claimed, without much exaggeration, that the US drive to isolate Iraq and to marginalise Iran has been the defining feature of political life in the Persian Gulf in the 1990s. The US strategy of the 1990s, 'dual containment' of Iran and Iraq, has provided the structure around which a range of issues relating to Gulf security, and relations between Iran and its Arab neighbours, have revolved. More broadly still, regional relations of the Gulf Cooperation Council (GCC) countries, and those of the European powers (the European Union countries as well as Russia) with the Persian Gulf region have all been subject to the impact that the US overarching strategy for this part of the world has had on its littoral states. The US, Western and Third World allies have at times faced stark choices: either to support the American quarantine policy, or be seen to be subverting it with every contact which they may have had with either Tehran or Baghdad.

Of the two 'containees', Iran's efforts to break free of the US straightjacket has been the more dramatic and persistent. It would appear that much of the foreign policy and substantial portions of the economic policy, of President Rafsanjani's second term of office (1993–7) were devoted to devising ways of minimising the impact of containment. In this struggle both parties can claim notable successes; Iran for having been able to breach the US-made barriers, and the US for its ability to force its allies to take note of its concerns. But for the neighbouring countries, this duel has been an expensive distraction from the real problems facing the region: lack of invesment, economic mismanagement, fiscal crises, political instability, environmental degradation, etc. The Tehran–Washington confrontation, moreover, also went a long way towards complicating the responses of Middle Eastern countries to the historic changes to the north of the region, in Central Asia and the Caucasus.

Amongst the Gulf countries it was only in the late 1990s that the strategic implications of the emergence of new hydrocarbon producers on their doorstep (in the Caspian Sea area) was considered. The realisation of possible competition in global markets from the hydrocarbon-rich republics of the former Soviet Union was accompanied by two other concerns: firstly, that it was the Western oil companies which were leading the charge to the Caspian; and, secondly, that the West, having dominated the Gulf, had now found a foothold in the territories north of Iran and Turkey as well, the new periphery that the Middle Eastern powers had wished to integrate into a larger 'Greater Middle East' structure.

The security, economic and political issues relating to the Caspian states, and the potential problems associated with the Central Asian republics' desire to break out of Russia's orbit, taxed no Middle Eastern country more than it did Iran. For, soon after the collapse of the Soviet Union, Iran had begun grooming itself as the strategic link, the 'bridge', between the landlocked Trans-Caspian region and the outside world, hoping in the process to be the party which would gain most from the division of the Soviet Union into its constituent parts. What is more, the Islamic Republic did not cherish the prospect of insecurity on its northern shores, and certainly not at the same time as having to respond to the entrenched position of the United States in the Gulf, where the US Fifth Fleet was becoming accustomed to navigating its 20 or so warships along Iran's southern shores. Thus, Iran's position vis-à-vis its neighbours and the Iranian–US relationship were to form the backdrop to the changing geopolitics of West Asia in general, and the post-Cold War political economy of oil exploration in this area in particular.

As so much has hinged on Iran, the question of the moment must be: has Washington's preoccupation with Iran been warranted?

Iran in the 1990s: a regional power or a marginal player?

It was fortuitous for Iran that President Rafsanjani emerged as the state's first executive president in 1989, just as the tremors in the international system were warning of the major earthquakes to come. His sharp departure from the policies of the Khomeini era seemed suited and responsive to the passing of the post-1945 international order. After all it was in 1990, his first year of presidency, that the earthquake in the international system occurred and the system started its rapid tranformation with the demise of the Warsaw Pact. Soon afterwards in December 1991, the Soviet superpower itself, Iran's neighbour of several generations, collapsed.

Nearer to home, Iraq's military defeat of 1991, the disarray in the ranks of the Arab states which followed the August 1990 attack on Kuwait, and the emergence of new republics in the Transcaucasian and Central Asian regions on Iran's northern doorstep also left a deep mark on Iran's regional policies. In the Gulf sub-region, and before the imposition of America's quarantine strategy in 1993, the eclipse of the Iraqi challenge to the security of the GCC states and Iran's improving image, as well as its economic and military reconstruction, contributed to President Rafsanjani's tentative attempts at sub-regional reassertion. Improved relations with its neighbours foretold of a more active and pragmatic Tehran, bent on recovering its position in the Middle East subsystem.

It is possible to chronicle the recovery of Iran as a major regional actor in the 1990s, and its potential to emerge as a significant regional power early in the twenty-first century.[1] After a decade in the cold, with revolution and war detracting from its ability to assert its strategic aims in the region, Iran has demonstrated since the cease-fire of its war with Iraq (1988), and more intensely since the Kuwait crisis, that it is once again both willing and able to draw upon its geopolitical deposits, as well as its ideological dynamic, to recommence play as a heavyweight regional actor and to mature into an influential regional power.

Such ambitions, however, although encouraged by better conditions at home and a myriad of improved opportunities abroad, have had to be set against a multitude of obstacles, not least of which have been outside pressures (dual containment for example), economic problems at home (high debt and inflation in the mid-1990s), and, perhaps most critically of all, a shortage of power projection capabilities.

Therefore, to talk of Iran becoming a major regional power may appear premature to some sceptics. Yet the potential remains, as well as the will and the investment. Domestic difficulties and external obstacles should not be assumed to be rigid certainties. Certainly there are still many pitfalls in the way of Iran emerging as the dominant actor, but it is very difficult to see in which direction a recharged and self-confident Iran would not influence the destiny of the region. And it is for these reasons that outside powers have little choice but to view Iran as a pivotal player in the Middle East subsystem. With its potential to emerge as the key balancer in the neighbouring oil-soaked regions of the Persian Gulf and the Caspian Sea, interested powers can choose it as a partner or view it as a rival; either way, they have to engage it and can no longer ignore it. This much has been acknowledged since 1996 by Washington insiders, many of whom have been conceding since Hojjatoleslam Khatami's election as Iran's president in May 1997 that a major review of US–Iran relations may be overdue.

For Iran itself, the outlying regions are full of challenges and opportunities. In the south, it is the perennial problem of security and the American naval presence which dominate Iran's agenda. Indeed, in view of positive messages arriving from virtually every GCC capital after the election, President Khatami's new Foreign Minister, Kamal Kharrazi, has made improving Tehran's relations with its southern neighbours a high priority. Despite many false dawns since 1989, however, it genuinely no longer seems to be a question of if, but when, Iran finds full accommodation with its Arab neighbours, Iraq included. In such circumstances, when virtually every US-friendly country is busy befriending Tehran, Washington's containment policy cannot be tenable and a complete overhaul of its policy towards Iran will have to be considered.

Ironically, the real obstacle to such an overhaul of policy towards the Islamic Republic may not be the situation in the Persian Gulf, where the US has a resident naval presence, but the more dynamic and unpredictable situation on Iran's northern border, around the oil-rich Caspian Sea.

In the north, Iran itself has been concerned not only with the impact of new regional players on its own security, but also with the consequences of its own diplomatic initiatives in Central Asia and the

Caucasus on its good relations with Russia and, to a lesser degree, on the Gulf Arab countries and on Turkey.[2] Also, as Iran's entire regional policy had thus far had an Arab focus, the results of the reorientation northwards of its diplomatic machinery had to be considered with some care.

In fact it was not until 1993 that Iran displayed a coherent policy towards its new northern neighbours. Firstly, with the Economic Cooperation Organisation (ECO) emerging as an important regional body, Iran was able to use this vehicle for advancing its own interests in the north, as well as using the structures offered by ECO to address existing tensions arising from it and Turkey following different lines in this region. Secondly, despite considerable American pressure and Russian indecisiveness after the collapse of the USSR, Iran was able to extract from Moscow a reaffirmation of its cooperation agreements with the Islamic Republic. Moscow had also begun showing an interest in cooperating with its Caspian neighbour in problems arising out of its 'near abroad'. A close relationship thus began to take shape, particularly after the Russian Foreign Minister Andrei Kozyrev's March 1993 trip to Tehran, during which he paved the way for joint Iranian–Russian action on such regional issues as the legal status of the Caspian Sea, ways of ending the Tajiki civil war, and the political crisis in Afghanistan.

Not surprisingly, it took Tehran some time to put its 'northern strategy' into gear. Iran's new initiatives surfaced in October 1993, during President Rafsanjani's second trip to the region at the head of a high-level delegation to four Central Asian republics (excluding Tajikistan) as well as to Azerbaijan. This trip was particularly significant for it laid the basis for Iranian–Central Asian cooperation (see below).

Significantly, President Rafsanjani was soon followed by the American Secretary of State, who was himself on a friendship mission to Central Asia, offering these states economic and diplomatic support. In an obvious gesture towards the most strategically placed of all these republics, Kazakhstan, Secretary Christopher increased the US bilateral aid package by $85 million, to $140 million a year, and offered it a further $15 million per year towards its project for reclamation of the Aral Sea.[3] Other republics also received American backing, particularly Uzbekistan and Turkmenistan.

Clearly, US policy since Christopher's high-level trip conforms with Washington's obsession with Tehran and fear of it developing a substantial foothold in Central Asia and Transcaucasia. The thrust of

American policy, however, cannot simply be seen as efforts to keep Iran out of Central Asia. A closer reading of Washington's diplomatic moves towards the Asian CIS would in fact reveal the emergence of a new American regional policy, which has been taking shape since 1995. This clearly goes well beyond the 'containment' of Iran.

The US strategy towards the Muslim republics of the former Soviet Union is based on two realities. Firstly, Washington appears no longer content to stay clear of Russia's self-declared zones of influence in its 'near abroad'. US behaviour shows that it is out to safeguard its own legitimate security and economic interests in Asia's heartland. As these interests have grown significantly since 1993, so Washington is having to formulate a comprehensive strategy for both protecting and advancing them. The US is prepared to protect its interests with Russia's assistance, but not at the expense of foregoing closer bilateral relations with the states of Central Asia and the Caucasus. Too much is at stake for that degree of cooperation to work. The new assertiveness in US policies towards these Asian republics also reflects two other realities: first, that Turkey alone does not seem capable of safeguarding US interests in Central Asia; and, second, that the smooth expansion of NATO eastwards in Europe can mean the extension of the West's security parameters to Central Asia as well.

Secondly, the act itself of Washington formulating a strategy speaks volumes for the importance the US administration has begun to attach to America's emerging interests in Central Asia and the Caucasus. While it is true that international politics dictates that the US, as the only superpower, ought to have a presence in the vast territories which stand between Russia, China and India (Asia's main continental powers) which it has now in fact secured, it seems to be America's very real interests (and growing stakes) in the Caspian's new hydrocarbon sources which is leading it to adopt a proactive posture in this region. Just as it was oil which drew it to the waters of the Persian Gulf in the 1930s, so it is again the same force which pulls the US towards this landlocked sea.

But, being practically a local power in the oil-rich region of the Gulf, it would have been quite unnatural for the US not to have made its presence felt around this newest fountain of oil and gas situated in the Middle East's backyard. And so it is that these new interests, championed by American oil companies and several governmental agencies, have been influencing Washington's more direct approach towards the countries of Central Asia and the Caucasus.

In the last analysis then, all the signs indicate that Washington is preparing for a long stay, which throws into sharp focus its problems with Iran, the potential power broker of the twenty-first century in Caspian–Persian Gulf energy zones. For, apart from Moscow's displeasure at America's growing presence around the Caspian Sea, the only immediate concern which Washington has displayed has been to do with Iran, the 'rogue' state *par excellence*. Iran is the only country which truly enjoys the advantages of geopolitics, but it also draws considerable strength from Russia's goodwill. The fact that Iran straddles the two energy zones which the US covets, and also that its territory provides the shortest and most direct geographical link between the two, adds to US dilemmas about Iran.

America's policies in the next few years, therefore, will have to reflect its attitude towards two developments: firstly, the reality that oil and natural gas will be flowing in reasonable quantities out of the Caspian basin towards OECD markets in Asia and Europe; and secondly, that the reliance of its NATO allies and the larger Far Eastern economies on Persian Gulf exports will have increased dramatically. Iran is uniquely placed either to smoothen the consumers' access to Caspian–Persian Gulf oil (which is in its own interest of course) in the twenty-first century, or to be intransigent and disrupt the flow by undermining the security of one or both of the oil zones along its shores. So, as far as links between the Persian Gulf and the Central Asian and Caucasian republics are concerned, most routes pass through Iran. This much is clear already, judging by Turkey's desire to cooperate with Iran in energy matters, and Kuwait's agreement in September 1997 to finance Turkmenistan's gas pipeline project through Iran to the Persian Gulf.

Central Asia and the Persian Gulf

The Central Asian republics themselves of course desire to befriend Western countries, particularly the United States. They want Western assistance to smooth the path towards an independent, market-based economy: in political economy jargon, to take them to the point of 'take-off'. The route might have appeared a short one to several of the Central Asian republics, as, in aggregate terms, their economies seemed in better shape than those of some of their non-Soviet neighbours. This (partial) truth is borne out by World Bank data for the mid-1990s, which showed that the GNP per capita of the post-Soviet Asian countries compared quite favourably with those of their southern neighbours: Turkmenistan's figure of $1,700, Azerbaijan's $1,670, Kyrgyzstan's $1,551, and Uzbekistan's $1,350 are not much smaller than the Turkish GNP per capita figure of $1,820; Iran's figure of $2,320 is smaller than Kazakhstan's $2,470. The GNP per capita of the Central Asian republics is many times greater than those of Afghanistan, Pakistan and India which are $250, $400 and $330 respectively. Only the four oil-rich states of Saudi Arabia, Kuwait, Qatar and the UAE have larger gross national products per head of population.[4]

So, a number of the Asian members of the Commonwealth of Independent States (CIS), particularly those blessed with oil and gas deposits, have been preparing themselves as candidates for the twenty-first century's fast-developing economies. It is my expectation that the national strategies of these potential 'rentier' states, assisted by the policies of the international oil companies which are their main Western economic partners, will determine the nature of regional relations in West Asia in the twenty-first century. One prediction puts the problem in quite dramatic terms: 'the strategic implications of this bonanza [Caspian oil deposits] hypnotise Western security planners as completely as the finances transfix oil executives. Once Caspian oil begins flowing, they dare to dream, they will never have to kowtow to OPEC or maneuver to prevent oil-thirsty nations from dealing with Iran and Iraq.'[5] A discussion of one or two scenarios will suffice to highlight how such dreams could turn into nightmares for the Persian Gulf oil producers.

It will not be too long before these new Caspian producers emerge as competitors of the OPEC countries in international oil markets. How such competition will affect these oil states' relations with each other is one part of the problem, as it could cause severe tensions between an OPEC intent on hanging on to its international market share, and the eager Caspian producers (and the oil companies who have invested heavily in the Caspian oil and gas sectors), who may wish to maximise the return on their hefty investments by maximising output.

Another part of the problem is that once the non-OPEC Caspian producers come on line, as it were, they could then be in a position to undercut the Gulf oil exporters on price and delivery terms. It should be remembered that, in sharp contrast to OPEC's practice, the pricing structures and output of the Caspian producers are being worked out in cooperation with the leading international oil companies – the same oil companies which in the recent past suffered the consequences of OPEC members' oil nationalisation policies and their 'independent' pricing strategies of the 1970s.

Furthermore, access to the hydrocarbon resources of the Caspian area has emerged as a main issue. The myriad of multi-billion dollar oil/gas pipeline projects for the Caspian region is an indication of the desire of both producers and consumers to create safe outlets for the Caspian's hydrocarbons. Whoever controls these outlets, of course, will influence the international politics of the region. Thus, Iran, Russia, Turkey, Georgia, Armenia, and Pakistan have found themselves sometimes in partnership and other times in competition with each other over the routing of these pipelines. Their competition in this regard is symptomatic of the problem; the route that these pipelines take will shape West Asia's geostrategic agenda for many years to come.

In addition, the position that international oil companies have managed to secure for themselves in the Caspian region speaks of their overwhelming power, and their desire and commitment to secure control of the hydrocarbon resources of Central Asia and the Caucasus. The flow of Caspian oil/gas in acceptable quantities under the direction of these companies will inevitably make OPEC members more vulnerable to international pressure, and also put huge pressures on them to review their already shaky output and pricing strategies. Such pressures could paralyse OPEC, or worse: in the probable free-for-all which could accompany the implosion of OPEC, oil prices could collapse. A price collapse would cause international chaos, throwing many countries into crisis, from Egypt and Yemen to Azerbaijan and Russia.

Furthermore, no OPEC member, bar one (Saudi Arabia), has the capacity to retaliate by declaring an oil war on the Caspian states and their international backers. Only Saudi Arabia has the technical ability to pump sufficient quantities of oil to cause a big enough glut in international markets to make Caspian oil production uneconomic. Not even Saudi Arabia, however, is in a position to absorb the financial losses that such a policy would bring. Certainly no other OPEC country can accept the heavy damage that 10 million barrels of Saudi oil output could inflict on their national economies.

Inevitably, in the stalemate which will follow a Persian Gulf–Caspian Sea oil confrontation, the ground will be prepared for many such crises as the Kuwait war of 1990-1, with even more drastic consequences for an already edgy region.

In more immediate terms, other problems associated with economic change around the Caspian Sea itself will have to be addressed. The very success of the oil-rich Caspian states could cause problems as it creates a multi-tier economic sphere in Asia's heartland. Such a development could act as a catalyst for political and military conflicts between the Central Asian republics themselves, and also amongst other interested powers. A situation might develop, therefore, resembling the current Arab system and the relations between rich and poor Arab states, where the elaborate efforts of the 'haves' to keep the Arab 'have-nots' from access to the oil bounty has increasingly come to cause tension between them. As is well known, largely thanks to oil wealth, the Arab world has become a highly polarised region in both economic and political terms – a situation that is at variance with the current position in Central Asia.

Of the eight states of Central Asia and the Transcaucasus only four have the basic ingredients for penetrating the global hydrocarbons market, of which only two, Azerbaijan and Kazakhstan (with nearly 25 million of the eight countries' total population of around 70 million), will be able to pump oil and natural gas in reasonably profitable quantities. The four oil states' output of an estimated 3.6 million barrels of oil per day in the year 2010 is unlikely to be outstripping that of the Persian Gulf states in the near future, since Iran's output alone in the mid-1990s was greater than the above target. It is worth noting that OPEC's estimate of its members' total output in 2010 is around 39.4 million barrels per day.[6] Such a total OPEC output, led by the Persian Gulf producers, will be a substantial barrier against the Caspian producers.

Nonetheless, as stated already, the Caspian region's hydrocarbon wealth is quite substantial in international terms. The combined reserves of Kazakhstan and Azerbaijan, for example, is said to exceed 50 billion barrels of oil.[7] Other oil experts, however, claim that such figures are gross underestimates: Azerbaijan's and Kazakhstan's deposits alone, they claim, could be as great as 200 billion barrels.[8] These figures also carry with them significant strategic implications for the five Caspian Sea countries, for the reserves of Azerbaijan and Kazakhstan would be sufficient to keep the industrialised world supplied for a considerable length of time, provide the United States with over thirty years of its energy requirements, or satisfy the energy needs of Asia's hungry economies (China in particular) for well over a generation. Such reserve figures will mean many billions of dollars in revenues, and may indeed herald a new oil bonanza. As it was in the Persian Gulf in the twentieth century, so it will probably be in the Caspian Sea area in the twenty-first: presence can mean global influence and will translate into huge economic and political power.

Not surprisingly, therefore, several Asian players have already embarked upon a strategy of engaging the new republics in new regional ventures. Turkey and Iran, as well as Pakistan, China, India, Saudi Arabia and South Korea, have all been very keen to help in moulding the Central Asian/Caucasus clay. The oil companies of Indonesia, China, Malaysia and Japan are busy players here, competing for a share of the hydrocarbons action with such well-established Western companies as Chevron, BP, Amoco, Exxon, Mobil, Shell and Bechtel.

Amongst the regional players, Iran and Turkey emerge as the key players. Before the fall of the USSR the Middle East was Arab-dominated with Iran and Turkey on its cultural and political margins. Now both Iran and Turkey have acquired greater freedom of action and manoeuvrability and have taken the opportunity to create a new regional subsystem around the states of Central Asia, with Tehran very much at its geopolitical nerve centre.

In geopolitical terms, Iran in the Cold War years acted as the resident gatekeeper of the strategically important Straits of Hormuz. From this role it was able to draw near-hegemonic status in the Persian Gulf. In West Asia's post-Cold War order, however, Iran's role has been enhanced, so that it is now the main gateway to Central Asia and its vast natural resources. Underpinning this strengthened geopolitical standing is easier economic and political access to the heartland of Asia. In practical terms, this has acquired two interconnected aspects: firstly, the rush to construct new oil and gas pipelines out of Central Asia and Transcaucasia; and secondly, the need to establish new road and rail networks southwards. In both cases, geography dictates that Iran be a vital link, literally the bridge, in these proposed transportation chains and networks in and out of these former USSR territories.

As Iran and its non-Arab neighbours have recognised, while the routes out of the region themselves may not be paved with gold, providing access can bring considerable geo-economic and political benefits to the countries chosen for this purpose. One country which has much at stake in this new 'Great Game' is Russia, still the area's undisputed imperial power.

Russia enters the fray

After a period of uncertainty in the immediate post-Cold War period, a more coherent Russian foreign policy has been in evidence in the second half of the 1990s, in which nationalism, territorial security, trade, and a pro-active approach towards potential regional issues play a part. Moscow has developed an acute sense of awareness of the 'near abroad' and how instabilities and disturbances there could undermine the federation's own territorial integrity. This has made Moscow more aware of the proximity of the old 'southern belt' countries to its near 'near abroad'.

Furthermore, since 1991, and more specifically with the Chechnya conflict in the northern part of the Caucasus, Moscow has developed a much keener sense of its outlying regions. This shift in emphasis is consistent with the transformation of the Russian state from a global superpower to a dominant regional power with a much more focused awareness of regional factors and balance of power and of the local and regional forces that can affect the federation's own interests. It is therefore possible to see where the Persian Gulf region would fit into Russia's overall priorities.

In the first instance, Russia needs to keep its hydrocarbons industry competitive and to maintain its export potential. In order to do this, however, Moscow needs to ensure that it has access to Western capital, and also that its relations with the main hydrocarbons exporters of the twenty-first century, which will probably be concentrated in the Persian Gulf–Caspian Sea zones, are more cordial now than they were in the decades before the end of the Cold War, when Moscow's diplomatic presence in the Gulf did not really go beyond Iran and Iraq.

Secondly, the Russian leadership has come to realise that it cannot hope to bring about a recovery in the country's weak economy without the participation of its large industrial and military-industrial complex. This much all Russian politicians agree on, but majority factions in the Duma have been demanding a policy of aggressively marketing Russian weapons systems, not only in those markets where the Soviet Union used to enjoy a monopoly, but globally. Russia's weapons sales drive started paying dividends soon after its launch; in 1995 alone, for instance, Russia signed new arms deals worth $9.1 billion, exceeding the US arms transfer agreements of $8.2 billion in the same year.[9] In East and Southeast Asia, China, India, Vietnam, Malaysia and Indonesia have emerged as large Russian weapons customers, purchasing advanced combat aircraft, missile systems, and ground warfare equipment. Russia has been so masterful in developing its niche in Asian markets that the authoritative Teal Group has estimated that the sale of just one type of its military aircraft, the Su-27 fighter-interceptor, is likely to reach 444 between 1997 and 2012, earning Russia $17 billion.[10] Few other regions, however, offer more lucrative markets for Russia's sophisticated weapons systems than the Persian Gulf, whose total arms markets exceeded the $100 billion mark in the 1990s.

In tandem with the development of its military relations, Russia's diplomatic presence has also become more vibrant. From the mid-1990s one detects a much more independent voice coming from Moscow, and with it a slowly emerging distance between Russia and the West in regional subsystems (such as the Middle East, South Asia and East Asia). Russia's forceful return to the Middle East, therefore, must be seen in the context of its general drive for international reassertion. Russia's presence in the Middle East has also improved, most notably since Primakov's appointment as the Russian Foreign Minister in January 1996. Not without good reason, his reassessment of Russia's Middle East policy has been followed by some tensions in relations with the US and with Israel over the Arab–Israeli peace process, of which Russia is a co-sponsor. But Russia's post-Cold War posture as a big regional power has also demanded that it try to contain potential threats to its security from nuclear weapons states such as Israel, whose programme has been 'unguarded' and not subject to any control regime, and which possesses the delivery systems to strike at Russian targets. As a first step, therefore, Moscow has tried to bring Israel's undeclared nuclear weapons force into the open, hoping eventually to create an internationally binding non-conventional arms control regime for the entire region. That Moscow's policies in this regard coincide with those of other Middle Eastern regional powers has complicated Israel's relations with Russia somewhat, in that Israel increasingly views Moscow as a potentially hostile rival determined to weaken Israel by sponsoring its regional enemies such as Iran and Syria.

The most visible aspects of the new Russian Middle East policy have been Moscow's positive gestures towards Syria and Egypt, and renewed involvement in the Arab–Israeli peace process on behalf of its erstwhile ally Syria. Primakov reaffirmed this during his high-profile tour of the Middle East in the autumn of 1996. The launch of joint Russian–Syrian anti-aircraft exercises in mid-September 1997, in response to the US-planned naval exercises with Turkey and Israel, provided the first evidence of Russia's re-entry into the Middle East. More tellingly still, these moves were followed by President Yeltsin's blunt criticism of Israel's regional policies in late September and the announcement of an agreement between Moscow and Cairo to sign a new friendship treaty.[11] The Israeli press began articulating the concerns of Israel and its main Western backer with comments such as, 'the Americans must make it clear that they will no longer provide Russia with economic aid, if – in exchange – the Russians resume the Cold War in the Middle East'.[12]

Moscow's relations with the Persian Gulf also fit into this same pattern, particularly its relations with Iran, which have blossomed since 1989. Not surprisingly, the nuclear cooperation and arms sales agreements with Iran have continued to feature highly in Russia's Persian Gulf policy, and have remained on the agenda of most meetings between American and Russian officials.[13] Since the early 1990s, Iran has served as a profitable market for Russia's military hardware and its military-related technologies and industries. The transfer of billions of dollars worth of Russian arms – three Kilo-class submarines, MiG-29 and MiG-31 fighters, Su-24 bombers and Su-27 fighter-interceptors, T-72 tanks, missiles and munitions – to Iran since 1990 has effectively re-equipped the entire Iranian armed forces with Russian arms. This fruitful military relationship with Moscow has prompted senior Iranian foreign ministry officials to refer to Russia as one of the Islamic Republic's 'strategic partners', a claim which, to the dismay of Israel and the US, Moscow has been reluctant to dismiss.

This, though, is not by any means the end of the story, for Moscow has managed to make inroads into the Western-dominated GCC countries as well. Qatar, Kuwait, the UAE and even Saudi Arabia have tested or purchased Russian military equipment, and several are expected to short-list Russian military aircraft for future contracts. Despite this, however, the real gains for Moscow in the Persian Gulf will only become apparent after the lifting of the UN sanctions against Iraq and the realisation of some $10 billion worth of military and civilian contracts with that country. The Iraqi armed forces have stated on several occasions that in a post-sanctions scenario their main priority will be to replenish their military stores with Russian weapons. Once Iraq's freedom of action is restored, therefore, Russia will be in the envious position of being the main military partner of both northern Gulf countries, a position not held by any power in modern times.

Although I have argued that Russia is now a *dominant* regional power, it nonetheless needs the support and goodwill of several of its Asian neighbours for the stability of its 'near abroad'. Further east, it is China and India which are the key neighbours, and in West Asia, it is Iran, Turkey and Saudi Arabia, which, for a range of economic, geopolitical and political reasons, feature most highly in Moscow's calculations. With Turkey Russia's trade is well in excess of $1.0 billion per year, but its political posture remains a competitive one. Russia's unusual friendship with Iran and Saudi Arabia has been all the more pronounced as access to its traditional and most important Gulf ally (and market), Iraq, has been denied it since 1990.

Finally, Russia's desire to have close relations with the Gulf states is consistent not only with its interests in the 'near abroad' and its security concerns in the potentially volatile northern Caucasus region, where several million non-Slavic Russian Muslims reside, but also with a determined desire to balance NATO's expansion into eastern Europe (and the West's penetration of the Caspian zone) with a presence in the West's own 'backyard', the Persian Gulf region. The prospect of a Russian–Iranian alliance, which could arguably bring Russian troops and possibly their tactical non-conventional weapons to the Strait of Hormuz, will surely be testing the Pentagon tacticians, one or two of whom will be reflecting on the irony that even in a post-Cold War setting Russia can still emerge as the main strategic rival of the United States in 'out of area' theatres.

Conclusion

I have argued elsewhere that, although one can find much evidence of political and economic activity in the territories of the former Soviet Union, the future of Eurasian regions, particularly Central Asia and the Caucasus, remains unclear.[14] It may take several decades before we can know with any certainty Russia's own fate, let alone that of its 'near abroad' republics. That some of these states may be reduced to peripheries of a powerful regional axis is a real possibility. Nor can the disappearance of one or two of them from the map be ruled out.

Furthermore, as we have seen, the fluid and unstable nature of inter-state relations in West Asia will suck in big players like the United States, which will have seen that the end of the Cold War has already spun unexpectedly friendly ties between several of Asia's future giants: Russia and Iran, Russia and China, India and Iran, Pakistan and China, Kazakhstan and Kyrgyzstan, and even Japan and China. With these powers so active on the Asian continent, it is impossible to believe that the geopolitical map of the whole region could not change in other ways as well. Let us consider the fate of China as a case in point. By the middle of the twenty-first century, China, with its 1.2 plus billion people, will be thirsty for both new territories and natural resources. Conceivably, parts of Central Asia could satisfy some of China's hunger; much of Central Asia is low in population, large in terms of territory (around 51 million people in 1995 and an area of 3,994,300 square kilometres) and very rich in primary inputs. If, in the coming years, numbers really do continue to dictate China's foreign policy, then the chances of Beijing giving in to the temptation of usurping some of the 'virgin' territories of Central Asia cannot ruled out. How such a Chinese policy might affect its Asian neighbours, let alone the United States, is anybody's guess. But it can be predicted with some certainty that it would not be welcomed, particularly if it were to be combined with China's expansionist drive into the Pacific rim.

Neither Russia, however weak, nor the United States could tolerate such a Chinese strategy. The China factor, therefore, could bring Moscow and Washington together in a new Euro-Atlantic alliance against Beijing. But such a natural and strategically significant alliance may not evolve unless one of the complicating factors, perhaps even an obstacle against its formation, is removed. That is to say, Russia and America could remain apart if the competitive framework which divides them in West Asia is not revised, compounded as it is by their quite serious policy differences in the Caspian and the Gulf oil zones.

Evidence so far indicates that Russia and the US are aware of potential regional dangers to their bilateral relations, but finding a *modus operandi* in regions of significant strategic value has not been easy. Two instances suffice to illustrate the point. The first, and not a very promising one, relates to the Middle East proper. Here, Israel has begun, with US assistance, the process of integrating its US-supplied F-15i fighter-bombers (with a range capable of reaching Iran) into its formidable air force, while Russia has been busy assisting the Islamic Republic with its development of new surface-to-surface missiles with enough power to strike at any Israeli target, as well as reaching the territories of China, India and several of America's European allies. With these highly dangerous military developments, and the posture that Moscow and Washington have been adopting, one could be forgiven for believing that the Cold War still prevailed in the Middle East, which perhaps is not too far from the truth!

And yet – and this is the second example, showing how the end of the global Cold War has transformed inter-state relations right across the world – in the summer of 1997 500 US troops travelled 12,000 kilometres to Kazakhstan to join another 1,200 or so soldiers from Russia (and several of its CIS allies) in joint military exercises in the heart of Asia.

The message that the US apparently wanted to get across – 'there is no nation on the face of the earth that we cannot get to'[15] – fuelled speculation that its military presence in Central Asia was no more than a reminder to Russia and others of the importance that Washington now attaches to the Transcaspian area, a perspective underlined by the strategic reality that around 55 per cent of America's oil needs were now being imported. Others, however, pointing to the volatility of West Asia and the prospect of some 3,000 ballistic missiles and several nuclear weapons states being let loose in the Middle East in the near future (by 2010), and the limited involvement of European and Japanese peacekeepers in the area, would prefer to give the US the benefit of the doubt and deepen its presence in West Asia. These pundits prefer to see the US remaining fully engaged in the Middle East and Transcaspia, arguing that, as in the Far East, America's self-interest can provide for future tranquility. What this chapter has tried to show is that, despite individual preferences, neither the US nor its regional adversaries have much choice in being engaged with post-Soviet republics east of the river Volga. It is not so much their presence which will decide the fate of the region, but the dynamics of their relations with each other and their strategy for dealing with the twenty-first century's new hydrocarbon producers – north and south of Iran.

NOTES

1 Anoushiravan Ehteshami, *After Khomeini: The Iranian Second Republic* (London: Routledge, 1995).
2 Mohiaddin Mesbahi, 'Iran's emerging partnership with Russia', *Middle East Insight,* XI:5 (July–August 1995), pp. 84–7; Philip Robins, 'The Middle East and Central Asia' in Peter Ferdinand (ed.), *The New States of Central Asia and their neighbours* (New York: Council on Foreign Relations Press, 1995), pp. 55–74.
3 *New York Times*, 24 October 1993.
4 The World Bank, *World Development Report* (various years).
5 Stephen Kinzer, 'A perilous new contest for the next oil prize', *The New York Times*, 21 September 1997.
6 Nadir Guerer and Fatih Birol, 'Assessing the future oil export potential in Transcaucasia and Central Asia', *OPEC Bulletin*, September 1995, pp. 8–15.
7 British Petroleum estimates.
8 *Associated Press*, 20 September 1997.
9 Richard F. Staar, 'Russia and the Islamic Middle East', *Mediterranean Quarterly*, 8:2 (Spring 1997), pp. 163–75.
10 *Finansovye Izvestia*, 31 July 1997.
11 RFE/RL, 23 September 1997.
12 *Maariv*, 18 September 1997.
13 The West fears that Russian scientists have aided Iran's long-range missiles and nuclear weapons programmes, for instance the Shahab 3 missile, which, with a range of 800 miles, can easily strike at targets in Israel.
14 The discussion in this section is based on my article, 'Iran and Central Asia: responding to regional change' in Mehi Mozaffari (ed.), *Security Politics in the Commonwealth of Independent States: The Southern Belt* (London: Macmillan, 1997).
15 Chief of US Atlantic Command, General John J. Sheehan, quoted in the *Wall Street Journal*, 16 September 1997.

7

Iran and the Newly Independent States of Central Asia

Mohammad Farhad Atai

The author charts the transitional process in the new republics of Central Asia, paying careful attention to the impact of economic, political and cultural crises on the process of nation-building. Just as they were not prepared for a suddenly acquired independence, similarly Iran was not ready for dealing with three neighbours on its northern borders instead of one. Here Atai discusses the process of Iran's adjustment to the reality of building relations with its new neighbours in Central Asia.

Introduction

The breakup of the Soviet Union in 1991 released the unprepared peoples of Central Asia into the international arena. They have had to face the challenge of living in independent nation-states, a predicament for which they have no or limited experience. For centuries these people pursued a nomadic existence on the vast steppes of Central Asia or lived in settled communities in the fertile Farghana valley and in Samarqand and Bukhara, ways of life in which loyalty to a nation-state with well-defined political borders was alien. During seventy years of communist rule Moscow managed, with reasonable success, to inculcate in the peoples of Central Asia a sense of their citizenship of the greater political unit of the Soviet Union. Stalin's arbitrary creation of distinct republics based on the ethnic character of each region tied ethnicity to land and to specific borders. Under the Soviet system, however, loyalty to an individual republic was overshadowed by the notion of citizenship of the Soviet Union. After the empire's collapse at the end of 1991, the legacy of Stalin's policy on nationalities, combined with a world order based on independent nation-states, forced these peoples to seek new national identities and to try to come to terms with their new status as citizens of independent states.

As the republics of Central Asia go through this transition, so the outside world is trying to understand the region and define its relationship with the new independent states. During the disintegration of the Soviet Union, the West's attention was focused on developments in Russia. Hence, whenever the term 'former Soviet Union' was mentioned, it usually meant Russia. This was because of the critical role that Moscow played both on the international scene and in the affairs of the other republics in the former Soviet Union. For some time, the emerging independent states, especially the Central Asian republics, were almost forgotten. Immediately after the breakup of the Soviet Union, the West's main concerns in Central Asia were:

(1) The threat of nuclear weapons left in the hands of governments such as Kazakhstan;
(2) the threat of radical Islam and the possible emergence of Islamic regimes in Central Asia;
(3) exploiting the natural resources and economic opportunities in a region freed from Soviet domination.

Denuclearising Central Asia

As early as 1991, attempts at denuclearising the former Soviet republics got under way. Subsequent to the adoption of a bill in Washington proposed by Senators Sam Nunn (Democrat) and Charles Lugar (Republican), the Security Assistance Program was introduced. It mandated the United States Department of Defense to allocate $400m of its 1992 budget for the dismantlement of nuclear weapons in the newly independent states of the former Soviet Union. The annual allocation of funds continued through 1995.[1] Kazakhstan, as the only nuclear power in Central Asia, was directly affected by policies in the West aimed at denuclearising the former Soviet republics. After independence, Almaty was faced with a crucial decision:

(1) Remaining a nuclear state gave Kazakhstan prestige in the region, balanced against the threats of becoming the target of nuclear attacks and, more immedidately, international sanctions should it decide to pursue a nuclear proliferation policy;

(2) foregoing the nuclear option would, among other things, bring the promise of considerable Western financial and technical assistance.

Almaty opted for the second alternative. Through 'Project Sapphire' in 1993, Kazakhstan's government agreed to transfer to Oakridge, Tennessee, close to 600 kg of nuclear material. There were further plans for the destruction of tactical nuclear weapons left over from the Soviet era and/or placing them under the operational command of Russia.[2] In separate agreements with the United States, Russia, and China, Kazakhstan was assured that it would not become the target of nuclear attacks. On 26 July 1994 it signed the Safeguard Agreement with the International Atomic Energy Agency and in April 1995, Kazakhstan's president, Nursultan Nazarbayev, reported to the United Nations Secretary-General that the transfer to Russia of all transcontinental ballistic missiles and the destruction of all underground nuclear warheads at the Semipalatinsk nuclear test site had been completed.[3] Western concerns about proliferation of nuclear weapons in Central Asia were thus alleviated.

Radical Islam

The concern here was that the Islamic Republic of Iran would be tempted to take advantage of the situation which had arisen, and encourage some sort of Islamic movement or campaign among the predominantly Muslim population of Central Asia, leading to further destabilisation of the region. Another concern was that, at this crucial juncture when the Central Asian people were about to lay the foundations of their newly independent states, Iran might be taken as a model. Yet another long-term concern, though less elaborated and expressed, was the possible emergence of an Islamic bloc, with a population of 300 million, that would stretch from the Mediterranean to the Indian Ocean.

As the region opened up to the outside world and more contact became possible, preoccupation with an Islamic threat was considerably reduced. It soon became clear that the peoples of Central Asia, though Muslim, did not have any inclination to follow Iran's version of Islam. Islam had spread in the region from the tenth century mainly by Sufis, who presented their particular understanding of the religion to Central Asia. Seventy years of communist rule many centuries later had further left an impact on the people's faith.

It turned out also that the West did not have vital strategic concerns in Central Asia. It was even argued that the West had only 'negative interests' in that region, i.e. as long as there was no major upheaval in the region leading to destabilisation of Central Asia, the West would be content.[4]

Exploiting economic opportunities

As regards exploiting the natural resources and economic opportunities in Central Asia, it seems that long-term investments were rated as uneconomical or risky relative to the newly emerging opportunities in Eastern Europe. The main area of interest for the West, then, was energy in which relatively short-term investments and high rates of return seemed to be guaranteed. It is these areas in which the bulk of Western investments have been concentrated. Exploration in Kazakhstan's oil fields in Tengiz, investment in Turkmenistan's natural gas and the creation of Azerbaijan's offshore oil consortium are all examples of this.

Iran and Central Asia

The developments of 1991 placed Iran in a unique and privileged strategic position, unmatched by that of any other country. This was due to various factors, the most important of which are the following:

(1) The Central Asia–Caspian region has emerged as one of the world's richest regions in oil and gas reserves. The Caspian region with 57.1 trillion cubic metres of gas (excluding that of Russia) has the richest reserves in the world,[5] and with 59.2 billion barrels of oil it has the third largest oil reserves on the globe, after the Persian Gulf and Siberia.[6] By 2010, it is estimated that the republics of Kazakhstan, Turkmenistan, Uzbekistan, and Azerbaijan will produce 5 million barrels of oil per day.[7]

(2) The newly independent states of Central Asia are land-locked with no access to open seas. They depend on their neighbours, including Iran, to transport commodities to and from the outside world.

(3) Iran is the bridge linking the world's two largest oil and gas reserves, the Persian Gulf and the Central Asia-Caspian regions.

> With 2000 miles of shore on the Persian Gulf, Iran is the shortest, and the most economical route for transportation of oil and gas from the Central Asia–Caspian region to Japan, and the Far East. The network of Iran's gas pipelines is already linked with Azerbaijan, and is within a short distance from Turkmenistan. A pipeline that can connect Kazakhstan and Turkmenistan to this network is at least four times shorter and cheaper than the proposed pipelines to the Mediterranean and the Black Sea.[8]

Common history and culture

Aside from the privileged position Iran enjoys in this geo-economic area, it shares a long and common history with Central Asia. Indeed, over seven centuries of Iran's past was centred on Central Asia as much as on the Middle East, outside its present day political borders. The Persian language spoken by the majority of Iranian people today was born in Central Asia, in today's Uzbekistan. From the Samanid dynasty in the tenth century to the Irano-Turkish dynasties of Ghaznawids, Seljukids, Khwarazmshahs and Timurids, the nexus of Iran's political power and culture lay in Central Asia.

For centuries Persian served as the language of *belle lettres* and poetry amongst the peoples of the region and Persian culture left a lasting impact on the lives of the Central Asian peoples. The decision by Kazakhstan's government to observe the Persian New Year, *naw ruz*, declaring it an official holiday, is a testimony to this claim. Despite vast differences in interpretation and inclination, the majority of the peoples of Central Asia, like the Iranians, are Muslim. This shared history, religion, and culture affords Iran the potential for forging a close relationship with the Central Asian republics.

The Iranian government's view of Central Asia

With the breakup of the Soviet Union the Iranian government, too, looked to Central Asia with interest. The Iranian view of its potential interests in the region proved as naive as those of the Western governments. Iran's hope was that, with the disappearance of the Soviet Union, the Muslim peoples of the region would follow Iran's footsteps and turn their newly formed governments into Islamic republics. One concern that soon emerged was the security of Iran's northern border, as the civil war in Tajikistan broke out and the dispute in the Nagorno-Karabakh region between Azerbaijan and Armenia resulted in thousands of refugees on Iran's northern border. In the spring of 1992 Abbas Maleki, Iran's Deputy Foreign Minister for Research and Training, in his address to China's Institute of International Relations, warned: 'The emergence of a handful of undeveloped and poor states that continuously face the threat of rebellion and drought would severely affect the security and stability of the borders of the neighbouring countries.'[9]

Interestingly enough, it seems that, unlike the other governments, the Islamic Republic's initial concern was not economic. Iran's perception of, and policy toward, Central Asia has evolved over recent years. It has gone through various stages. The first stage can be characterised by the belief that the people of Central Asia would be inclined to go back to their roots and hopefully create their own Islamic states. In 1992, such a hope was hinted at by Dr Ali Akbar Velayati, the then Iranian Foreign Minister:

> The true cultural identity in this region of the world is a combination of valuable Islamic principles and ancient national traditions amongst these peoples . . . With the rich history of this region in mind, we are determined to provide the means for Central Asia and the Caucasus to once again join the main current of world culture and civilization.[10]

It was assumed that this would be the natural consequence of the changing geopolitics of the region, rather than a result of any particular initiative by the Islamic Republic of Iran. In his speech to China's Institute of International Affairs, the Iranian Deputy Foreign Minister Abbas Maleki explained:

> With the breakup of the Soviet Union, the region's subsystem has been altered completely. The Middle Eastern subsystem was such that, politically and culturally, Iran stood at its periphery. That subsystem had basically an Arabic character, its main economic feature being the presence of huge oil reserves, a strategic commodity; whereas the recent developments have expelled Iran from the Middle Eastern system and introduced it into a new subsystem that includes the newly independent states of Central Asia and the Caucasus. The main feature of this subsystem, from the economic and cultural point of view, is its non-Arabic nature and lack of any transactable strategic commodity at the international level, such as oil.[11]

This belief was greatly reinforced by an almost total lack of knowledge about the region, its emerging governments, and the wishes of its peoples. With little insight into the nature of the developments in Central Asia, the Islamic government offered verbal support to trends and groups that were not necessarily in harmony with Iran's interests. An example of this was the support offered to the government in Tajikistan that took power after independence. Though labelled Islamic, it was in fact an awkward coalition between Islamists and a group of intellectuals and academicians. The excesses carried out by that regime alienated a great number of Tajiks and brought to power the present pro-Russian, pro-Uzbek government in Dushanbe, with an anti-Islamic attitude and opposing Tajik nationalist tendencies. It later turned out that the main support for the 'Islamic regime' came from the Saudi government, whereas Iran's involvement with that regime did not go beyond verbal support.

The second stage came with the realisation that the peoples of Central Asia, and especially their governments, had no enthusiasm for creating an Islamic state. This became increasingly apparent as diplomatic and commercial contacts between Iran and Central Asia developed.[12] Furthermore, the Russians – who still hold considerable political power in the region and see it as their own backyard – would not tolerate the creation of such states in their former south.

Finally, perceptions have become realistic, giving priority to maintaining peace and security in the region, with an emphasis on economic and cultural cooperation. This was reiterated by Foreign Minister Velayati in his address at the seminar on 'Security and Foreign Policy in Central Asia and the Caucasus' in January 1996 in Tehran:

> The Islamic Republic of Iran is convinced that its security lies in preservation of peace and tranquillity in the region and it is in this context that her policies vis-à-vis the Persian Gulf, the neighbouring countries, and Central Asia evolve."[13]

A very important aspect of this policy has been the recognition that Russia's influence and interests in the region cannot be ignored. This is an important point worth elaborating. Having been isolated on the international scene, mainly because of the efforts of the United States and European acquiescence, Iran is gradually tilting towards Russia – a former superpower and still the major power in the region – for support.

At the Irano-Russian Roundtable held in Moscow in October 1995, Deputy Foreign Minister Maleki spoke of 'the dawn of a new era of greater cooperation and friendship' between the two countries. 'The recent thrust of the Irano-Russian bilateral relations,' he said, 'though in an embryonic stage, has channelled events in the right direction . . . The road ahead seems stable and steady.' Referring to Russia's intransigence in the face of international pressure and Iran's insistence on maintaining her 'special relations' with Russia, he stated: 'Russia and Iran have rejected the groundless accusations of Washington, resisting the spread of unwarranted approaches on the international scene.'[14] This, it seems, has meant avoiding actions and comments that might annoy Moscow. Thus, President Hashemi Rafsanjani, addressing the conference on Security and Foreign Policy in Central Asia and the Caucasus, held in Tehran in the summer of 1996, noted:

> Many of their [Central Asia] needs are in Russia. Railroads, industries, communications, and their academic expertise is in Russia. [Outside] powers and governments should not attempt to create conflicts between them and Russia. We must try lest the sincerity between them and Russia disappears. The United States, for example, should not, for the sake of its own presence [in the region], think of severing its relations with Russia. Here is not the place for this sort of competition . . . They must work with them so that gradually their dependence on Russia would be reduced. This is what Iran is doing.[15]

The Iranian government's position on Bosnia-Herzegovina may also be an indication. Even though Russia has been by far the most important backer of the Serbs, Iran decided to turn a blind eye to Moscow's stance and blame the US government as the main culprit in the Bosnian tragedy.

Increasingly, Iran is looking to the Economic Cooperation Organisation (ECO)[16] as a vehicle for cooperation and gaining influence in the region. However, as long as the member states continue to prefer bilateral economic relations with Russia or the developed countries in the West, ECO's potential as a powerful regional organization integrating the economies of the region remains in doubt.

Impediments to the development of long-term relations

Iran faces a number of obstacles, both internal and external, in forging a long-term relationship with its neighbours. Internally, these obstacles are as follows:

(1) Proper understanding of the region is lacking, though this is gradually improving.

(2) There is a lack of a coherent foreign policy towards the region, in part a result of Iran's deep-rooted leaning towards the West. Prior to the revolution, during the Pahlavi regime, such an inclination was understandable, given the regime's close ties with the West. It seems, however, that underestimating the importance of Iran's neighbours, both in Central Asia and the Middle East, in formulating its foreign policy persists to this day. Central Asia is still handled in the Ministry of Foreign Affairs by the department responsible for Europe and America.

(3) The legacy of the past when the region was under Soviet domination and treated as part of a European country has persisted. The fact that the more competent members of Iran's diplomatic core are sent to Western capitals may be another indication of this inclination. But the confusion over who should handle the affairs of Central Asia and the Caucasus in executive circles of government has not been limited to the Islamic Republic of Iran. In the United States, aside from uncertainty over that country's proper goals and policies in the region, there emerged a competition between the departments that were in charge of the former Soviet Union and those that handled the Middle East.[17] Whereas for most other countries Central Asia is not a vital region, for Iran, as her immediate neighbour, the region is of great importance and a clear policy towards it is conducive to the development of long-term friendly relations.

(4) There is an absence of modern ideas and innovative thinking in the execution of Iran's policies in the region. The Islamic Republic's major tool for gaining influence in Central Asia in the past few years has been sending books in the Persian script to the region – and that mainly to Tajikistan – despite the fact that very few people in Central Asia can read any script other than Cyrillic. This is in sharp contrast to Turkey, for instance, which broadcasts 18 hours of satellite programmes daily all over Central Asia, has founded many

schools in the new republics, and in 1992-3 alone offered scholarships to over 7000 students from the region to study in Turkish universities and other vocational and educational institutions.[18]

(5) Iran has had limited success in gaining the trust of Central Asian leaders.

(6) 18 years after its revolution, Iran is still suffering from weaknesses common to revolutionary regimes; key positions and policy decisions are the prerogative of the ideologues of the Islamic Republic, leaving the specialists and experts outside the decision making process. This has meant vacillations and repeated policy changes resulting in confusion.[19]

There are also external factors that have hampered Iran's efforts in gaining her objectives in the region. These include:

(1) The suspicion that Central Asian leaders have of the Iranian government. There is a view that the presence of the Islamic Republic in the region is a source of instability, both through its backing of radical Islam and through providing a model of government for the predominantly Muslim peoples of Central Asia. Iran's image in the world as an outlaw state that condones terrorism and Islamic fundamentalism is mainly a product of the major Western governments and the Western media with their own agendas vis-à-vis the Islamic Republic of Iran.[20] Yet, increasingly, the rest of the world, including Central Asia, depends on this media, and hence its views are shaped by them.

(2) The persistence of the old Soviet mentality among many of the Central Asian leaders that distrust foreigners.

(3) Political antagonism by the United States. The United States has used its power and influence against Iran, blocking Iran's initiatives in the Nagorno-Karabakh dispute and blocking the National Iranian Oil Company's membership in the Azerbaijani Oil Consortium despite Iran's entitlement to join as a legitimate partner in the enterprise.

Conclusion

Iran faces a good deal of competition in Central Asia. Russia still enjoys considerable clout in the region as well as political influence and an economic advantage. Turkey, which sees the twenty-first century as the century of the Turks, has already embarked on a long-term initiative in Central Asia and the Caucasus. China, with a long border with the region and an expanding export capability, has not hesitated to lay the grounds for exploiting the commercial and economic opportunities in Central Asia.

Despite tremendous potential, Iran's level of influence in the region remains relatively small. In order to improve its position, Iran needs to enhance its diplomatic activity in the region and mount a public relations campaign aimed at changing its image as a potential troublemaker and an untrustworthy neighbour. All the same, it may be argued that Iran has pursued a rational and positive course of action in Central Asia and the Caucasus. In spite of lingering radicalism among some circles in the Islamic government since the breakup of the Soviet Union, Iran has been an advocate of Islamic unity and economic cooperation based on a common history and culture rather than radical Islam. It needs to remind these countries' leaders of this reality and that long-term economic, political, and cultural relations with Iran can be beneficial to all the states in the region.

More important still is for Iran to show that it is committed to serious long-term foreign policies and is unaffected by short-term domestic political considerations. Between 1992 and 1995 alone more than 60 visits by heads of states and ministers took place between Iran and the Central Asian countries, in each of which at least one memorandum of understanding, agreement, or contract was signed in economic, trade, cultural, and scientific fields. Yet the outcome of such intense diplomatic activity has been minimal as many of these have not moved beyond the signing ceremonies. Iran must see to it that these will actually materialise and become the basis for further cooperation in the region.

Finally, the present antagonism between the governments of Iran and the United States has its roots more in domestic political expediency for both countries than in real, substantial differences between the two nations. Whatever short-term political benefits the leaders of the two countries might gain domestically through bashing each other's governments, the national and international costs are considerable. Whereas the United States as a superpower can absorb the national cost, Iran, with diminishing resources and a weak economy, is bound to find it increasingly difficult to sustain such a hostile posture towards the

United States. Central Asia is but one region where the antagonism between these countries has taken its toll of Iran's national interests. The costs in terms of lost opportunities (construction of the oil pipeline to the Persian Gulf, membership in the Azerbaijani oil consortium, etc.) may be too high to justify continuation of the present policy.

Iran should rethink its policy towards the United States and embark on the initiatives outlined above.

NOTES

1 'Factlife-US security assistance to the former Soviet Union', *Arms Control Today*, 25:3 (April 1995), pp. 24–5; see also Sherman W. Garnnet, 'Ukraine's decision to join the NPT', *Arms Control Today*, 25:1 (January–February, 1995), pp. 7–12; and Sa'ideh Lotfian, 'Kazakhstan's nuclear status and regional security', *Amu Darya*, 1:2 (1996), p. 254.
2 Ibid., p. 247.
3 Ibid., pp. 252–3; see also 'Kazakhstan is nuclear free', *Jane's Defense Weekly*, 29 July 1995.
4 See Seyyed Mohammad Kazem Sajjadpour, 'Negaresh-ha-ye mowjud dar Gharb darbarah-ye raftar-e Iran ba jomhuri-ha-ye Shawravi-ye sabeq' (The West's views on Iran's behaviour towards the republics of the former Soviet Union), *Motale'at-e Asiya-e Markazi va Qafqaz (MAMQ)* (Central Asia and the Caucasus Review), 1:2 (Autumn 1992), p. 101.
5 Piruz Mojtahedzadeh, 'Didgahha-ye Iran dar Rabeteh ba Darya-ye Khazar, Asiya-ye Markazi, Khalij-e Fars, wa Khavar-e Miyaneh' (Iran's views on the Caspian Sea, Central Asia, the Persian Gulf, and the Middle East), *Ettila'at-e Siasi-Eqtisadi*, 9:11/12 (1995), p. 8.
6 International Energy Agency's report (September 1993).
7 See Faridun Barkashli, 'Mulahizati darbareh-ye esteratejiha-ye mantaqah'i-ye Jumhuri-ye Eslami-ye Iran' (Some notes on the Islamic Republic of Iran's regional strategies) in Seyyed Rasul Musawi (ed.), *Manabe va zarfiyatha-ye eqtesadi-e Asiya-ye Markazi va Qafqaz* (Tehran: Ministry of Foreign Affairs) (1995).
8 Mojtahedzadeh, 'Didgahha-ye Iran'.
9 Abbas Maleki's address to China's Institute of International Affairs in June 1992, 'Ravabet-e Iran va Jomhuriha-ye Asiya-ye Markazi' (Iran's relations with the Republics of Central Asia), *MAMQ*, 1:1 (1992), p. 5.
10 *MAMQ*, 1:1 (Summer 1992), p. 4.
11 Maleki, 'Ravabet-e Iran', pp. 9–10. Apparently, he had not yet been aware of the huge gas reserves under Turkmenistan and the oil reserves in Kazakhstan and Azerbaijan.
12 Extensive interviews during six weeks of stay for a related project in Central Asia in the autumn of 1994 clearly demonstrated this to the author. Also see N.

Lubin, 'Islam and ethnic identity in Central Asia: a view from below' in Y. Ro'i (ed.), *Muslim Eurasia: Conflicting Legacies*, (London: Frank Cass, the Cummings Centre Series, 1995).

13 The inaugural speech delivered by Dr Velayati at the seminar on 'Security and foreign policy in Central Asia and the Caucasus', held at I.P.I.S., Tehran, 14–16 January 1996. For the text of the speech see 'The constructive role of the Islamic Republic of Iran in maintaining regional security', *Amu Darya*, 1:2 (1996), pp. 183–9.

14 Abbas Maleki, Deputy Foreign Minister for Research and Training, addressing the Irano-Russian Round Table in Moscow, 4–5 October 1995. In an obvious reference to the United States, he correctly observed: 'In the so-called "new world order", they have gone as far as redefining the interests of nations and entire continents and even the Central Asian states within their "security sphere".' For the text of the speech, see 'The prospects of Irano-Russian relations till the Year 2000', *Amu Darya*, 1:2 (Fall 1996), pp. 191–9.

15 President Hashemi Rafsanjani's address to the conference on 'Security and foreign policy in Central Asia and the Caucasus', held at I.P.I.S., Tehran, 13–15 January 1995. See 'Jomhuri-ye Eslami-ye Iran va keshvarha-ye jadid ol-bonyad' (The Islamic Republic of Iran and the newly founded states), *MAMQ*, 5:13 (1995), p. 9.

16 After the Islamic Revolution, the RCD, a regional organisation whose members were Iran, Turkey, and Pakistan, was changed to ECO on Iran's initiative. After the breakup of the Soviet Union, the Central Asian states were invited to join the organisation.

17 At the Pentagon, for instance, both the Middle East and NATO commands requested to take over responsibility for the region.

18 Turkey's Ministry of Culture State Bureau of Statistics 1993 cited in Na'ini Haydarzadeh, *Ahromha-ye nofuz-e Torkiyeh dar Asiya-ye Miyneh* (Turkey's means of penetration in Central Asia) (Tehran, 1995), p. 32, unpublished. Turkey has long-term plans for expanding its relations and influence in Central Asia and the Caucasus.

19 A case in point is the frequent changes in Iran's export and import policies. After the breakup of the Soviet Union Iranian entrepreneurs managed to gain a foothold in food and clothing markets of Kazakhstan, Turkmenistan, and Kyrgyzstan. The severely restrictive currency policy adopted by Tehran in 1995 wiped out the Iranian commercial presence in Central Asia in a matter of months.

20 See Mahmud Sariolqalam, 'Shenakht-e esterategi-ye Amrika nesbat be Iran va Khavar-e Miyaneh' (American strategy in Iran and the Middle East), *Faslname-ye Khavar-e Miyaneh*, 2:2 (Summer 1995), pp. 304–5; see also Sajjadpour, *MAMQ* (Summer 1992), pp. 104–5.

8

Afghanistan's Relations with Iran, Pakistan and the Central Asian Countries

Alam Payind

This chapter discusses the developments in the Afghan civil war since the early 1990s, and Afghanistan's relations with its neighbours. The information in this chapter is based on the interviews that the author carried out in Afghanistan prior to 1994. His purpose was to explore the future direction of Afghanistan's policy towards its neighbours. Today, over 90 per cent of Afghan towns and villages are under the control of Taleban forces whose relations with Iran are extremely tense. Since the assassination of nine Iranian diplomats and the mass killing of Shia Muslims in areas under their control in 1998, the Taleban have been on the brink of war with Iran.

The background

It has been the unhappy fate of Afghanistan to be the stage for numerous internal conflicts and foreign invasions. While many of these conflicts have been generated within Afghanistan or within the region itself, others have been provoked from without. Just in the past hundred years, Afghanistan was invaded either partially or completely six times by outsiders. Contemporary Afghans recognise that in the absence of a legitimate and effective central authority, their country will continue to serve as a battlefield where the conflicting interests of various Afghan ethnic and linguistic groups and of Afghanistan's neighbours converge. They also recognise the ways in which these conflicts and wars have forced changes in traditional relations among various Afghan ethnic and linguistic communities.

This chapter on the perceptions of Afghans about their country's relations with its neighbours is based on views gathered through interviews conducted both inside and outside Afghanistan between 1992 and

1994. More than 110 Afghans were interviewed, representing a broad spectrum of Afghan ethnic and class groups. The aim of the interviews was to assess attitudes towards recent political developments in Afghanistan. Specifically, how do the Afghan *awam* (general public) perceive their vital interests and how do their perceptions coincide with or differ from the views of the Afghan armed groups or the political leaders of China, Iran, Russia, Saudi Arabia, Tajikistan, Turkmenistan, the United States, and Uzbekistan? Ghulam Hassan, a Hazara scholar, summarised the views of many Afghans on the situation in Afghanistan:

> When Afghans as a front line people were fighting against the Soviet occupying forces and their clients for 14 years, and were absorbing the blood of over one million casualties, the United States, Pakistan, Iran, and the Arab Gulf States were saying 'Well done, we are with you.' They labelled Afghanistan, 'a country of unbending, freedom-loving heroes'.
>
> Praises accompanied by weapons and money poured into the resistance camps. But when the Soviet troops, after devastating Afghanistan, retreated from it, outsiders, including those who supported Afghans in their 14 years of resistance, abandoned them. The country which burned for 14 years in the flames of the Cold War between the superpowers is now burning in the flames of a less known Cold War waged among lower-level powers such as Iran, Pakistan, Saudi Arabia and the Central Asian countries, the latter still ruled by former communists. What a fateful reward for yesterday's heroes?[1]

Ghulam Hassan rather poetically expressed a common theme of the Afghan *awam* since the Soviet invasion of their country in 1979. 'Most major armed groups inside Afghanistan have formed close associations with foreign powers, especially Pakistan.'[2] These cosy relationships with, and dependence on, outside – especially neighbouring – countries have deprived the warring factions of legitimacy in Afghanistan. Pakistan, due to its geopolitical situation and its involvement in Afghanistan's ongoing conflicts, continues to be in a unique position. During the Soviet occupation of Afghanistan, 3.5 million Afghans sought refuge in Pakistan. Although Afghans generally appreciate the hospitality, support and cooperation extended by the Pakistani people, they resent the domineering tendencies of the Pakistani military. Afghanistan's Interim Government (AIG), comprised of members of pro-Pakistan *mujahedin tanzims* (Pakistan-supported political parties), not only was formed in Pakistan, but according to many Afghan and Pakistani scholars was created by the Pakistani military.[3] Moreover, all the major accords among Afghan warring factions were signed under the watchful eyes of the military. Pakistan under the late President Zia ul-Haq set a pattern of supporting only Pakistan-based *mujahedin tanzims* and undercut the formation of nationalist, traditionalist, moderate and democratic organisations and movements among the Afghan resistance and refugee groups. There is consensus among Afghans that even in the post-Soviet era the Pakistani military has continued to pursue Zia's model of supporting the monopoly and control of only pro-Pakistani Islamist *mujahedin tanzims* over arms and political power. Referring to the government changes since Zia's death, one scholar has argued: 'The personnel change did not, in fact, lead to the anticipated modifications of Pakistan's Afghan policies. The military resisted any diminution of the ISI's (Inter Services Intelligence) power.'[4]

Indian strategists and security experts watch Pakistan's continued support for only pro-Pakistani Afghan factions with great concern. They view this development as a *mujahedin*–Islamabad alliance against Indian security interests in the region. While criticising Pakistan's interference in Afghan affairs, India still maintains its own close relations with the remnants of the Soviet-supported People's Democratic Party of Afghanistan (PDPA). In a similar fashion, Pakistani analysts criticise Russian–PDPA–Indian relations as an attempt to resuscitate 'the failed Moscow–Kabul–Delhi axis'.[5] Some Afghan and Pakistani analysts even argue that India pursues its own crude version of a 'triple containment' with respect to Afghanistan, Pakistan, and Kashmir.[6]

Iran, because of its own internal and external conflicts during the Iran–Iraq War, was initially more cautious than Pakistan in its support of Afghan resistance groups. It supported only those Afghan Shia political parties it believed were ideologically closest to it and thus could help to export the Iranian revolution and strengthen Iranian influence in Afghanistan.[7]

Two pro-Iran Afghan Shia groups, Nasr and Sepah, became the major recipients of Iranian assistance. Shaykh Asif Muhsini, although a prominent Shia scholar and resistance leader from Kandahar and an Afghan nationalist, not only was prevented from supporting anti-Soviet Afghan refugees and resistance groups based in Iran, but also was forced to move the centre of his resistance activities to Pakistan. While in Pakistan, Muhsini discovered that his Afghan nationalistic views were not tolerated by the Pakistani military either. Eventually, he and his associates felt compelled to move their headquarters back inside Afghanistan. Among warring Afghan factions, Iran also supported the Northern Alliance of armed groups. Many members of this alliance, such as the Ismaili Shia leader Jaffar Naderi, the Hezbi-Wahdat leader Abdul Ali Mazari, and the Jamiat-i Islami leaders Ahmad Shah Masoud, Ismail Khan and Burhanuddin Rabbani, received political and moral assistance from Iran.

Just as pro-Pakistan and pro-Iran *mujahedin* parties were and are the recipients of weapons from their respective supporters, General Rashid Dostum, a former Soviet-trained Uzbek militia commander, has received his share of weapons, spare parts, and fuel through and from Uzbekistan since 1992. Moreover, under current post-Soviet relationships, any Uzbek–Tajik conflict to the north of the Amu Darya affects the Uzbek–Tajik relations on the Afghan side of Amu Darya.

Azizullah Wasifi, a former cabinet member and the last president of the *loya jirgah* (the Afghan Grand National Council) before the Soviet invasion of Afghanistan, stated:

> It is true that the Soviet troops have left Afghanistan in disgrace, but the physical and social devastation that resulted from the 10-year occupation and subsequent conflicts are very difficult to repair. It is not the end of the story. Yeltsin's Russia under its policy towards its 'near abroad' and the former *nomenklatura* who rule in Tashkent, Almata, Ashkabad, Dushanbe and Dishkik, all want to influence developments in Afghanistan to their liking.[8]

The newly independent but landlocked Muslim countries of Central Asia need stability and peace in Afghanistan, which could serve as a link to international markets for them and reduce their dependency on Russia. However, the secular leaders of these predominantly Muslim states feel insecure and are therefore fearful of any possible adverse impact from the perceived threat of an 'Islamic Comintern' based in Afghanistan. For instance, President Islam Karimov of Uzbekistan apparently considers all forms of political activity by Muslims as 'Islamic fundamentalism' dedicated to reviving, in his words, 'medieval horror'. He has declared that no Islamic movement should be tolerated in the region and he has denounced the various political activities and movements of Muslims regardless of their root causes and targets, as links in the same chain of extremism, with an ideology of expansionism.[9]

In Moscow, policy-makers, who hope to attract US and European cooperation in perpetuating Russian hegemony over its 'near abroad', sound like Western academics such as Samuel Huntington and Bernard Lewis, for whom the 'clashes of civilisation' between 'the West and the rest' is a reality.[10] Vladimir Zhirinovsky, leader of the Russian ultra-nationalist Liberal Democratic Party, in his November 1994 California speech warned his American audience 'to watch out for those Chinese and Muslims'.[11] According to Azizullah Wasifi, Afghan experts who study nationalist movements among non-Russians of the former Soviet Union were not surprised when the Russian government and media labelled the Chechen uprising a movement of bandits, criminals and Islamic fundamentalists.[12]

Russian leaders and their Tajik, Turkmen and Uzbek counterparts seem to believe that Islam is the primary cause of social unrest in predominantly Muslim areas. In reality the root cause of the problems and conflicts lies in chronic oppression, authoritarian regimes, crises of legitimacy, and extremism, both religious or secular. However, former communists, like authoritarian leaders in Egypt, Morocco, Syria, and Tunisia, often have magnified the threat of religious movements to obscure more pressing political, social and economic problems.

Most people in Afghanistan and many international observers view the ongoing war and its consequences as a reflection of the incompatible political and economic interests of the Afghan warlords and foreign powers, especially neighbouring countries. The clash of these interests caused the disruption of the delicate balance of ethnic, linguistic, tribal and *mudhabi* Sunni–Shia relationships that prevailed in Afghanistan prior to 1979. A Tajik scholar who conducts research on Tajikistan and Afghanistan states:

> The fighting in Afghanistan has been going on for 15 years. It is the continuation of a Cold War tragedy now being played out by several actors. Inside Afghanistan, the main actors are: (1) the Pakistan-supported Jamiat-i Islami of Burhannuddin Rabbani; (2) the Hezb-i Islami of Gulbuddin Hekmatyar, also supported by Pakistan; and (3) the formerly Soviet-supported and now Uzbekistan-supported General Rashid Dostum. Other actors are Pakistan, Iran, Saudi

> Arabia and the rulers of newly-independent Central Asian countries who are former communists and continue to follow directions from Moscow.[13]

An Afghan scholar, Hafizullah Emadi, agrees with this assessment. The main thesis of his book, which was written before the Soviet withdrawal in 1989, is that the United States, Pakistan, Iran, and Saudi Arabia provided financial and military support only to so-called Islamic parties in the hope that, after overthrowing the Afghan communist leadership, these parties would serve their respective interests in Afghanistan and in the region. Emadi further argues that, from the beginning of the popular uprising against the Soviet occupation, some of the recipients of assistance, under the pretext of fighting communism, carried out repressive policies against traditionalists, intellectuals, nationalists, and democrats throughout Afghanistan and the refugee camps in Pakistan. These policies of repression, along with the pervasive corruption within the ranks of the self-declared Islamic parties, have isolated them from the people.[14]

Many foreign observers have noted the transformation of the *mujahedin* into groups interested only in pursuing the personal ambitions of their respective leaders. The support of outside powers has facilitated this process. For example, Stephen Masty, an American who has worked for years with Afghan relief programmes, said: 'The United States was not responsible for the Soviet Union invading Afghanistan, but we [Americans] were responsible for arming the *mujahedin* groups that grew to be Frankensteins.'[15]

In August 1992, five months after the collapse of the Najibullah government and during the second Pakistan-engineered *mujahedin* administration of Burhanuddin Rabbani, one of the disillusioned field commanders commented:

> The fall of Najib sharpened the rivalries and ambitions among Pakistan, Iran, and Central Asian countries as well as among different *mujahedin* parties supported by these countries. Instead of promoting reconciliation among *mujahedin* and between *mujahedin* and common Afghans, the Pakistani, Iranian, Saudi and Central Asian governments are aggravating the division among Afghans by favouring one political party or one group over the others. What is more, all parties are heavily armed and continue to receive arms and money from their foreign supporters.[16]

Both serious and casual observers of Afghanistan who visited the country after the fall of the Najibullah government witnessed the diminishing popularity of the foreign-supported *mujahedin* parties, fighting with each other for the control of Kabul and other provinces. Since 1979, the leaders and commanders of Pakistan-based *mujahedin* parties and Pakistani war profiteers have accumulated power and wealth beyond their wildest dreams. They do not seem to be willing to give up their newly acquired power. At the risk of becoming marginalised, these leaders and other Afghan, Pakistani, and Iranian war profiteers have resisted adjustment to the new realities of a post-Soviet Afghanistan. An Afghan observer summed up this dilemma in two sentences: 'Before we had one king in Afghanistan. Now a Soviet-made Rashid Dostum, Pakistan-made *mujahedin* leaders and Saudi-sponsored Wahhabis all behave like kings.'[17] To make his point clear, he quoted the Persian proverb: 'The legacy of the dead bear is now acquired by hyenas.'[18]

After a decade of resistance (1979–89) against Soviet occupying forces and more than six years of ruthless fighting among the warlords since 1989, Afghans have lost hope of a reconciliation among foreign-supported *tanzims*. This resentment of the arrogant and corrupt behaviour of the warlords and a hunger for peace among the Afghan *awam* has paved the way for the surprising success of a new force in Afghanistan, the Taleban (translated as students of religious institutions). According to the Taleban leaders, their objectives are to eliminate oppressive *tanzim* warlords and establish a united Islamic government in Afghanistan. This new force captured nearly half of Afghanistan in only five months, beginning in September 1994. Later, in the autumn of 1995, the Taleban captured all of Western Afghanistan, thus bringing under unified control a greater area of the country than at any time since the Soviet occupation began in December 1979.[19] Reports from inside Afghanistan indicate that the Taleban have disarmed most of the warring factions and have established relative calm in areas under their control.

In early 1995, the Taleban began an offensive to capture the capital, Kabul, but this move was blocked until September 1996 by stiff government resistance. The capital and northern Afghanistan have become testing areas for the Taleban forces, which were halted five miles from Kabul. The Rabbani government's propaganda against the Taleban, labelling them clients of a foreign country, succeeded for a short period in areas under government control.[20] In September 1996, both Jalalabad and Kabul were captured by Taleban forces. After their defeat in Kabul, the deposed president, Burhanuddin Rabbani, and his chief military commander, Ahmad Shah Masoud, formed alliances with some of their bitter enemies, for example, Rashid Dostum and the Hazara warlords, against the Taleban. As of January 1997, the Taleban have expanded their control over two-thirds of Afghanistan. Many Afghans speculate that the Taleban, like their predecessors, the seven Pakistan-based *mujahedin tanzims*, are also supported by the Pakistani government. The difference is that the *mujahedin tanzims* of Said Ali Gailani, Gul Buddin Hekmatyar, Younis Khalis, Mohammad Nabi Mohammadi, Sibghatullah Mujjaddedi, Burhanuddin Rabbani, and Abdul Rab Sayaf were under the control of the Pakistani ISI while the Taleban are supported primarily by the Pakistani ministry of interior under the leadership of retired General Nasirullah Babur. Several Pakistani newspapers including the *Muslim,* the *News* and the *Frontier Post* have published articles about the ongoing relationship between the Pakistani government and the leaders of the Taleban.[21] A US magazine quoted Pakistani and foreign sources referring to Pakistan's role in this dangerous 'game'.[22] In an interview with the *WUFA* newspaper, General Nasirullah Babur denied that Pakistan was supporting the Taleban forces in Afghanistan.[23]

One solution suggested by most Afghans to their country is the convening of a *loya jirgah,* under the auspices of the United Nations and the Organisation of the Islamic Conference (OIC). For nearly 300 years, the *loya jirgah* has proved to be an effective forum for negotiation during many crises.[24] The devastating results of the 10-year Soviet occupation and the continuing infighting among *tanzims* have compelled the traditionally self-reliant and xenophobic Afghan *awam* to welcome the United Nations peace-making initiatives. Because Pakistan, Iran and Saudi Arabia have all involved themselves in the inter-*tanzim* conflicts, many Afghans view their involvement in the peace negotiations with suspicion.

Supporters of the idea of convening a *loya jirgah* argue that a primary reason for the ongoing crisis in Afghanistan can be found in the exclusion of the general Afghan public from all negotiations, accords and discussions since 1979. This exclusion of the general Afghan public has resulted in a lack of popular support for foreign-supported formulations. Consequently, six presidents have failed to acquire a token *bai'at* (legitimacy), a very high rate of failure even by Afghan standards. It is important to note that all six presidents since 1978 (Nur Mohammed Taraki,

Hafizullah Amin, Babrak Karmal, Najibullah, Sibghatullah Mojaddedi, and Burhanuddin Rabbani) have been viewed by the general Afghan public as foreign-imposed or foreign-supported.

Supporters of the idea of convening a *loya jirgah* under the auspices of the UN and OIC range from The Writers Union of Free Afghanistan to popular public figures such as the late Abdul Rahman Pazwak, Said Shamsuddin Majrooh, Said Qasim Rishtiya, many prominent Afghan ulama, former elected members of the Afghan parliament, and the former king, Zahir Shah. However when Benon Seven and Mehmud Misteri, the United Nations special envoys to Afghanistan, tried to include independent or non-*tanzim* moderate Afghans in peace-making efforts, their plans were sabotaged by the extremist *tanzims*. After these failures, most Afghans have concluded that the militant *tanzim* leaders have pushed Afghanistan to a dangerous level of civil war, purely for personal ambition. Moreover, Afghans believe that as long as the *tanzim* leaders suffer no consequences for sabotaging peace plans, the *tanzims* and their supporters will continue to violate all peace efforts.

Many Afghan observers and United Nations diplomats fear the further deterioration of the Afghan crisis to the level of ethnic cleansing. If such a tragedy were to happen, neither Pakistan, Iran, nor the Central Asian countries could remain immune from the consequences. Even Iranian leaders who in the past criticised the UN role have come to support the peace-making efforts of Mehmud Misteri. For example, Alaeddin Boroujerdi, Iranian Deputy Foreign Minister, expressed support for the UN plan to send a special envoy to Afghanistan, declaring: 'The implementation of such a plan would be a major step toward the peaceful settlement of the Afghan crisis.'[25]

The British in the nineteenth and early twentieth centuries, and the Soviets in the 1980s, learned that too much meddling in Afghanistan's internal affairs invites disaster. Nevertheless, it is difficult to predict when Pakistan, Iran, Saudi Arabia and the Central Asian countries will understand that their meddling in Afghanistan's internal affairs is counter-productive.

The challenge faced by those involved in Afghan affairs seems to be to achieve a better understanding of the history and complex realities of the country and its neighbours. It appears that, after paying the heaviest cost in history for independence, the Afghan general public will not be satisfied with a government which is 'foreign-supported, oppressive and, worst of all, mediocre'.[26] Popular sentiment with regard to the current state of affairs in Afghanistan is often expressed by educated, Pashto-speaking Afghans who recite the seventeenth century Afghan poet and leader, Khushal Khan Khattak:

> The fame of Bahlol, and of Sher Shah too, resoundeth in my ears.
> Afghan Emperors of India, who swayed its sceptre effectively and well.
> For six or seven generations did they govern so wisely that all their people were filled with admiration of them.
>
> Whether those Afghans were different, or these have greatly changed.
> Other otherwise, at present, such is the Almighty's decree,
> If the Afghans shall acquire the gift of concord and unity. Old Khushal shall, a second time, grow young therefrom.
>
> . . . .
>
> Let it not be, that every bad rider should mount fortune's steed:
> If it be ridden by anyone, at least a good horseman let him be.[27]

Similarly, Dari-speaking Afghans often recite Shaykh Sa'di's following 'story-in-verse' to described the selfishness and greed common among Afghan warring factions and their foreign backers:

> I heard [a fable] that a sheep had been rescued by a great man from the jaws of a wolf. When the evening fell, the rescuer pressed his sharp knife against the sheep's throat. Whereon the soul of the sheep complained to the man: 'You have snatched me away from the claws of a wolf, but at last I saw that you turned out to be the ultimate wolf.'[28]

The search for peace in Afghanistan continues and the warring factions are still far from achieving sustainable peace in a united Afghanistan, despite all the attempts being employed by Iran to bring peace to its eastern border. At the very end of the twentieth century mankind is witnessing a brutal factionalist war that is supported and abetted by various foreign states in the region.

NOTES

1 Interview, Jalalabad, Afghanistan, 25 August 1992.
2 John Fullerton, 'A rift among rebels,' *Far Eastern Economic Review*, 29 October 1982, p. 20.
3 Mushahid Hussain, 'Prospect for the peaceful settlement,' *Seminar Report on Afghanistan* (Islamabad: Institute of Strategic Studies, December 1990), p. 8.
4 Marvin G. Weinbaum, *Pakistan and Afghanistan: Resistance and Reconstruction* (Boulder, Colo.: Westview Press, 1994).
5 Interview with a former sociology Professor at Kabul University, who resides and conducts research in Pakistan and prefers to remain anonymous, August 1993.
6 Ibid.
7 *Sudur-i-inqilab* (exporting revolution) has been a proclaimed major objective of Iranian foreign policy since the establishment of the Islamic Republic in 1979.
8 Interview, California, June 1994.
9 *The Times*, 25 July 1994, p. 21.
10 Richard E. Rubenstei and Farle Crocker, 'Challenging Huntington', *Foreign Policy*, no. 96, (Fall 1994), p. 114; see also Samuel P. Huntington, 'The clash of civilizations', *Foreign Affairs*, 72:3 (Summer 1993), pp. 21–39.
11 *The New York Times*, 9 November 1994, p. A6.
12 Interview with Azizullah Wasifi, California, June 1994; see also *The Message*, 20:3 (September 1995), p. 13.
13 Interview with a Tajik visiting professor, who preferred to remain anonymous, Columbus, Ohio, 19 March 1994.
14 Hafizullah Emadi, *State, Revolution and Superpowers in Afghanistan* (New York: Praeger, 1990), p. 11.
15 *The New York Times*, 28 February 1994.
16 Alam Payind, 'Evolving alternative views on the future of Afghanistan', *Asian Survey*, 235:9 (September 1993), p. 927.
17 Interview with Ghulam Hassan, Jalalabad, Afghanistan, 25 August 1992.
18 Ibid.
19 *The New York Times*, 16 February 1995.
20 Mohammad Zahid, 'The Taleban and Afghan imbroglio', *The Writers' Union of Free Afghanistan (WUFA)* (Peshawar, Pakistan), no. 6 (December 1995), p. 26.
21 See, for example, *The Frontier Post* (Peshawar, Pakistan), 11 December 1994.
22 *US News and World Report*, 6 March 1995, p. 66.
23 *WUFA*, November 1994, p. 6.
24 Sayid Qasim Rishtiya, 'The right way out of the current dangerous crisis in Afghanistan is to resort to the will of the general public in Afghanistan under UN observation', *WUFA*, 23 May 1993.
25 *Ettela'at*, 21 November 1995.
26 Interview with Azizullah Wasifi, California, 30 June 1994.
27 Khushal Khan Khattak, *Collected Works* (Peshawar, Pakistan, 1952), pp. 214–5.
28 From the *Gulistan* (Rose Garden) of Shaikh Sadi Shirazi (d. 1291 AD), *Kulliyati Sadi* (Tehran: Feroghi, 1988), p. 75.

9

A Historical Perspective on Iran–Afghan Relations

Ali A. Jalali

This chapter reviews the historical background of Iran–Afghan relations with a closer look at the impact of recent changes in the region on bilateral ties between Iran and Afghanistan. It also examines the factors that could influence future development of relations between the two countries.

Introductory note

Despite the deep-rooted historical ties and extensive cultural relationship between Iran and Afghanistan, the two neighbours' foreign policies have been dominated for most of this century by their interaction with other countries in the region and outside powers. A notable shift in the pattern has come into view in the past twenty years, as both nations were embroiled, almost simultaneously, in major political upheavals. The collapse of old regimes in both countries by revolutionary governments with contrasting ideologies opened a period of continued instability in the region. The communist coup in Afghanistan in 1978, followed by the Soviet invasion of the country in December 1979, coincided with the downfall of the Shah and victory of the Islamic revolution in Iran. During the subsequent years, while the Moscow-backed government in Kabul and the Soviet occupation forces faced a nationwide armed resistance in Afghanistan, Iran was locked in a devastating war with Iraq. The Soviet forces began pulling out of Afghanistan (15 May 1988) almost at the same time Iran's war with Iraq ended (August 1988).

These events came at a time of fundamental global changes culminating in the breakup of the Soviet empire and the end of the Cold War. The situation brought deep alterations in the conventional norms, which governed traditional ties between Iran and Afghanistan. The two countries, which for long were mostly engaged with other outside powers, suddenly found themselves directly involved in fast-paced developments inspired by the changing geopolitics in the area or caused by political turmoil in the region.

During the past two decades, Iran and Pakistan have been competing for influence in Afghanistan by supporting rival factions in the Afghan civil war. However, while Pakistan has campaigned for the emergence of a pro-Islamabad government in Afghanistan, Iran has been struggling to secure a balanced role for the Shia minority in Afghan politics and avert the establishment of a hostile regime in Kabul. The two neighbours' distinct strategic aspirations stem from their varying level of influence over Afghan developments, their political priorities and the geopolitics of the region.

The background

People living in the present territories of Iran and Afghanistan have been bound by deep-rooted historical and cultural ties. The relationship has been shaped by shared cultural values and common historical experience. At the same time, geographic diversity and shifting geopolitics in the region have significantly affected the lives of social communities settled in different parts of the massive land. From ancient times, great empires, with shifting centres, straddled the current boundaries between Iran and Afghanistan. Dynastic borders and identities were mostly carved in the minds of ruling powers that controlled the area rather than in the hearts of the people who lived there. Extensive cultural commonalities coloured by distinctive regional peculiarities have characterized the evolving sub-national, national and supra-national identities in the multi-ethnic region. Meanwhile, changing geo-strategic motives tended to pull Afghanistan-based dynasties to the east while Iran-centered powers were mostly drawn to the west and southern peripheries of the Iranian plateau. The north, with its traditional vulnerability to conquering nomadic hordes of the steppes, has been the source of invasion against the whole area.[1] The top concern for the dynasties ruling the western and eastern parts of the Iranian landmass was often the outside threats from opposing directions leaving the inter-dynastic boundaries less volatile.

At the beginning of the sixteenth century, Iran's official adherence to Shiism under the Safavid dynasty marked a cultural divide between the

Iranians and the dominantly Sunni inhabitants living in Afghanistan and Central Asia. State-sanctioned crackdown on Sunnis during the early years of the Safavid rule forced many non-Shia intellectuals to emigrate to Central Asia and India while Shia theologians from Arab lands streamed into Iran.[2] During the following two centuries – when Afghanistan was divided between the Mughal Empire of India and the Safavids of Iran – the sectarian schism left an enduring impact on relations between social communities in the region. Religious persecution by Safavid authorities that was relaxed for some time was resumed in a more violent form during the reign of Shah Sultan Hussein (d. 1726) under the influence of the renowned Shia theologian Shaikh-ul-Islam Mohammad Baqer Majlisi. The uprising of Hotakis and Abdalis of western Afghanistan in the early eighteenth century, leading to the invasion of Iran by the Afghans (1722–9), was partly motivated by sectarian disputes.[3]

Relations between the modern states of Iran and Afghanistan have been influenced more by external factors than bilateral issues. In the eighteenth and early nineteenth centuries, the Afghan state under Ahmad Shah Durrani and his successors was mostly engaged in the Indian subcontinent, while Iran was struggling to deal with the expanding Russian Empire and the Ottomans in the West.[4]

This was immediately followed by the entanglement of both Iran and Afghanistan in the power struggle waged in the region by European powers. Fleeting threats by Napoleon and sustaining expansionist schemes of czarist Russia against the British power in India drew Iran and Afghanistan into the so-called 'Great Game' politics. Britain blocked a renewed Afghan invasion of India under Zaman Shah Durrani (the grandson of Ahmad Shah Durrani) at the end of the seventeenth century through cooperation with Fath'ali Shah Qajar of Iran. The Iranian ruler instigated Zaman Shah's brother Mahmoud, the governor of Herat, to move against the capital and helped him with men and money in his bid for the throne of Kabul. Mahmoud's threat frustrated Zaman Shah's plans for the Indian invasion and he was forced to return home to deal with his domestic problem.[5] About forty years later Iran moved against Afghanistan under the Russian influence. Inspired by Russia, Mohammad Shah Qajar of Iran laid siege to Heart in 1837.[6] Considering the move a threat to India, the British government reacted politically and militarily, which led to the first British invasion of Afghanistan (1839–42). Continued Anglo-Russian rivalry during the rest of the nineteenth and early twentieth centuries, influenced virtually every aspect of relations between the Qajar government of Iran and the Barakzai rulers of Afghanistan. The current boundaries of Afghanistan were drawn by the British and the Russians during this period.

The first half of the twentieth century saw Iran and Afghanistan painfully coping with increasing domestic challenges and foreign interference. In June 1921, two years after the restoration of full independence of Afghanistan from Britain, Kabul signed a treaty of neutrality and friendship with the Qajar government of Iran. The accord was reconfirmed in a friendship and security treaty of 1927 following the establishment of the Pahlavi dynasty in Iran. Ten years later, Kabul and Tehran signed the Saadabad treaty of non-aggression and cooperation between the two nations. During the Second World War Iran's occupation by the Allies and Afghanistan's adherence to its traditional neutrality offered little potential for wider Iran-Afghan interaction.

Cold War politics

During the eventful years of the Cold War, relations of the two neighbours with the outside world took diverging turns. Iran joined the US-led regional security alliance and Afghanistan maintained its traditional neutrality – trading the 'buffer state' epithet of the Great Game era to the 'non-aligned state' designation of the Cold War period. Nevertheless, in the 1950s Kabul's political dispute with the newly created state of Pakistan, an ally of the West, forced the Afghan government to turn to the Soviet Union for military and economic assistance. In the following three decades, the Soviet Union was the main military supplier and trade partner of Afghanistan while the United States forged a close strategic partnership with Iran. During this period when the two neighbours were preoccupied with external powers and other states, their bilateral dealings were mostly placed on the 'back-burner.' However, Iran and Afghanistan managed to maintain friendly ties and resolve their dispute over distribution of water from the Helmand River in the early 1970s (13 March 1973).

A notable shift in Iran–Afghan relations came into view following Mohammad Daud's 1973 coup d'état against King Mohammad Zaher Shah in Afghanistan. The new Afghan regime, which was initially promoted by a Moscow-backed Communist faction (Parcham), received significant support from the Soviet Union. The situation raised fears of increased Moscow influence in Afghanistan at the expense of the country's traditional neutrality. Encouraged by the United States, the Shah's regime in Iran launched a systematic effort to offset Moscow's influence in Afghanistan through expanding economic and political ties with Kabul.[7] Iran offered a two-billion-dollar economic aid programme over a ten years period to Afghanistan. At the same time, Iran participated in channelling covert aid to underground anti-Daud Islamic groups who were fighting the Soviet influence in Afghanistan.[8] Iran's dual-track policy was aimed at blocking the expansion of the Soviet power in the region.[9] During the next few years the Afghan government clamped down on pro-Moscow leftist elements in the administration, took steps to resolve its long-standing political dispute with Pakistan, and forged closer ties with Iran and some other Islamic countries in the region.[10] Meanwhile, disturbed by Daud's independent policies, Moscow stepped up its interaction with Afghan Communist factions mediating their merger in 1977, less than a year before the bloody Communist coup against the Daud regime (27 April 1978).

In terms of policy content and goals, one can see three phases in Iran–Afghan relations during the past twenty years. The first phase spans the first ten years (1979–89) during which Tehran's dealing with Afghanistan was inspired by a revolutionary Islamic ideology. The second phase (1989–92) covers the period between the Soviet military withdrawal from Afghanistan and the fall of the Communist regime in the country. Iran shifted to a more pragmatic approach trying to unite the fragmented Shia factions and enhance their influence in the post-Soviet Afghan politics. The third phase, which began right after the collapse of the Communist regime in Afghanistan (April 1992), has been dominated by an intense struggle for power by ethnically led Afghan factions with extensive foreign competition for influence in the country.

Iran and the Afghan 'jihad'

During the initial years of the Islamic revolution, Iran's ideology-based foreign policy faced an awkward situation in Afghanistan. The United States and the Soviet Union, both vilified in Iran's revolutionary world-view, were supporting the opposing sides in a war that pitted the Islamic-led Mujahedin forces against a repressive Communist government. The

Soviet invasion of Afghanistan in December 1979 sharpened the ideological contraposition that dominated the Afghan jihad. Iran was extremely vociferous in condemning the Moscow-backed Kabul regime and supporting the Afghan Mujahedin in their jihad against the Soviet occupation. But Tehran's actual commitment to the policy hardly matched the rhetoric. The policy was influenced by Tehran's hostility to the United States, the Iran–Iraq war and the ideological world-view of the Iranian revolutionaries.

Iran's anti-American and anti-Western hostility limited its dealing with the US-backed Afghan Mujahedin. This made Pakistan the sole conduit of the multi-billion dollar US-led international military assistance to the Afghan resistance forces. The trend provided Islamabad with a significant political leverage in influencing Afghan politics long after the Soviets' withdrawal. Consequently, Iranian support of the Mujahedin, which was merely verbal until 1981,[11] was too limited to match the continuous flow of military hardware and funds extended to Pakistani-sponsored resistance factions.

The war with Iraq had drained a significant portion of Iran's resources leaving little flexibility for Tehran to get fully engaged in Afghanistan. Further, the war discouraged Iran from risking its stability on the east by getting too much involved in anti-Soviet activities in Afghanistan. Iran, after all, did not feel threatened by the Soviet invasion of Afghanistan at the same level as Pakistan did. Beginning in 1981, the Moscow-backed Democratic Republic of Afghanistan (DRA) launched a major effort to normalize relations with Tehran. It voiced support for Khomeini's anti-American stance which the DRA also shared.[12] The policy continued until 1984 when Iran flatly rejected any relationship with Kabul and stressed its support of the Afghan Mujahedin.[13] Nevertheless, as the war with Iraq and domestic problems began to de-radicalise Iran's foreign policy, Tehran embarked on efforts to improve relations with the Soviet Union by signing a wide-ranging economic protocol with Moscow in 1986. It was argued that the move might discourage Moscow from aiding Iraq and encourage Soviet withdrawal from Afghanistan.[14] Iran has claimed that it never compromised its commitment to support the Afghan Mujahedin despite Moscow's overtures that 'it would halt the sale of long-range missile and jet fighters to Iraq, provided the Iranians would turn a blind eye on developments in Afghanistan'.[15]

Iran's ideological solidarity with the Islamic-led Afghan resistance against the Soviet invaders was constrained by the requirements of Tehran's grand revolutionary strategy. The ideological appeal of the Afghan 'jihad' was eclipsed by Iran's political exigencies. Iranian revolutionaries paid more attention to the Palestinians than the Afghan Mujahedin and favoured Lebanese Shias over their Afghan co-religionists.[16] As an Iranian observer of the Afghan scene notes, Tehran's failure to adopt a comprehensive policy on Afghanistan had a lasting effect on its ability to influence the turbulent development in the war-devastated country.[17] The ambivalence of Iran's policy has been attributed to its continuing course correction along the revolutionary path. Consequently, Iran has been reacting to emerging situations rather than pursuing a proactive policy in Afghanistan.

Thus, Iran's policy on Afghanistan was narrow in scope and sectarian in nature. It mostly targeted the country's Shia minority living in the central Afghan mountainous area of Hazarajat. Iran's ideological crusade in the Hazara land added fuel to internal strife in the area, which was undergoing a profound social upheaval sparked by a power struggle between the traditional establishment and the reformist forces.

Iranian influence fostered fragmentation of a united front of Shia Afghans who in September 1979 formed in Hazarajat a *Shura* – the 'Revolutionary Council of Islamic Union of Afghanistan'.[18] The *Shura* led by Sayed Ali Beheshti – with Sayed Mohammad Hassan (known as Sayed Jaglan) its military commander – organised the administration of the central Afghan mountainous region into nine provinces (*wilayat*) where the government had lost control.[19] The absence of direct threats from the government and Soviet forces to the Hazara hinterland brought to the open a simmering power struggle among the local leaders. The discord split the *Shura* into three factions – one moderate and two extremist. The traditionalists and clerics (Mullahs and Sayeds), who retained control of the *Shura,* were challenged by the Shaykhs-dominated radical Islamists, who supported the Iranian revolution. The leftist elements, mostly of Maoist orientations, which had joined the defeated local tribal figures (mirs and Arabs), were forced out to Quetta.[20]

In 1980-1, the National Liberation Movements Department of Iran's Revolutionary Guards Corps, which supervised relations with the Afghan parties, helped set up the pro-Khomeini Nasr party (*Sazman-e Nasr*) which recruited its members from the young Hazaras trained in Iran. Iran supported the *Nasr* in its bid to seize the leadership of the Hazarajat *Shura*, which was pursuing a more independent policy. This was followed two years later (1983) by the creation of another pro-Iranian Islamist group, the Guardians of the Afghan Islamic jihad (Sepah-e Pasdaran-e jihad-e Islami Afghanistan), under direct control of Iran's Revolutionary Guard Corps.[21] The intra-Shia rivalry led to bloody clashes in 1983–4 that spread unbridled violence across the region, forcing the *Shura* out of its base in Waras and domination of two-third, of Hazarajat by the pro-Iranian *Nasr* and *Sepah* factions.[22] *Nasr* and *Sepah's* repressive policies and their brutal treatment of local landowners and supporters of the *Shura* drove out thousands of Hazaras to refugee camps in Pakistan or other Afghan provinces.

Iran also supported a number of other pro-Khomeini parties including the Hezbollah of Afghanistan, which was active in the western Afghan province of Herat and along the Iranian border. Further, influential Iranian clerics and revolutionary freelancers tried to create their own client revolutionary cells in Hazarajat to bolster their influence in domestic politics. Consequently, in a short time, dozens of pro-Iranian mini-factions mushroomed in the area.[23] These groups, who in their mountainous hideouts were relatively safe from threats by Kabul or the Soviet forces, were mostly involved in internal power struggles. The Kabul regime and its Soviet backers saw the internal strife in Hazarajat to their advantage since it allowed concentration of their forces against the Mujahedin in other areas.[24]

The Iranian policy of favouring selective Afghan factions weakened Tehran's influence over Afghan politics. A number of Shia groups forged coalitions with Pakistan-based Sunni Mujahedin factions. One of the most effective Islamist factions, the Harakat-e Islami of Shaykh Asef Mohseni, the only Shia party which really fought against the Soviets in Hazarajat's border areas and some towns, broke ties with Tehran and shifted its main headquarters to Pakistan. Some other Afghan groups turned down Iranian offers for assistance because of the conditions attached to them, including support of Iran's anti-Western policy.[25]

Iran did allow most of the non-Shia Afghan parties to open offices in Iran, and even tolerated the use of its territory by selected Mujahedin groups as a staging area for cross-border military operations. Some of the groups were getting military supplies from Iran in exchange for the delivery of an equal amount of material from their Pakistani bases to

Iran-backed groups in the Hazarajat which Iran could not supply directly.[26] However, Iran imposed restrictions on the shipment of arms from Pakistan to the Mujahedin bases in western Afghanistan through its territory. Iran allowed only small arms while every convoy was checked, inspected and escorted by the Revolutionary Guards.[27] It was during one of these transfers that Iran got hold of Stinger missiles from a shipment destined for a group in Western Afghanistan.[28]

Iran accepted an estimated 2.35 million Afghan refugees, mostly from the western and southwestern provinces of Afghanistan such as Heart, Farah, Ghor, Nimroz, Badghis, Kandahar and Hazarajat. The politics of the Iran–Iraq war discouraged many international donors from providing funds and facilities to help Tehran deal with the refugees the same way as Pakistan did. Iran generously allowed the Afghans to be integrated locally and get employment in different parts of the country.[29] However, the refugees who were involved in low-wage manual work in Iran were looked down upon by the locals and usually stereotyped as nefarious elements. The resulting discontent among the refugees weakened Iran's political and cultural influence over them. The situation was different in Pakistan where Pakistani patronage of religious schools (*madrasa*) along the Afghan–Pakistani border provided thousands of Afghan refugee children with religious education and political indoctrination. Many of the students later constituted the core of the Pakistani-backed Taleban movement.[30] Iran did train a large number of Afghan Shia refugees, who mostly were engaged in internal strife in Afghanistan in special training centres. Some of the trainees were sent to the battlefronts with Iraq.[31]

Meanwhile Pakistan's influence over the major Mujahedin parties based in Peshawar increased. After many alignments and realignments over the years, Islamabad brokered the formation of the Seven Party Alliance in 1985[32] and dealt with them through a well-organised structure.[33] This gave political weight to Pakistan in the Geneva peace process in which Islamabad was a party to the so-called 'proximity talks.' Iran refused to participate in the Geneva negotiations on the grounds that the Afghan resistance was not represented. However, Iran agreed to be briefed by the UN mediator on the progress of the talks. The Geneva agreement was signed by the DRA and Pakistan, and guaranteed by the United States and the Soviet Union. The accord stipulated a phased withdrawal of the Soviet forces from Afghanistan between 15 May 1988 and 15 February 1989.[34] A bilateral agreement on the voluntary return of refugees was signed between the DRA and Pakistan. The agreement did not include Iran despite the fact that there were about 2.35 million Afghan refugees in Iran.[35]

After the Soviet withdrawal

The period between the Soviet military pullout and the fall of the Moscow-backed government in Kabul (1989–92) was marked by unsuccessful efforts by the Mujahedin to form an all-inclusive government to replace the Communist regime in Kabul, which was expected to fall following the complete withdrawal of the Soviet forces from Afghanistan. UN efforts to mediate the formation of a broad-based government in Afghanistan, which would include some elements of the Moscow-backed Najibullah regime, met strong resistance by the Mujahedin parties and their foreign backers. Islamabad saw a military victory by pro-Pakistani Mujahedin parties within their grasp once the Soviet forces pulled out. Iran on the other side was trying to secure a fair share for the Iran-based Afghan groups in any settlement.[36]

As factional competition with ethnic underpinnings intensified, Iran encouraged the unification of fragmented Afghan Shia parties to enhance their political weight in post-communist Afghan politics. In stark contrast with its doctrinaire approach in earlier years of the revolution, Iran took a pragmatic stance, encouraging the alliance of all Afghan Shia factions regardless of their political orientations. The move led to the formation of a nine-party alliance in December 1987.[37] Known as the Coalition Council of the Afghan Islamic Revolution,[38] the group represented the Shia population of Afghanistan in the Islamabad assembly (Shura) convened in January 1989 to form what was dubbed as the Afghan Interim Government (AIG). However, differences over the level of Shias' participation in the government led to the Iran-based coalition's boycott of the Shura.

About six months later (July 1989), Iran-based parties were fully integrated into a unified Islamic Unity Party (Hezb-e Wahdat-e Islami) led by Abdul Ali Mazari. The new party included all elements of the nine-party coalition except Ayatullah Mohseni's Islamic Movement (Harakat-e Islami) which remained independent and allied with Sunni factions.[39] The leftist Afghan Oppressed Mujahedin Party (Sazman-e Mujahedin-e Mustaz'afin-e Afghanistan) also joined the Wahdat marking a major turn in intra-Shia politics. Two years later in July 1991, Iranian Foreign Minister Ali Akbar Velayati and Pakistani Secretary of Foreign Affairs Akram Zaki mediated renewed talks in Islamabad between Iranian-based Mujahedin and their Pakistan-based counterparts to reach a settlement on an interim power sharing mechanism that would rule Afghanistan before elections. The negotiations failed again.

The diplomatic setbacks came against the backdrop of a changing political landscape in Afghanistan. As the Soviet withdrawal and the end of the Cold War eroded the ideology-based unity among the Mujahedin groups, rival factions began to invoke regional and ethnic references to legitimise their claim on power in the emerging post-Communist state structure. Using the traditional tribal/ethnic connections, competing Mujahedin groups tried to forge alliances with elements of the toppling government in Kabul who too were eager to cut self-interested deals with separate Mujahedin factions. Such a marriage of convenience was epitomised in the failed military coup in 1990 (6 March) by General Tanai, Kabul's Defence Minister, in collaboration with Gulbuddin Hekmatyar, the leader of the fundamentalist Hezb-e Islami party. Sharing the same Pashtun ethnicity, the two men had little in common politically. The ethnic card became so prominent in Afghan politics that in 1991 the idea of a 'Pashtun solution' to the Afghan crisis was floating in Kabul.[40] There were speculations that Najibullah might transfer power to a Pashtun leader in the resistance. In fact, Najibullah did send emissaries to the former Afghan king Mohammad Zaher Shah to return from exile in Rome and head a coalition government in Afghanistan. Zaher Shah turned down the offer.[41] Reaction to such a scenario was strong among the Afghan Mujahedin in Iran who suggested Iran's intervention to foil the concept.[42] Exactly two years after the Hekmatyar–Tanai failed coup, a coalition of non-Pashtun elements successfully challenged and effected the downfall of the Najibullah regime. The alliance grouped the Mujahedin forces under the Tajik commander, Ahmad Shah Masoud, and Iran-backed Hezb-e Wahdat, with well-armed units of the Communist regime's Uzbek militia commander, Rashid Dostum, and a number of Ismaili and Tajik militias affiliated with the Kabul regime. The rebellion thwarted a UN arrangement for peaceful transfer of power from the Najibullah regime to a transitional administration that was endorsed by the majority of Mujahedin parties.

The Afghan civil war

The period immediately following the collapse of the Communist regime in Afghanistan (April 1992) has been dominated by an intense struggle for power by ethnically led factions with extensive foreign involvement. As the central government fell a hastily formed interim administration with rotational leadership took over in Kabul. The Pakistan-sponsored arrangement called for a two-month presidential term for Sebghatullah Mujaddedi followed by a four-month mandate of Burhanuddin Rabbani, who was to hand over power to a transitional administration selected for 18 months by an assembly of elders and influential figures (Shura-ye Ahl-e Hal-o-ʿaqd). But the central government failed to establish its authority over the country, and competing Mujahedin factions raced to seize control of the provinces and carved up the devastated country into an odd assortment of fiefdoms. The situation had an unsettling impact on national and international peace efforts. The collapse of the state, and emergence of a new elite, who invoked infra-political references to legitimise their claim on power, spawned new power bases, de facto mini-states, political freebooters and warlords. Factional mini-armies were reluctant to desist from waging a low-cost war of attrition in support of their factional interests. Since such a war was more destructive to the civilian population than the combatants, the warring factions had little incentive to opt for a peace that did not favour their corporate agenda.

As the frontline states and hosts to millions of Afghan refugees, and patrons of the Mujahedin factions, Iran and Pakistan have been heavily involved in Afghan politics during the post-Communist civil war. The Afghan situation has a direct impact on the two neighbours' geo-strategic, political and economic interests in the region. Although contrasting in scope and primacy, these interests did not clash until recent times.

Maintaining a strong influence in Afghanistan has been the hallmark of Pakistan's Afghan policy. Islamabad's quest for a westward strategic depth to counter India's geopolitical edge has been one of the underlying principles of the strategy. Pakistan was also eager to compensate its waning post-Cold War strategic significance by marketing itself as a stabilising power in a potentially unstable Afghanistan and Central Asia.[43] The gravity of the goals inspired Islamabad to pursue a deliberate policy of active involvement in Afghanistan and influence the country's political developments. On the other hand Iran has been seeking a secure and stable backyard to the east, and therefore its Afghan policy has been limited in scope. Tehran did not want to see a hostile government in Afghanistan. However, Tehran failed to pursue a clear and well-defined strategy. Its policy to promote the Iranian culture in Afghanistan was confrontational and lacked focus, while its commitment to support the Shia minority was too narrow and biased to influence non-Shia parties. The split in Hezb-e Wahdat, confronting the ethnic-based faction of Abdul Ali Mazari with the religiously oriented group of Hujatul-Islam Akbari, and continued hostility between Mazari and the Tajik-led government of Burhanuddin Rabbani, means that the Iranian policy faced with new challenges. The added confusion made it even more difficult to make effective policy choices.

A stable and peaceful Afghanistan was considered to serve the economic interests of both Iran and Pakistan, including their trade with the newly independent states in Central Asia. Further, restoration of peace to Afghanistan could pave the way for the return of nearly three million remaining refugees in Iran and Pakistan. However, the two countries have not always agreed on the details. The differences mostly stemmed from the competing factional interests of Tehran and Islamabad's Afghan clients, mutual mistrust between the two neighbours and the interests of other foreign players in the region.

So long as their interests did not clash, Iran and Pakistan genuinely worked together to find a peaceful solution to the Afghan civil war. During his visit to Islamabad in September 1992, Iranian President Ali Akbar Hashemi Rafsanjani dismissed the idea that Iran and Pakistan were engaged in a rivalry in Afghanistan. Rafsanjani indicated that neither country gained from meddling in Afghan affairs. He said one must be 'crazy and want to lose his life' to interfere in Afghanistan.[44] Other Iranian officials too have echoed the same statement.[45] However, Iran had no illusions about the depth of Pakistan's connections with Afghan political forces and its influence on Afghan developments. Nevertheless, despite its limitations Iran could not afford to be absent from the Afghan political scene, albeit not playing the leading role.

As rival factions in Afghanistan became embroiled in a bloody factional war, Iran and Pakistan cooperated to foster the establishment of a broad-based government in the country. A power-sharing arrangement mediated by Pakistan in March 1993 awarded the post of President to Burhanuddin Rabbani for eighteen months and confirmed his rival Gulbuddin Hekmatyar as the Prime Minister. Other parties including the

Shia Hezb-e Wahdat and Harakat-e Islami parties were also represented in the government. However, the settlement did not hold long. Several factions objected to what was considered as efforts by the Tajik-led Jam'iyat-e Islami faction of President Burhanuddin Rabbani and Ahmad Shah Masoud to monopolize power. The dissidents, including Hekmatyar's Hezb-e Islami, Mazari's Hezb-e Wahdat faction, and the National Islamic Movement of the Uzbek strongman Rashid Dostum, joined hands in armed opposition in January 1994 against the Rabbani administration. The fighting continued at different levels of intensity until the orthodox Islamic movement of Taleban burst into power and defied all factions by the spring of 1995.

Emergence of the Taleban

The sudden appearance of the Islamic student movement of the Taleban in September 1994, and its swift development into a viable military force in Afghanistan, have been the subject of different interpretations, speculations and conspiracy theories. Whether Pakistani intelligence had a role in its creation or it evolved from a local vigilante group challenging the corrupt warlords, the puritanical Sunni militia found extensive support among the masses who had been victimized by continued infighting and lawlessness. Riding a wave of public discontent, the Taleban embarked on a major drive aimed at unifying the country and disarming the warring factions. The Taleban's stated commitment to a popular mission of fighting corruption and chaos won them enormous support. Thousands of young recruits from the refugee *madrasa*s across the border in Pakistan swelled their ranks. Many ex-army officers and dissatisfied former Mujahedin commanders who resented the continued infighting among the Mujahedin groups also joined the emerging force.

In a northward movement from their birthplace of Kandahar, Taleban forces made a lightning advance, reaching the gates of Kabul by mid-February 1995. The move broke former Prime Minister Golbuddin Hekmatyar's three-year military siege of Kabul, and dislodged the Iranian-backed Wahdat faction from southwest precincts of Kabul following the killing of its leader Abdul Ali Mazari by the Taleban, whose military victories resulted in far-reaching political consequences. The development intensified ethnic polarisation of Afghan factional politics, and moved

Iran and Pakistan further apart as their Afghan policies gradually took a divergent turn.

The Taleban movement found extensive support among the Pashtuns, the largest ethnic community in the country. Domination of the government by the Tajik-led coalition of President Burhanuddin Rabbani, who unilaterally extended his mandate several times, had caused discontent and a sense of downfall among the Pashtuns, who have been the traditional ruling group in Afghanistan since 1747. Even Pashtun intellectuals in the West, who seriously differ with the Taleban on many issues, expressed support for the movement on ethnic grounds. On the other hand, fears of political and cultural hegemony of Pashtuns under the Taleban, particularly after the fall of Kabul to the student militia in September 1996, precipitated a political alliance of Tajik, Uzbek and Shia factions in an anti-Taleban coalition.

The Taleban's enforcement of a rigid and pre-modern interpretation of Islam, which prevailed mostly in Pashtun rural areas, clashed with accepted norms in the cities and areas inhibited by Shia and other non-Pashtun communities. In the areas under their control, the Taleban enforced a rigorous Islamic social order including a religious dress code for both men and women, the wearing of beards by men and full veiling for women. The Taleban barred women from work outside the home and closed girls' schools. It also banned listening to music and watching TV and videos, and some other forms of entertainment. Supporters of the Taleban see the restrictions as an acceptable price for the peaceful conditions and security established under the militia rule.

The Taleban factor impaired the spirit of cooperation between Pakistan and Iran in finding a solution to the Afghan crisis. Inspired by competing interests in the Afghan conflict, the two countries chose to back rival factions in the war. Pakistan hoped that the Taleban's military victory would lead to the restoration of Pashtun preeminence in Afghanistan and the security of trade routes to Central Asia. Islamabad saw both as supportive of its long-term geopolitical aims. Consequently Pakistan patronised the religious militia from the early days of its inception, providing it with organissational and logistical support and 'volunteers.'

But, Iran viewed the Taleban as an anti-Shia and anti-Iranian fundamentalist Sunni movement supported by hostile forces. The movement's close ties with Pakistani anti-Shia groups, its links with Saudi Wahabis, and the alleged Washington backing of the militia in support of its anti-Iranian policy were the source of Iran's distrust and fear. Taleban's sectarian and ethnic parochialism, with its tendency to marginalize Iran-backed non-Pashtun factions and their ousting of the Rabbani government, added to the distrust. Iran saw the victory of the Taleban as part of a plot by Sunnis and the United States to isolate Iran.[46] Iran improved the logistical infrastructure of anti-Taleban forces and set up five training camps near the Afghan border for thousands of pro-Rabbani troops.[47] After the fall of Kabul, Iran continued to send supplies to the Rabbani-led anti-Taleban alliance through Central Asia.[48]

Polarisation of the Afghan political scene upset continued UN peace mediation aimed at ending the war and the formation of a broad-based government. The United Nations complained that foreign backing of rival camps left little incentive for the warring factions to accommodate the peace process.[49] Separate diplomatic efforts by Tehran and Islamabad made little headway. Iran's shuttle diplomacy, led by Deputy Foreign Minister Alauddin Boroujardi, met a major setback in September 1996 when the Taleban army captured Kabul and ousted the government of Burhanuddin Rabbani. Boroujardi was trying to improve relations between Rabbani and the opposing factions, and resolve differences between Kabul and Islamabad. The following month a new anti-Taleban alliance composed of former enemies was formed in the north of the country, grouping all major Tajik, Uzbek, Shia and Ismaili factions. The group included Ahmad Shah Masoud's Shura-ye Nezar, Dostum's Junbesh-e Mili Islami, Karim Khalili's and Akbari's factions of Hezb-e Wahdat, and the Ismaili militia. Known as the Northern Alliance, the coalition was headed by the ousted President Burhanuddin Rabbani who continued to be internationally recognised as the president of Afghanistan. Despite facing a common enemy, the coalition failed to develop into a cohesive military power and end constant intra-factional disputes over areas of influence.

After the fall of Kabul, Islamabad focused on the Taleban's military and political dominance as the basis of its legitimacy, while Iran emphasised the international unpopularity of the militia and its potential threat to stability in the region. The Taleban's poor human rights record, their condoning of drug production and sheltering of wanted terrorists cost them international recognition. Fearing the spread of Taleban-inspired Islamic extremism and political instability, the Central Asian neighbours of Afghanistan joined Iran in opposing the Taleban policies. In a two-day regional conference in Tehran in October 1996, which Pakistan did not attend because of India's presence, Iranian foreign minister Ali Akbar Velayati hoped that the gathering would mark the first step toward 'universal efforts' to end the fighting in Afghanistan.[50] Pakistani officials later accused Russia, Iran and India of not wanting a return of peace to Afghanistan because it was not in their economic interest.[51]

Competing economic interests of outside powers have long been alleged to be a reason for foreign involvement in Afghanistan. The Taleban and their foreign supporters have argued that Iran favours continuation of instability in Afghanistan to deter international companies from building oil and gas pipelines that would transport Central Asia's energy resources to the Indian Ocean through Afghanistan and Pakistan. On the other hand, Iran and Iranian-backed Afghan factions have alleged that the US government, the American oil company UNOCAL and Saudi Arabia's Delta oil firm support the Taleban grip on power to facilitate the construction of an oil and gas pipeline from Turkmenistan to outside markets avoiding Iran. Iran's concerns were reflected in an article published in *The Washington Post* by its ambassador to the United Nations, Kamal Kharazi, who is now Iran's foreign minister. Kharazi accused US administrations of efforts to isolate and contain Iran at all costs. He further wrote that, according to the strategic scheme of American policy makers, 'if a semblance of security can be maintained in Afghanistan, then the proposition to build a gas and oil pipeline from the Central Asian republics through Afghanistan and Pakistan to the Indian Ocean gains credibility. By marginalising Iran in Afghanistan and by bypassing Iran as a route for an oil and gas pipeline, US strategists assume they stand a better chance to contain Iran.'[52] Disputing the validity of the assumption, Kharazi doubted that peace and security would be maintained in Afghanistan through use of force in defiance of broad support from all Afghan groups. Iran also denied its opposition to an Afghan pipeline.

The Taleban's short-lived military inroads in the north during the spring of 1997 spurred further polarisation of Afghan politics. However, the Taleban's disastrous failure to sustain their brief hold on the northern city of Mazar-e Sharif, the seat of power of the Northern Alliance, coincided with a major diplomatic move in their favour. Prompted by the Taleban's short-lived victory, Pakistan, followed by Saudi Arabia and the United Arab Emirates, extended official recognition to the Taleban government. Iran and other neighbours of Afghanistan continued to honour the credentials of the ousted government of Burhanuddin Rabbani, which had kept its official representation at the United Nations. About 14 months later Taleban's decisive victory in capturing Mazar-e Sharif (8 August 1998) preceded a significant political setback for the militia. Less than two weeks later (20 August), the United States launched cruise missile strikes on suspected terrorist bases in Afghanistan. These bases were affiliated with Saudi militant Osama bin Laden who was linked by Washington to the bombing of two US embassies in Africa earlier that month.

Iran–Afghan military stand-off

The dramatic turn of events in August 1998, leading to the fall of Mazar-e Sharif to the Taleban, came as a surprise to Iran. Internal discord among the northern allies contributed to the dashing military success of the student militia. The disappearance of an Iranian journalist and seven people who, Iran says, were diplomats in Mazar-e Sharif, came as a shock to Tehran. Meanwhile the international human rights groups claimed that Taleban forces had killed thousands of civilians following their take over of Mazar-e Sharif. Amnesty International said that Taleban fighters systematically and deliberately massacred thousands of ethnic Shia Hazara civilians during the first three days of their take-over.[53] The killings were apparently to avenge the massacre of the Taleban fighters who failed in their bid to take Mazar-e Sharif in May 1997.[54]

Responding to a nationwide outrage over the incident, on 26 August Iran announced large scale military manoeuvres (Ashura-3) by 70,000 Revolutionary Guard troops near Turbat-e Jam close to the Afghan border. The Taleban responded by moving troops to the border and deploying missile units there. The tension further escalated when on 10 September, the Taleban admitted that the Iranian diplomats were killed by renegade Taleban fighters acting without orders. The Taleban promised to punish the killers. Five days later (15 September), the bodies of Iranian diplomats and a journalist were brought back to emotional scenes of mass anger and grief in Tehran. The event coincided with the fall of Bamian, the last major town held by the Iranian-backed Shia group Hezb-e Wahdat. Amnesty International issued warnings of the possible massacre of the

Shias in the city. With public outrage and emotion running high in Iran, the Supreme Leader Ayatollah Khamene'i put the country's military on alert, although a week earlier (6 September) he had ruled out military confrontation with the Taleban. The following day Iran announced that another nine divisions, some 200,000 troops, were on the way to conduct further military exercises following the Ashura-3 manoeuvres which had taken place at the beginning of the month. This led to the deployment of about half of Iran's armed forces on the Afghan border.[55] During the same week (18 September), Iranian Foreign Minister Kamal Kharazi warned his visiting Pakistani counterpart, Sartaj Aziz, that people in Iran were pushing for military action to avenge the killing.[56]

The Iran–Afghan military stand-off raised the spectre of armed confrontation in a region already devastated by war and internal strife. However, underneath the rhetoric Iran's policy was governed by rational calculations and hard-nosed strategic consideration. The risks involved in the use of force were too high to warrant an armed showdown. Avenging the death of Iranian diplomats was not a pressing reason to take the risk of military conflict, and empowering Iran's Afghan allies by defeating the Taleban was hardly an achievable goal. Despite the reports that Iran had concentrated half of its standing armed forces on the Afghan border, the real number of troops was believed to be a fraction of that. Further, logistical support of a military invasion would need months of preparation. An Iranian invasion would also rally support in Afghanistan behind the Taleban, who vowed to target Iranian cities for missile attacks. This brought to mind the harrowing images of the Iran–Iraq war which most of the population in Iran did not want to repeat. Militarily, there was little chance of success in an armed confrontation with Afghanistan. As an Iranian analyst argued, 'Afghanistan is like a swamp and once we get in we will never get out.'[57]

The potential consequences of a war with the Taleban were also believed to include serious effects on Iran's domestic politics. The reform-minded forces feared that the hardliners might see a limited war to their advantage to consolidate their power in the face of growing challenges to their authority. Ayatollah Khamene'i's address on 15 September, putting the Iranian armed forces on alert, focused more anger on Iran's relatively liberal media than the vilified Taleban. The next day, one of the leading independent newspapers, *Tous* was shut down and the editors sent to jail. Iranian Defence Minister Ali Shamkhani argued that the international outcry against the Taleban policies lent support to military action by Iran.[58] However supporters of Iran's moderate President Mohammad Khatami maintained that international sympathy would fade if Iran, which held the presidency of the Organisation of Islamic Conference (OIC), invaded Afghanistan to punish the Taleban. The Khatami team welcomed condemnation of the Taleban's behaviour by the international community, including the United States, Saudi Arabia, and the United Nations. Khatami's supporters believed these would blunt the bellicose mood of the public. In his address to the United Nations on 21 September, President Khatami dismissed a military solution of the Afghan crisis and called for UN-sponsored talks among the Afghan factions to form a broad-based government in Kabul.[59]

While a full-scale war was too risky, Iran also considered that punitive air strikes against the Taleban would be militarily ineffective and politically damaging. Arming Afghan refugees to fight the Taleban would also be a lengthy process. So, Iran opted for diplomatic persuasion backed by the threat of force. This strategy was aimed at deterring the Taleban and their foreign backers from further military action against Iran's allies in Afghanistan. When the initial deployment of the Revolutionary Guard troops failed to deter the Taleban from launching a successful assault on Bamian, Tehran moved another 200,000 troops to the border and staged more military 'manoeuvres'. Iranian military build-up on the border also tied up a large number of Taleban forces, relieving pressure on Commander Ahmad Shah Masoud who still held his ground in northeastern provinces and north of Kabul. The Taleban announced that they had deployed 20,000 fighters, half of the estimated size of the militia's standing army.[60] At the same time Iran wanted to pressurise the Taleban into sharing power with other ethnic factions in a broad-based government.

UN mediation in October eased the tension along the Iran–Afghan border and the Taleban released the last group of Iranians held in Afghanistan. However, Iran continues to demand that the Taleban hand over or punish the killers of Iranian diplomats and share power with other ethnic groups in Afghanistan. Meanwhile, Tehran maintains a large force on the border and continues to provide military support to the anti-Taleban forces in Afghanistan.

The outlook

Iran has vital interests in the restoration of peace and stability to Afghanistan under a government not hostile to Iran. Currently, the military balance inside Afghanistan is in favor of the Taleban, which Iran considers a hostile anti-Shia and anti-Iranian Sunni fundamentalist movement. But, the tide of regional politics disfavours the Taleban and their stated policies. As a short-term option, Iran is expected to continue helping the anti-Taleban forces inside the country and maximise regional opposition to the Taleban by pressurising their foreign backers to stop supporting the militia's government.

However, it may not be possible for Iran to bring about profound changes in the situation merely through cooperation with the anti-Taleban forces and sub-national dealings in Afghanistan. A long-term strategy would require a far more comprehensive approach involving the international community, the regional powers and the Afghan factions including the Taleban. The objective and content of such a strategy will depend on the extent of possible changes in Afghan politics, Iran's political clout in the region and relations between outside powers and major players on the Afghan political scene.

Three issues are important: perceptions of extraterritorial threats from Afghanistan; the political cost of waging a proxy war involving outside powers for influence in Afghanistan; and the national interests of the Afghan people, which have often been ignored in the political dealings of the warring factions with their foreign supporters.

The extraterritorial threat of Taleban-inspired religious extremism has been exaggerated by some governments in the region mainly to justify their unpopular domestic policies. Russia has used the perceived threat to stress the need for its presence in Central Asia. It is notable that the Taleban's vision of Islam is closely connected with the social conditions of rural Pashtun communities in Afghanistan and thus hardly exportable. It is hard to imagine that the Taleban model will find many supporters beyond the Afghan borders. The movement lacks a cohesive political framework and a militant foreign policy. This has allowed flexibility in the militia's dealings with foreign partners. Fears of a refugee exodus to Central Asia as a result of the extension of the Taleban's control to northern Afghanistan have not been materialised. The situation is changing Central Asians' assessment of the security threat from across the border. This year (9 April 1999), Uzbekistan protested at Tajikistan's plans to allow the establishment of a Russian military base on its territory to deter the threats from Afghanistan. Turkmenistan has followed a relatively neutral policy and has not hesitated to pursue a working relationship with the Taleban. On 10 October 1998, Kyrgyzstan blocked the transfer of 700 tons of ammunition supplies covertly sent from Iran to the anti-Taleban forces of Ahmad Shah Masoud in northern Afghanistan.

Meanwhile, growing domestic and international pressure may erode the Taleban's political and military influence. The very ethnic and political factors that helped the movement seize control of about 80 per cent of the country in less than four years may foil their efforts to establish a reactionary religious government in Afghanistan. The Taleban's restrictive policies coupled with their lack of administrative skills and economic failure make them an anachronistic force incapable of meeting the challenges of modern life. Even if the movement extends its control over the entire country, it might not be able to bring stability to the nation unless it broadens its base, reforms its policies and attends to the concerns of other ethnic groups. An unreformed Taleban regime facing domestic and foreign challenges will not have the capacity to engage in extraterritorial adventures, while a more responsible and moderate regime in Kabul will have no ambitions to project influence and power beyond its borders.

Iran's perception of the Taleban threat may also change as the Islamic Republic further opens up to the outside world. Instead of continuing its current reactive posture, Iran can play a more active role in bringing peace to Afghanistan using its improved political clout in the region. The Central Asian neighbours of Afghanistan no longer view Iran as the exporter of Islamic fundamentalism, while Pakistan and Afghanistan are seen as the potential source of Sunni extremism, loosely dubbed in the region as Wahhabism.[61] The growing movement for democratic change in Iran and prospects of US–Iran rapprochement will add weight to Iran's role in regional politics. Further, Saudi Arabia's warming up to Iran, at a time when Riyadh has downgraded its ties with the Taleban over the militia's sheltering of the Saudi militant Osama bin Laden, may alleviate Iran's sense of being encircled by hostile powers.

The mounting political costs of waging a proxy war in Afghanistan may contribute to regional cooperation in finding solutions to the Afghan imbroglio. Foreign sponsors of Afghan factions might find association with them politically too costly to afford. Saudi Arabia has already downgraded its diplomatic relations with the Taleban, and Iran is not likely to stand behind the Northern Alliance at all costs. There are signs of a divergence of interests between Islamabad and Kabul making it difficult for Pakistan to control the Taleban. The Taleban are closely woven into the *madrasa* network and its religious support system across the border in Pakistan. A militant Taleban movement can cause threats to Pakistan's stability more than to any other country in the region. Further, an unpopular Taleban regime may prove to become a liability rather than an asset for Pakistan's dreams of adding a westward 'strategic depth' to its position. Pakistan might not be able to establish viable political and economic relations with Central Asia by siding with the Taleban at any cost.

And finally, what have often been ignored amidst the fog of the civil war in Afghanistan are the national interests of the Afghan people. So far, conditions for a peaceful solution to the Afghan crisis have been linked to the ambitions of foreign powers and the factional interests of their clients in Afghanistan. Such trends have intensified foreign competition for influence in the war-devastated country. Unless the legitimate interests of Afghans as a nation are guaranteed, no peace arrangements can endure and no stable relations can be established between Afghanistan and the outside powers.

Iran and Afghanistan are interrelated parts of an increasingly important and changing region. Given the geopolitics of the area, strained relations between the two nations do not serve the national interests of either one. What the two countries can gain from cooperation might be synergistically far greater than what they can achieve at the expense of each other. However, much depends on the restoration of peace and stability in Afghanistan. Unless the Taleban and forces opposing them reach a peaceful settlement, no major shifts in Iran–Afghan relations is likely to take place.

NOTES

1 For example, the Achaemenids (6th–4th century BC), Parthians (3rd century BC–2nd century AD), Sassanids (3rd–7th century AD), Buyids (10th–11th century AD) and Saljuqs (11th–13th century AD) were mostly engaged in the Near Eastern and the Gulf region's political and military developments. On the other hand, the Graeco-Bactrians (3rd–1st century BC), the Kushans (1st–3rd century AD), Hephtalites (5th–6th century AD), Ghaznavids (10th–12th century AD), Ghorids (12th–13th century AD), Babur and his dynasty (16th–18th Century AD) were mostly drawn to the events of Central and South Asia.
2 See E.G. Browne, *A Literary History of Persia* (Cambridge University Press, 1928), vol. 4, pp. 50–5; and Said Amir Arjomand, *The Turban for the Crown* (Oxford University Press, 1988), pp. 11–13.
3 Rostam-ul-Hokama, *Rustam-u-Tawarikh,* ed. Mohammad Moshiri (Tehran, 1965), pp. 115–18; see also Said Amir Arjomand, *The Shadow of God and the Hidden Imam* (Chicago University Press, 1984), pp. 190–1; and Ralph Magnus and Eden Naby, *Afghanistan: Mullah, Marx, and Mujahid* (Boulder, Colo.: Westview Press, 1998), pp. 28–9.
4 Ali Ahmad Jalali, *Motali'aye tarikh-e Afghanistan az negah-e askari* (Kabul, 1967), vol. 2, pp. 508–11.
5 John William Kaye, *The History of War in Afghanistan* (London, Richard Bentley, 1851), vol. 1, pp. 4–7.
6 Ibid., pp. ; see also John H. Waller, *Beyond the Kyber Pass* (New York, Random House, 1990), pp. 106–8 and 112–18.
7 Diego Cordovez and Selig S. Harrison, *Out of Afghanistan* (Oxford University Press, 1995), pp. 15–16.
8 Ibid., p. 16.
9 See Shahram Chubin and Sepehr Zabih, *The Foreign Relations of Iran* (Berkeley, Calif.: University of California Press, 1974), pp. 309–10.
10 See Abdul Samad Ghaus, *The Fall of Afghanistan* (Washington DC: Pergamon Brassey's, 1988), pp. 174–9.
11 J. Bruce Amstutz, *Afghanistan: The First Five Years of Soviet Occupation* (Washington DC: National Defense University, 1986), p. 109.
12 The move was in stark contrast with DRA's pre-Soviet invasion stance on Iran. A year earlier, during the Herat uprising (March 1979) which was publicly supported by Iran's Ayatollah Shari'atmadari, Kabul accused Iran of masterminding the revolt and sending troops to the western Afghan city. In a pejorative tone, Kabul media called Shari'atmadari 'da Shri'at-madari' which in Pashto means 'the con man of the Shari'a'. Now a year later, Karmal government used all kinds of respected titles for Iranian clerics.
13 Amstutz, *Afghanistan: The First Five Years*, pp. 360–1.
14 See Jerrold D. Green, 'Ideology and pragmatism in Iranian foreign policy', *Journal of South Asian and Middle Eastern Studies*, xvii:1 (Fall 1993), pp. 60–1.
15 Documents of Iran's Ministry of Foreign Affairs quoted by Ali Khorram in 'Afghanistan and the National Security of the Islamic Republic of Iran', *Amu Darya*, 1:2 (Summer and Fall 1996).

16 Tschanguiz Pahlavan, *Afghanistan: 'asr-e Mujahedin ve baramadan-e Taleban* (The era of Mujahedin and the rise of Taleban), (Tehran, 1999), p. 467.
17 Tschanguiz Pahlavan, 'Afghanistan emtedad-e hayat-e farhangi mast' (Afghanistan is the extension of our cultural life), *Donya-ye Sokhan*, (January 1992).
18 *Shura-ye enqelabi-ye etifaq-e Islami-ye Afghanistan.*
19 These included the provinces (*welayat*) of Jaghori, Nawor, Behsud, Waras, Lal-o Sarjangal, Yakaolang, Balkhab, Darra-ye Souf and Deykundi.
20 Author's interview with Wahdat Party's senior political figure, Dr Taleb, Washington, April 1999. Also see Olivier Roy, *Islam and Resistance in Afghanistan* (Cambridge University Press, 1986), pp. 141–2.
21 Roy, *Islam and Resistance*, pp. 143–4. See also Jeans-Jose Puig quoted in Amstutz, *Afghanistan: The First Five Years*, pp. 109–10.
22 Ali Ahmad Jalali, 'Fero-pashi sakhtar-e davlat der Afghanistan' (The breakup of the state structure in Afghanistan), *Mehragan*, (Summer 1998), pp. 53–4.
23 *A Review of Political Movements in Afghanistan*, a chart published in the early 1980s by the Peshawar branch of the *Hezbollah* of Afghanistan.
24 Arthur Bonner, *Among the Afghans* (Durham, NC: Duke University Press, 1987), pp. 126, 327. See also Roy, *Islam and Resistance*, p. 145.
25 Amstutz, *Afghanistan: The First Five Years*, pp. 109 and 359–60.
26 Author's interview with Colonel Azizullah, an Iran-based Mujahedin commander, Quetta, October 1986.
27 Brigadier Mohammad Yusaf and Major Mark Adkin, *The Bear Trap* (Lahore: Jang Publishers, 1992), pp. 110–12.
28 Cordovez and Harrison, *Out of Afghanistan*, p. 198. Author's conversation with officials of *Hezb-e Islami* of Khales, 1987.
29 *Consolidated Report of the Office of the United Nations Co-ordinator for Humanitarian and Economic Assistance Programs Relating to Afghanistan* (Geneva, September 1988), p. 60.
30 Kamal Matinuddin, *The Taleban Phenomenon: Afghanistan 1994–97* (Karachi: Oxford University Press, 1999), pp. 12–20.
31 Hafizullah Emadi, 'Exporting Iran's revolution: the radicalisation of the Shi'a movement in Afghanistan', *Middle Eastern Studies*, 31:1 (January 1995), p. 8.
32 Known as the Islamic Alliance of Afghan Mujahedin (Etehad-e Islami Mujahedin-e Afghanistan), the coalition grouped the Islamic Party (Hezb-e Islami) of Golbuddin Hekmatyar, the Islamic Society (Jam'iyat-e Islami) of Burhanuddin Rabbani, the Islamic Party (Hezb-e Islami) of Mawlawi Mohammad Yunus Khales, the Islamic Unity (Etehad-e Islami) of Abdurrab Rasul Sayyaf, the Islamic Revolutionary Movement (Harakat-e Enqelab-e Islami) of Mawlawi Mohammad Nabi Mohammadi, The National Islamic Front (Mahaz-e Mili Islami) of Sayed Ahmad Gailani, and the National Liberation Front of Afghanistan (Jabha-ye Mili Nejat-e Afghanistan) of Sebghatullah Mujaddedi. The first four groups were known as Islamist or Islamic fundamentalist parties. The last three groups were identified as traditionalist Islamic factions.
33 Pakistan Inter-Services Intelligence Directorate (ISI) was maintaining liaison with the Afghan Mujahedin parties and assisted in coordination of their activity. It also provided training and transferred internationally provided supplies to the Mujahedin groups. The ISI's Afghan Bureau met regularly with the military

representatives of all parties to make joint decisions on planning, coordinating and conducting military operations in Afghanistan. The ISI leadership was coordinating overall political issues with the leaders of the alliance. See Yusaf and Adkin, *The Bear Trap*, pp. 38–43.

34 The Geneva Accords, 14 April 1988.

35 See *Consolidate Report Relating to Afghanistan*, (September 1988), pp. 60–4.

36 Cordovez and Harrison, *Out of Afghanistan*, p. 371.

37 Alexander Lekhovski, *Traggediya i doblest Afgana* (Afghan tragedy and valour) (Moscow, 1995), pp. 217–20.

38 *Shura-ye etelafi enqelab-e Islami Afghanistan*. The alliance included Sazman-e Nasr led by a collective leadership with Abdul Ali Mazari, Abdul Karim Khalili and Mohammad Mohaqeq its main figures; Sazman-e Pasdaran-e jihad-e Islami led by a secretive collective leadership with Sadeqi Nili, Alijan Zahedi, Akbari and Mohammad Ali Ehsani its major figures; Hezbollah led by Qari Ahmad Yakdast; Jabha-ye Motahed-e Enqelab-e Islami led by Akhlaqi and Hasan Ruhullah (an alliance of several smaller groups including Rouhaniat-e Jawan-e Afghanistan, Islam Maktab-e Tawhid, Fedayiyan-e Islam, Reja, Jonbesh-e Mostaz'afin); Harakat-e Islami Afghanistan led by Ayatullah Shaykh Asef Mohseni; Shura-ye Enqelabi Etefaq-e Islami Afghanistan led by Sayed Ali Beheshti; Nahzat-e Islami Afghanistan led by Es-haq Akhlaqi; Sazman-e Neyro-ye Islami Afghanistan led by Sayed Zaher Mohaqeq; and Da'wat-e Islami Afghanistan led by Mohammad Hussein Shaykh-Zada and Ramazan Ali Mohaqeq. The list is based on author's conversation with officials of the Wahdat Party in Peshawar, October 1996; Lt Gen (Rtd) Kamal Matinuddin, *Power Struggle in the Hindukush* (Lahore, 1991), pp. 75–9; Lekhovski, *Traggediya*, pp. 217–20; *A Review of Political Movements in Afghanistan* and Cordovez and Harrison, *Out of Afghanistan*, pp. 371 and 385. Except Kamal Matinuddin, other authors mistakenly called the group a coalition of eight parties while it was in fact an alliance of nine factions.

39 Author's interview with Dr Taleb, Washington, April 1999.

40 Steve Coll reporting from Kabul, *The Washington Post*, 20 October 1991.

41 Author's conversation with Sanator Abdul Qodous Barakzai (Washington DC, September 1992) who took Najibullah's message to Zaher Shah earlier that year.

42 Changiz Pahlavan, 'Afghanistan emtedad-e hayat-e farhangi mast' (Afghanistan is the extension of our cultural life), *Donya-ye Sokhan* (January 1992).

43 See Hafeez Malik, 'Pakistan and Central Asia hinterland option: the race for regional security and development', *Journal of South Asian and Middle Eastern Studies* (Fall 1993).

44 Rafsanjani's press conference in Islamabad, *VOA News*, 7 September 1992.

45 Author's conversation with Iran's Deputy Foreign Minister Mahmoud Wa'ezi at a press conference in Dushanbe, May 1995.

46 Naby and Magnus, *Afghanistan: Mullah, Marx, and Mujahid*, p. 190.

47 Ahmad Rashid, 'The new proxy war', *Far Eastern Economic Review*, 1 February 1996.

48 *AFP*, 21 April 1997.

49 Author's conversation with the head of the UN Peace Mission to Afghanistan, Ambassador Mahmoud Mistiri, February 1996.

50 Ali Akbar Velayati's opening remarks to the meeting on 29 October 1996.

51 Mark Huban, 'Russia warns of Afghan intervention', *Financial Times*, 18 December 1996.
52 Kammal Kharazi, 'What we want in Afghanistan', *The Washington Post*, 4 November 1996.
53 Amnesty International Press Release, 3 September 1998.
54 According to Amnesty International, about 2,000 bodies discovered in mass graves in northern Afghanistan were those of the Taleban militia who had been dispatched to capture the city of Mazar-e Sharif in May 1997. Amnesty International Report, *Afghanistan: Reports of Mass Graves of Taleban Militia*, ASA 11/11/97 (November 1997).
55 The total strength of Iran's active armed forces is estimated to be over half a million troops (545,000). The country can also mobilise a 350,000-strong reserve force and 70,000 paramilitary troops. See Anthony Cordesman, *Military Trends in Iran* (CSIS, February 1998), p. 22.
56 BBC News, 18 September.
57 Sadiq Zebakalam, political scientist at Tehran University, quoted by Scott Peterson in his article, 'Iran split over how to punish Afghans', *Christian Science Monitor*, 30 September 1998.
58 Ibid.
59 CNN and BBC News, 21 September 1998.
60 Associated Press, 28 September.
61 See Olivier Roy, 'L'Iran, l'Asie Centrale et l'Afghanistan', *Geopolitique*, 64 (January 1999), pp. 34–5.

10

Chechnya and the Impact of the Chechen Conflict on Russia, the CIS and Iran

Gholam-Reza Sabri-Tabrizi

This chapter examines aspects of the historical tensions between the Chechen people and the Russian empire in its various forms, tsarist, communist and post-Soviet. Sabri-Tabrizi discusses the recent development of independence movements in Chechnya and the neighbouring states of the Russian Federation. Another issue that Sabri-Tabrizi emphasises is the role of the Islamic government of Iran in religious and cultural movements in Central Asia and in those Russian states which have decided not to be part of the greater Russian Federation.

The background

The Chechens, a mountain people of just over a million, are indigenous to the Caucasus and speak a language unique to the region and closely related only to the neighbouring Ingush. They have recently adopted the Latin alphabet, although throughout the Soviet period they wrote in Cyrillic. They are Sunni Muslims with Sufi-influenced customs and education. The Chechen warrior cry of Allahu Akbar (Allah is Great) is not an imported fundamentalist Muslim slogan from which the present Russian government has to save Western civilisation, but it is part of a long tradition of Chechen culture.

Chechnya comprises only around 16,000 square kilometres. It has a great deal of oil, constituting a considerable asset for such a small state. Although the oil reserves are estimated at 5m tonnes, the economic importance of this for Russia is minimal compared to the value of the vast oilfields of Siberia. Of more significance are the oil pipelines running through Chechnya into Russia from Azerbaijan and the Central Asian Republics.

Chechnya is mostly mountainous pastureland. Tax revenues from local agriculture and industry are largely insignificant for the Russian budget which has such immense riches and lands at its disposal. So one might well ask what was the real motivation behind the Russian decision to take military actions against Chechnya?

The Russians regard Chechnya as their route to the Caucasus and Central Asia. If Chechnya wins its freedom from the Russian Federation, then other regions in the Caucasus and Central Asia will perhaps follow suit. It is for these reasons that the Russians have suppressed current and previous Chechen freedom movements. But Chechnya is not the only region which refused to participate in the 1992 Federation treaty with Russia.

Tataristan, one of the most industrially advanced areas of the Federation's heartland, accounting for 26 per cent of the Federation's total oil output and having the second largest populated area, with an approximately 50 per cent Turkic and 50 per cent Slavic population, confirmed its independence from Russia. Having declined to join the Federation treaty, Tataristan insisted that its relations with Moscow be built on a separate bilateral agreement. It maintained that it did not want secession from Russia, but nonetheless it is possible that this move might be the first step in that direction. Disagreements with Turkic Bashkortostan, another large territory of significant industrial capacity, were smoothed over at the last moment before the treaty of 1992 was signed.[1]

Moscow's heavy military pressure on Chechnya stemmed from its deep fear of the establishment of a Turkic–Muslim unity against Russian leadership. The conflict in Chechnya has strengthened the religious and ethnic solidarity in Tataristan, Bashkortostan, Azerbaijan and Turkmenistan against what they saw as Yeltsin's genocide in Chechnya. Moscow might have been temporarily successful in suppressing the freedom movement in Chechnya and killing the movement's leaders, but this has not diminished religious and nationalist feelings among Turkic and non-Turkic nationals in the former Soviet Union.

The first significant military incursion by the Russians into the northern Caucasus occurred during the years between 1785 and 1791, when the Chechens achieved remarkable successes against a powerful

Russia. In the nineteenth century, further resistance against Russian forces in the northern Caucasus was led by the legendary Chechen leader Shamil, and lasted for several decades. Eventually, many Chechens were expelled from Imperial Russia, and today their descendants are dispersed throughout Central Asia and the Middle East. In 1944, almost the entire Chechen population was deported to these regions and to Siberia by Stalin, and a significant number of them perished en route to exile.[2]

Russian historical records and literary works present a misleading picture of these conflicts, both during Tsarist rule and Soviet domination. The Imperial Court regarded the Chechens as uncivilised mountain people in rebellion against Russian civilisation. The Soviet government regarded the Chechen fighters as mountain peasants stubbornly clinging to the feudal system and rebelling against communist rule. A closer study, however, of the history, beliefs and aspirations of the Chechen people shows that the nature of their struggle has been quite different from that portrayed by their Russian rulers. Today, the Russians are still making similar accusations, describing Chechen resistance fighters as Mafia bandits and their leaders such as Shamil and Dudayev, as Mafia chiefs.

Shamil and the resistance to Russia in the nineteenth century

Shamil was an enlightened Muslim of the Naqshbandiyya Sufi order. He was both the spiritual and political chief of his people, regarded as a shaykh or *murshid* (religious leader), his followers being sufi disciples known as *murids*. Through prayer, spiritual exercise and ascetic practice, *murids* seek progress along the mystical path (*tariqa*) towards union with God, union with mankind, and union with their mountain landscape and nature. A *murshid* is a guiding light or star on a dark night, and is in possession of an imagination which can create his world within himself.

Shamil was the very epitome of what may be called a living imagination. He held all Chechnya within his own vision or soul, and saw himself as being part of all Chechnya and the people as members of one body and one soul, united in God, who was active in both the *murshid* himself and his *murids*. It was this unifying creative imagination which inspired him to defeat renowned Russian generals and enabled him and his followers to resist the superior power of the Russian army.

They knew the Chechen mountains, indeed every corner of Chechnya, intimately, whereas to a Russian general those same mountains would have been a forbidding mass of rock to be conquered only by the relentless use of heavy artillery.

Throughout the Muslim world, such versions of mystical Sufism, sometimes called popular Islam, challenged the orthodoxy of the urban ulama (doctors of religion). In the first half of the nineteenth century, for example, followers of Mohammad ibn Abd al-Wahhab contested Ottoman rule in Central Arabia, and in Iran, Sayyid Jamal al-Din al-Afghani protested against Nasir al-Din Shah Qajar and the orthodoxy of the Shia ulama. Even in the twentieth century, Afghan mujahedin have fought against Russian invading forces, and the religious thinker Dr Ali Shariati resisted in a like revolutionary spirit the Shah's rule and the orthodoxy of the urban ulama in Iran.

After the capture of Shamil in 1859 and the decimation of the Naqshbandiyya by Russian troops, the Qadiriyya quickly filled the vacuum left by the absence of Shamil. The Qadiriyya, a Sufi order dating from the twelfth century, was introduced into the northern Caucasus in the 1850s by a Kumyk shepherd named Kunta Haji Kishiev.[3] Shamil and the Sufi orders of the northern Caucasus were thus part of these broader historical movements of Islamic renewal, and of contact and conflict between new empires and old, and between revolutionary and conservative forces.

Shamil fought against the Russian forces when he was still in his youth and defeated distinguished commanders such as Count Vorontsov. Vorontsov was appointed as viceroy of the Caucasus and commander-in-chief of all the forces in the Caucasus in January 1845.[4] He had already achieved fame as Governor of New Russia (Southern Ukraine), making it one of the most important economic and cultural regions of the empire. According to Count Tolstoy, Viceroy Vorontsov, as the son of a Russian ambassador, had been 'educated in England and possessed a European education quite exceptional among the higher Russian officials of his day . . . He had obtained all the highest ranks . . . and was looked upon as a clever commander, and even as a conqueror of Napoleon at Craonne.'

There is much similarity between the 1993–6 conflict in Chechnya and the conflict of more than a century ago occasioned by similar Russian military policies. In the past, the Chechens, under the leadership of

Shamil, fought against Nicholas I's army, and until recently were fighting under the leadership of Dudayev against President Yeltsin. In both cases, the Russians believed that the Russian army could conquer the Caucasus in a matter of weeks. The first time that they tried to do so, they were proved mistaken, and the conflict lasted for decades. The recent conflict lasted approximately three years, and in the summer of 1999 it started up again and on present evidence shows that the future is uncertain.

The background of Vorontsov's appointment was the failure in 1844 of the huge Russian forces concentrated in the Caucasus to conquer Andi and deal a mortal blow to Shamil. Unwilling to believe that it was impossible to conquer Daghestan and Chechnya at one stroke, the Tsar blamed Neidhardt, the governor of the Caucasus and commander-in-chief there, for the failure of the expedition. He therefore replaced him with Vorontsov, giving the latter greater authority. The condition for the new viceroy's appointment was that he must continue the campaign in which Neidhardt had failed.

Very self-confident, and impressed by the huge forces concentrated in the Caucasus, Vorontsov felt sure that even if the campaign did not achieve all its aims, it could cause no serious damage to the forces under his command. Thus, on 15 June he started his campaign with an army of over 22,000 men, 42 pieces of artillery and a battery of rockets. He did indeed succeed in reaching Andi and Danghiyya, but both had been burnt and abandoned by Shamil. The losses on the Russian side were heavy. All in all, Vorontsov lost 984 soldiers, including three generals, with 2,753 wounded, and 179 unaccounted for. Also lost was a large amount of gold coins, brought along by Vorontsov, and some supplies. His biggest mistake was his underestimation of either his opponent or the difficulties of the terrain. The entire expedition started off as a picnic rather than a military campaign. Vorontsov's tendency not to take Shamil in earnest cost him several defeats and eventually his retirement from the army.

On 25 April 1846, for example, Shamil invaded Gharbata in an attempt to stir up the Gharbatians and Circassians against the Russians. Vorontsov was convinced that Shamil's chief objective was Agusha in central Daghestan, and so certain was the Russian commander-in-chief of this supposition that, remaining himself in Shamakha in the south, he sent orders to Freytag, the commander of the left flank of the Caucasian line, expressly forbidding him to delay the homeward march of the Fifth

Army Corps battalions.[5] Even after being informed of Shamil's campaign in Gharbata, Vorontsov insisted that it was only a diversion, and that Shamil would attack Agusha. Only on 3 May was he persuaded that Gharbata was indeed Shamil's main concern. By then, however, it was too late. Still overconfident and still underestimating Shamil's skill and the hostile nature of the terrain, Vorontsov intended to achieve three objectives in the three months between May and July 1847: to capture Girgil and build a fort there; to destroy Saltah and Sughur; and, if necessary and possible, to destroy Irih.

In June 1847, Vorontsov himself led a force of 12,000 men against Girgil. He bombarded it for two days and then gave the order to storm it. The attack was repelled with heavy casualties. Determined to gain some success that year, even if it meant resorting to a scorched earth policy, he decided to attack Saltah. After a 51-day siege, the garrison withdrew undefeated. This long siege of Saltah cost the Russians 2,700 killed and thousands of wounded, an exceptionally high price for the capture of a village only in order to destroy it.[6] The two attempts to capture Girgil were a waste of time, effort, money and lives, 1,232 of Vorontsov's men being killed. Vorontsov's insistence on the conquest and destruction of the village can be attributed first and foremost to the fact that he came to view the battle as a fight for his honour, a question of prestige and a challenge to the whole of Mother Russia. It is worth noting that the recent policy of the Russian state towards Chechnya is similar to that of tsarist Russia in this respect.

But by the autumn of 1847, Vorontsov must have realised that the subjugation of this region and its leader Shamil would be a lengthy process, and so he tried diplomacy. According to Musa Kundukh, a native officer in Russian service, Vorontsov instructed him in 1848 to negotiate peace with Shamil. Shamil demanded independence from Russia for all the mountain dwellers then under his rule, but Vorontsov could not agree such a peace plan and resigned himself to a slow campaign of pacification. The growing tension between Russia and the Ottoman Empire during 1853, followed by the outbreak of the Crimean War, and finally Vorontsov's resignation, resulted in the suspension of all offensive operations against Shamil.

In 1853 Shamil, having fought the Russian forces for several decades, spelt out the difficulty of his position in a letter to the Ottoman

Sultan: 'Now we have no [more] force to bring against our enemies. We are deprived of [all] means and are, as of now, in a difficult position.'[7]

The legacy of Shamil's struggle for independence from Russia remains a powerful example in modern Chechnya. As will become clear, the recent conflict under the leadership of Dzhokar Dudayev, was very similar to Shamil's struggle, though there are some fundamental differences. Shamil belonged to a culture with deep religious convictions. Dudayev belonged to a new generation with modern views on freedom, democracy and social change. But both were well known for their integrity and courage, not only among the Chechens but also in the Ukraine, Azerbaijan and elsewhere.

The origins of the 1993–6 conflict

In 1991, after the disintegration of the Soviet Union, Chechnya and many other former Soviet republics started calling for independence from the Russian state. In October of 1991, Dzhokhar Dudayev was elected president of Chechnya and four days later declared Chechen independence.

Tensions built up between Dudayev and Russian President Boris Yeltsin. In April 1993 fighting broke out between pro- and anti-Dudayev forces in Grozny, with Moscow supporting the latter. In November of that year, Russian helicopter gunships attacked pro-Dudayev positions near Grozny, and Yeltsin told the Chechens to lay down their arms or face direct Russian intervention. Russian jets then bombed Grozny.

In December, Russian tanks and about 40,000 troops moved into Chechnya. In the following weeks Russia launched extensive air attacks, destroying many Chechen towns. But it took the Russian troops several weeks to recapture Grozny. Boris Yeltsin came under attack from the Russian political opposition with the accusation that an unpopular military campaign was being bungled and that the Kremlin was suffering loss of prestige. Following this development, the Russian media started featuring the events in Checheno-Ingushetia more extensively, and articles were published explaining the background to them. *Isvestia* reported:

> More than 200,000 people in the republic do not have jobs. In certain areas the unemployment rate is 80–90 per cent . . . Checheno-Ingushetia occupies the last place on almost all vitally important

> criteria . . . The oil extracted and refined in Checheno-Ingushetia did not . . . become a source of wealth, but of a terrible ecological disaster.

This same article then cites S. Gadaev, a Petersburg lawyer, whose integrity the reporting journalist 'absolutely believes in', describing Dudayev as 'an honest man not connected with our corrupt system'. It added: 'Only such energetic and unselfish people can change this life.'[8]

A similar article appeared a few days later in *Pravda*. Mentioning first the poor living conditions and the general poverty in the republic, it commented:

> It is fully understandable that the Chechens' triumph of September 1991 was a taste of freedom which, after Moscow's rather harsh challenge, made without a second thought and seeming to be a virtual diktat, quickly changed to a defensive reaction, a readiness to die rather than to lose that which is most valuable to any citizen, freedom. Alas, Moscow did not act wisely in this situation . . . Up to now the conflicting sides in the republic have had one thing in common – [the attitude that] all matters of controversy must be solved without the interference of Moscow.[9]

This conveyed the feelings of the majority of Russians who opposed Boris Yeltsin's military campaign in Chechnya.

In April 1995, having driven the rebel fighters from most Chechen towns, Yeltsin ordered a unilateral cease-fire. Sporadic fighting continued. In June 1995, dozens of pro-Dudayev rebels attacked the southern Russian city of Budyonnovsk, taking 2,000 civilians hostage in a hospital. The Russian troops twice attempted to storm the hospital but failed. Russian Prime Minister Viktor Chernomyrdin negotiated with the rebel leader of the Chechens, who then freed the hostages and escaped into the mountains. Peace talks began in Grozny, with the negotiators calling for a cease-fire.

In July 1995, the negotiators signed a military agreement on troop withdrawals and the disarmament of the rebel fighters, but the movement to implement the agreement stalled over the following months as clashes continued. In December 1995, while the Moscow-backed elections were taking place, fierce fighting broke out in Chechnya's second largest city, Gudermes. The Russians succeeded in driving the rebels from the city, but at the cost of heavy casualties among their troops. The Russian government censored reports of Russian casualties in the Chechen conflict, and Russian mothers were even misled concerning the whereabouts of their sons. They kept sending letters month after month without receiving any reply. Some of them even travelled to Chechnya, hoping to find their sons. After enduring a difficult journey to Chechnya and bribing Russian officers and Chechen fighters, more often than not their search ended with the discovery that their sons had been killed. There was widespread resistance to the conflict among Russian families with men of conscription age, and Russian mothers staged several demonstrations against the war in Chechnya. The news of heavy casualties among the Russian soldiers seriously weakened Yeltsin's position.

On 23 February 1996, Boris Yeltsin in his State of the Nation Speech dismissed as 'irresponsibly radical' the calls for a complete withdrawal from the breakaway republic of Chechnya. He said that Russia was ready for compromise and would talk to anyone, but he again attacked the separatist leader, Dzhokhar Dudayev, and Dudayev's supporters, calling them bandits.[10] On 6 March 1996, Yeltsin assured female deputies of the Russian State Duma that the war in Chechnya would end in April or May. But failing to defeat Dudayev and his supporters, he, like Viceroy Count Vorontsov in the nineteenth century, resorted to a scorched earth policy. Several villages and cities in Chechnya were reduced to rubble by continuous bombardment.

'Poll forces Yeltsin to halt Chechen battle,' wrote Richard Beeston, the *Times* correspondent in Moscow on 27 March 1996.

> A long and bloody offensive by Russian forces against Chechen rebels will draw to an end in the coming days, when President Yeltsin announces a new peace plan to halt the fifteen-month conflict in the breakaway republic.
>
> According to General Pavel Grachev, the then Russian Defence Minister, the Russian military would halt its operations, characterised in previous weeks by air and artillery attacks. 'Military actions alone cannot step up the process of resolving the situation in Chechnya,' he said in Grozny, the capital of Chechnya. His remarks were the clearest sign yet about the contents of Mr Yeltsin's long-awaited peace plan.
>
> The change in approach is linked to Russia's presidential poll on June 16. Mr Yeltsin has admitted that, without peace in Chechnya, his re-election hopes are doomed. Yeltsin is locked in an uphill race against his Communist and nationalist opponents.

In his State of the Nation Speech in the Kremlin, Yeltsin's anxiety about the situation in Chechnya came to the surface. Earlier in July 1995 angry parliamentary deputies passed a vote of no confidence in the government and called on President Yeltsin to dismiss the defence and interior minister for 'the Kremlin's handling of the Chechen incursion'.[11]

Yeltsin had not learned the lesson of Russian history. He was well aware of the Soviet experience in Afghanistan from 1978 onwards, which, observers believe, acted as a catalyst in the breakup of the Soviet Union into 15 republics. Similarly, the Russian war in Chechnya contributed to the weakening of the Yeltsin regime, despite the West's support for Yeltsin and its offer to his government of $10bn from the International Monetary Fund as a pre-election morale booster. The then German Chancellor, Helmut Kohl, and the then US Secretary of State, Warren Christopher, who both made visits to Moscow, failed to bring up the subject of Chechnya with the Russians. Indeed, Helmut Kohl was to face strong criticism at home as a result. James Meek, correspondent for *The Guardian* in Moscow, wrote on 23 March 1996: 'Both Mr Kohl and Mr Christopher are thought to be trying to avoid giving ammunition to Mr Yeltsin's opponents in the months before the presidential election in June.'

The impact of the conflict of 1993–6 on the CIS

Taras Kuzio wote in 1995:

> The conflict in Chechnya has large security ramifications for Ukraine and the remainder of the near abroad. Unlike the majority of official Western comments, Ukraine and the other former Soviet republics, both in government and outside, do not look at the Chechnya crisis in isolation from other developments in the Commonwealth of Independent States (CIS).[12]

Firstly, the Chechen crisis was perceived as part of a trend in Russian security policy, which was becoming more assertive and nationalistic. Secondly, many outside the government viewed the Chechen crisis as a positive factor for the Ukraine and other former Soviet republics, in the belief that 'the worse for Russia the better', and domestic crises in Russia were perceived as distracting Moscow's attention from interference in the CIS.

The military intervention in Chechnya and the massive infringement of human rights there severely dented Russia's democratic image in the West and in the CIS. Thousands of innocent people were killed in the cities and villages of Chechnya. This action on the part of the Russian army angered humanitarian institutions and individual politicians in the West, but Western governments supported Boris Yeltsin both politically and economically. Statements made by these governments contained imprecise information that reflected the official Russian view rather than independent voices.

Throughout the three-year period, the Chechens and Dudayev asked for negotiations. Before the fighting a report put out by International Alert contained a copy of a letter asking for talks. These talks, however, had to be without preconditions, the idea being that Chechnya could not negotiate for autonomy and independence when neither were on Russia's agenda. There was no armed struggle at the time, no terrorist acts against the Russian state; talks would not have been seen as a climb-down by Russia. The fact is that the offer of talks from Dudayev was not taken seriously by the Russian government. Yeltsin launched his so-called peace initiative on 31 March 1996, after recognising that the continued loss of Russian troops was harming his campaign in Russia's presidential election. The irony of this 'peace initiative' was not only that the attacks on Chechen villages by Russian forces continued, but that three weeks later, on 21 April, Dudayev died in a rocket attack as he stood in a field talking by satellite telephone to a foreign intermediary about starting peace talks with Yeltsin. He was a brilliant military strategist, who held out against the largest army in Europe for 16 months. He was buried in secret in a village cemetery, and is regarded as a martyr by the Chechen nation. Over 40,000 civilians died in the conflict, and the country was devastated by the Russian army. In the run-up to the June 1996 presidential election, Boris Yeltsin renewed his peace initiative with the Chechens' newly elected leader, Zelimkhan Yandarbiyev.

Most of the CIS members have openly supported Chechnya's struggle for independence. The Ukrainian media and the Estonian media have portrayed Dudayev in a favourable light, part of the overall sympathetic image of the Chechens as underdogs – one which most Ukrainians and Estonians can readily associate with. President Kuchma acknowledged that Russia's actions in Chechnya had a negative impact on Ukrainian public opinion. The majority of Ukrainians could not remain indifferent towards developments there due to the large number of deaths occurring. In Kuchma's view, Chechnya proved that military force could not be used to solve domestic problems. Taras Kuzio observed: 'The Chechnya crisis was condemned by the entire cross-section of Ukrainian political parties immediately after the launch of the covert war to topple President Dudayev in the summer of 1994.[13]

The Baltic republics have been at the forefront of both official and unofficial condemnation of Russia's military intervention in Chechnya. The Chechen determination in their struggle against Russia was an inspiration to the three Baltic republics, which also feared Russian attempts to reassert its hegemony. Many compared it to Mikhail Gorbachev's vain attempt to crush the Baltic states and Azerbaijan in January 1990.

In Central Asia, the Kazakh parliament adopted an appeal to the State Duma and Federation Council at the start of the hostilities on 13 December 1995, asking it to resolve the Chechen conflict by peaceful means. Members of the Chechen population of Kazakhstan and the Kazakh nationalist Azat movement had demonstrated outside the Russian embassy in Almaty on 11 December, where they had handed in a protest note calling for the Chechens to be allowed 'to decide their own path of development by themselves'. The protest note was read out in the Kazakh parliament, and called on President Yeltsin to prevent mass genocide and stop financial support for the Chechen opposition. The Chechens should be allowed to decide their own future through a referendum.

Kazakh President Nursultan Nazarbayev offered his services as a mediator to end the conflict by peaceful means and through mutual concessions. He was motivated in this desire by the strength of public opinion in Kazakhstan, including that of the Chechen community.

Kyrgyz Foreign Minister Roza Otunhayeva called for a peaceful settlement of the Chechnya crisis through compromise and suggested the CIS should be used as a forum to help resolve such conflicts. Uzbek President Islam Karimov, on a two-day visit to Poland, also condemned the use of violence by Russia in Chechnya. 'We are for a stable Russia, but military force cannot be used against innocent people,' Karimov said. 'The results of the tragedy may have a negative effect on the other countries in the region,' he warned, adding that 'armed forces must not be used against a nation'. As for Armenia, Taras Kuzio wrote:

> The Armenians, Russia's traditional allies in the Caucasus, whose support for separatism in Nagorno-Karabakh has been backed by Moscow, have largely refrained from any commentary on the Chechnya crisis. The Armenian authorities have stuck to the opinion that it is an internal Russian affair and that they would refrain from adopting any resolutions on Chechnya.[14]

The Azerbaijan authorities, on the other hand, were most critical of Russia's military intervention. Russia repeatedly accused Azerbaijan of recruiting pro-Dudayev mercenaries, and the Azeri authorities repeatedly denied any official involvement in the recruitment of volunteers for Dudayev. Although the Azeri ministry of defence denied a Russian report that it had sent a 'military contingent' to Chechnya, observers believed that Azerbaijan and Ukrainian democratic forces were nonetheless involved, though unofficially, on Dudayev's side. Russia's criticism that Afghan pro-Dudayev volunteers were crossing the Azeri–Iranian border on their way to fight in Chechnya was also disputed by the Azeri authorities. It was unlikely that Iran, which backed an anti-Azeri and pro-Russian position in the Caucasus, would allow Afghan mercenaries to cross its territory on their way to Chechnya. In return for recognising Russia's predominance in the Caucasus, Iran was able to purchase conventional weapons and nuclear reactor technology from Russia. Another reason for Russia's criticism that Azerbaijan was incapable of patrolling its borders was to pressurise it to accept the return of CIS/Russian border troops to the former Soviet external frontiers. This persistent Russian demand has been rejected by both Ukraine and Azerbaijan.

Can Iran play a key role in Russian and CIS policy?

Some in Chechen-Ingushetia and Tartaristan have raised the possibility of the Iranian model of government. Moscow wants Iran to restrain fundamentalists in both the CIS and Afghanistan and to allow Russia to gain political access in the Persian Gulf region. In return, Moscow has had to accept Iranian economic, political and religious influence in Afghanistan and Central Asia. Russia and the CIS need Iran in order to enter the Gulf, and Iran needs Russian and CIS political and military support. In Central Asia and Afghanistan, Russia and, to a lesser extent, the Central Asian republics need Iran's support, either to maintain stability or for assistance in the fields of culture, religion, economics or energy.

In Chechnya, as in Afghanistan and elsewhere, Iran's considerable capacity for stirring up trouble, and Russia's fears for CIS internal security, make Iran a key figure in Russian and CIS policy. Russia cannot easily or painlessly reject Iran merely to please the United States. This extremely delicate and mutually beneficial relationship is also being tested by Iran's efforts to spread its influence in the countries of the CIS. This point also applies to Iran's position on Persian Gulf security. Russia supports Iran's position that Gulf security cannot be maintained without all the littoral states participating. Russia sees 'little local benefit in excluding Iran and is also determined to continue to play a great role in Iranian foreign relations.' But at the same time it seeks an alliance with Iran's possible enemies and is susceptible to pressure to join a US-led security system.

Geographically and geopolitically, Iran enjoys a unique position in both the CIS and the Persian Gulf and can utilise this for a mutually beneficial relationship with Russia by a long-term realistic policy geared to the improvement of security in the region and of economic and social conditions. The new railway track which connects Mashhad in Iran to Tedzhen in Turkmenistan is the shortest overland route between the Persian Gulf and Central Asia. Iran, still subject to a United States embargo, is hailing the new link as the first concrete achievement in a strategy to enhance its role as a regional economic power.

NOTES

1 Mikhail Konarovsky, 'Russia and the emerging geopolitical order in Central Asia' in Ali Banuazizi and Myron Weiner (eds.), *The New Geopolitics of Central Asia and its Borderlands* (London and New York: I. B. Tauris, 1994), p. 201.
2 Tamara Dragadze, 'Report on Chechnya', *Central Asian Survey*, 14:3 (1995), pp. 463–71.
3 Austin Lee Jersild, 'Who was Shamil? Russian colonial rule and Sufi Islam in the North Caucasus, 1859–1917', *Central Asian Survey*, 14:2 (1995), p. 205–23.
4 Moshe Gammer, 'The Conqueror of Napoleon in the Caucasus', *Central Asian Survey*, 12:3 (1993), p. 253–63.
5 Quoted by Moshe Gammer, ibid., p. 254.
6 Ibid., p. 258.
7 Ibid., p. 262.
8 *Isvestia*, 1 November 1991.
9 *Pravda*, 4 November 1991.
10 Reported by Sergei Shargorodsky, writer for the Associated Press.

11 John Kohn, 'Breakaway dancing', *Time Magazine*, 15 March 1993.
12 Taras Kuzio, 'The Chechnya crisis and the "near abroad"', *Central Asian Survey*, 14:4 (1995), p. 553–72.
13 Ibid., p. 560.
14 Ibid., p. 567.

11

A Hellenic Bridge between Iran, the Middle East, Eurasia and the European Union

George A. Petrochilos

This chapter focuses on the relationship of Iran and the European Union from the Greek perspective. The Western image of Iran, shaped by its media, tends to be one of a state inciting people to commit murder, exporting terrorism, and encouraging and financing various extremist and terrorist groups in the Middle East and elsewhere. Is it perhaps the case that, because an unrepresentative group of people wields so much power in Iran, rapprochement with the outside world becomes very difficult, if not impossible? However, there is also evidence to suggest that there are people in the Iranian government interested in dialogue with the outside world, and, it is in this context that the author examines the link that Greece can provide.

The background

The main argument in this chapter is that Greece with her political, diplomatic, economic and cultural policies can provide a link between the countries of the Middle East, the Balkans and the Black Sea, on the one hand, and the European Union, on the other. Of course other countries too, bigger and more powerful than Greece, can operate in the same field. So what makes a small, peripheral nation like Greece likely to succeed in this game? First of all, the Greek efforts are not opposed, but rather complementary, to action and policies pursued by other countries. Secondly, the answer may very well be found precisely in the small size of Greece. Its interlocutors know that Greece is small and, consequently, its actions do not arouse suspicions of dominance. Greek businessmen and politicians are not seen as arrogant, economic imperialists trying to impose themselves in the way their American, Japanese, German and other Western counterparts are seen. Particularly in areas such as the Balkans, where Greek businessmen are already active in trade and foreign direct investment, nascent local capitalists do not feel threatened by Greek partners. Finally, the area in question is one where the Greeks have been active politically, economically and culturally during their long history and, therefore, they know it better than any of their Western partners. Similarly, the other peoples of that region know the Greeks well and, generally, sentiments of mutual trust and friendliness have developed over the centuries. Consequently, Greece forms a natural link between this area and the West, and Graeco-Iranian relations are best considered as part of this general framework.

It must also be added that some of Greece's actions and policies regarding the former Yugoslavia have left Greece compromised and with considerable fence-mending to do, which however is in the process of being achieved. Not only has this soured Greece's relations with its EU partners, but there is an Iranian connection too.

The EU–Iran 'critical dialogue' and the role of Greece

The EU–Iran relationship is underlined by the so-called 'critical dialogue'. At the European Council meeting in Edinburgh in December 1992, the heads of governments in the EU decided to initiate a dialogue with Iran rather than isolate it, one which seeks to put pressure on Iran to change its behaviour, but not to corner it. It was considered unwise to isolate a country of considerable strategic and regional importance by treating it as a pariah, otherwise, an important and volatile area of the world might become unsettled beyond control.

Despite occasional utterances to the contrary, the present situation in Iran has become susceptible to careful pressure. Relations between Greece and Iran have been traditionally friendly and Greece, as a member of various important international organisations, can play the role of a broker between Iran and the outside world. The Bosnian problem provides a suitable example of this. It will be recalled that efforts were made to involve Iran in a dialogue with the Contact Group regarding the conflict in former Yugoslavia, because of its support for, and the influence it could exercise on, the government of Bosnia. Greece, during its presidency of the EU Council in 1994 and as a member of the Contact Group, contributed to the formulation of the proposal of the Contact

Group on the Bosnian question. Within this framework tripartite talks were held between the foreign ministers of Bosnia, Iran and Greece on a number of occasions. In fact, it may not be an exaggeration to say that the only meetings the Iranians had with Western ministers during 1995 were those with Greek Foreign Minister Papoulias and his Cypriot counterpart Michaelides. In addition, the Iranian Deputy Foreign Minister paid an official visit to Copenhagen. In this respect, and as if to underline the complexity of international relations, the Iranian authorities may have done the Greek government a favour in facilitating the latter's contacts with the Bosnian government, for despite the fact that the Greeks had maintained contact with all parties in the Yugoslav conflict, in some quarters their traditional friendship with Serbia was nevertheless seen as an obstacle to their efforts at mediation.

However, in an even greater ironic twist, the Iranians did the Americans in particular, and the West generally, an even bigger favour. By clandestinely supplying the Bosnian government with arms, at a time when there was a UN-inspired embargo on such supplies to the various combatants in the former Yugoslavia, they helped the Bosnians to stabilise their positions and then take the offensive. The West, aware of these goings-on and reluctant to be directly involved themselves in arming the Bosnians, but wishing to see them armed, simply decided to turn a blind eye and let the Iranians (and others), do the work. Meanwhile the Western media conveniently saw nothing and reported nothing untoward, but instead concentrated their attention on reporting on the occasional barge sailing up the Danube and breaking the oil embargo on Serbia! However, such sensibilities vanished in the case of Croatia, which the Americans and Germans openly armed, thus making possible the Croatian gains in the summer of 1995. It is common knowledge that the condemnation of violations depends not on principles but on political alignments between states. Thus, states often condemn the behaviour by their opponents whilst turning a blind eye to similar behaviour by their friends. Of course, what this did to the UN embargo and UN credibility is another matter. By and large, the changes brought about in the military field – as a result of the arming of Bosnia and Croatia – and the mediating efforts of the Contact Group, together with the considerable pressure that the US administration brought to bear on all parties, culminated in the signing of the Dayton Accord.

The 'critical dialogue' had not been equally and wholeheartedly accepted by all members of the EU, because of their different approaches and attitudes to a number of issues regarding Iran; but, nevertheless, it was thought to be the best available option for a way forward, and Greece was one of the few EU states which kept it going with official and unofficial contacts. Currently, the 'critical dialogue' has again come under stress as some of the EU members began to feel frustrated at the lack of progress and angry at Iran's attitude towards the latest bombings in Israel. This, together with possible pressure from the more hardline US approach, has led them to question the value of the 'critical dialogue', but are failing to produce adequate alternatives to the policy of isolation, which did not work in the past and is very unlikely to work in the future. What has to be remembered is that in the Middle East, as elsewhere, long-standing and deep-seated feuds and differences are such that there are no angels or demons and few, if any, emerge with any credit. Thus, the policy of trying to isolate one of the parties in a dispute may turn out to be counter-productive.

Graeco-Iranian economic relations

Turning to economic relations between Greece and Iran, it can be observed that, during the past twenty years or so, the friendly relations mentioned earlier did not seem to translate into close economic ties. Such relations as there were, took the form of trade (mostly crude oil from Iran) and a number of construction projects undertaken by Greek companies in Iran during the time of the Shah. These two aspects were interconnected, as will be seen later. Also, it must be emphasised that, traditionally, Greece has a chronic deficit in its visible trade, reflecting the structural weakness of its economy and the small size of its manufacturing base. It therefore relies to a large extent on trade in invisibles, primarily tourism and shipping, and in recent years on transfers from the EU, to reduce its balance-of-payments deficit to manageable proportions. Accordingly, up to the end of the 1980s total Greek visible exports financed around 40 per cent of total Greek visible imports, but in the 1990s there has been a further deterioration, as column 4 of Table 1 clearly indicates. Therefore, Graeco-Iranian trading relations must be seen within this context, though in the period 1976–93 these have been characterised by a see-saw movement, without much of a discernible pattern.

Table 1 provides a summary picture of trade in visible exports between Greece and Iran as well as the percentages of exports over imports for the trade between the two countries and, for comparison purposes, of the corresponding percentages for total world trade and for the OPEC group. It is clear that for only four out of 18 years has Greece had a positive trade balance with Iran and that for most of the period the sums involved were very small indeed, thus making a mockery of the figures in column 3. These are out of step not only with those of column 4 for total foreign trade in visibles, but also with the more comparable figures of column 5 showing the corresponding trade between Greece and the OPEC group. However, since 1989 Iranian exports (practically all of them oil) to Greece have assumed significance for both countries compared to earlier years, since for Greece they represent between one quarter and one third of its total crude oil requirements and for Iran a sizeable part of its oil revenue. On the other hand, Greek exports to Iran since 1986 have all but disappeared.

There may be a number of explanations for this phenomenon. The obvious one may be the inability of Greek producers to export, but this is rather too simplistic. If Iran were following the general pattern, Greek exports would be expected to be between 30 and 40 per cent of imports from Iran, or, if the OPEC pattern were more applicable, they would represent something of the order of between 15 and 20 per cent. However, Iran is not a typical case, for during the period under review, Iran went through a revolution and a bloody and protracted war, and was subjected to a US-inspired, but rather unsuccessful, trade embargo. Consequently, its trade could not possibly follow a 'normal' pattern. In fact, between 1976 and 1979 the Graeco-Iranian trade pattern conformed to what has been suggested. The wide fluctuations are probably due not only to the small amounts involved for most of the period, but, more significantly, to the fact that during the Shah's regime a number of Greek construction companies had undertaken large projects in Iran, which, for whatever reason, were not continued when the Islamic Republic of Iran replaced the monarchy. This left a bitter legacy, and, clearly, it did not go unnoticed by Greek exporters, who may have reasonably felt that the benefits of trade with Iran did not justify the risks involved, particularly in the absence of any exports guarantee scheme. In fact, it is only in recent years that the Greek government has set up the Export Credit Guarantee Organisation, which covers investment, construction

TABLE 1
Trade in visibles between Greece and Iran
($ million)

Year	Exports to Iran (1)	Imports from Iran (2)	(1) as % of (2)	% of visible Greek exports to imports	
				World	OPEC
1976	21.8	51.0	42.7	40.1	45.9
1977	22.2	93.5	23.7	39.3	52.7
1978	15.8	191.3	8.3	40.8	48.6
1979	18.5	67.1	27.6	38.9	27.7
1980	73.6	1.8	4,088.9	37.6	21.2
1981	75.1	3.6	2,086.1	41.6	22.3
1982	14.1	2.0	705.1	41.1	22.5
1983	33.4	102.3	32.6	43.3	39.1
1984	18.3	24.5	74.7	45.1	24.9
1985	33.2	54.2	61.3	40.7	20.6
1986	5.4	3.5	154.3	44.3	36.6
1987	1.3	23.4	5.6	44.7	15.2
1988	0.8	78.1	1.0	43.7	22.5
1989	2.1	441.7	0.5	39.7	16.7
1990	6.1	881.4	0.7	34.1	9.7
1991	31.4	584.3	5.4	35.5	11.5
1992	8.3	684.7	1.2	30.2	9.7
1993	1.3	509.4	0.3	28.6	8.5

Source: Bank of Greece, *Monthly Statistical Bulletin*, various issues.

and technical contracts, in addition to exports. The insurance covers political, not commercial, risks and offers protection against wars, coups, nationalisation, devaluations and problems with currency transfers.

The larger than usual Greek exports of the early 1980s must surely have consisted of military equipment; and once the war was over they dried up. In addition, the strict import restrictions instituted by Iran in recent years, to economise on foreign exchange and help to meet the repayments on its foreign debts, partially explain this state of affairs.

Greece and the the Arab world

As mentioned earlier, the Arab world, encompassing both North Africa and South-West Asia, is a region where Greeks have always had close relations with the indigenous peoples. Since the Arab conquests in the seventh century, such relations have essentially become Graeco-Arab. The religious differences between Christianity and Islam have never been an obstacle to close relations, and the emergence in this century of a number of independent Arab states has led to the establishment of close relations between each of them and Greece. Such relations are characterised by friendship and mutual respect, and a commonality of interests among the Arab states allows one to speak of Graeco-Arab relations in general. Such commonality found expression in attempts at uniting some of these Arab states in confederations or other groupings, albeit not very successfully. Nevertheless, this sense of unity led to the establishment in 1945 of the Arab League which initially encompassed Egypt, Syria, Iraq, Saudi Arabia, Jordan, Lebanon, and later was to grow to include 21 Arab states. It is interesting to note that during the whole of this period the Arab League has maintained contacts with all Greek governments and there has never been a period of unfriendly relations.[1]

The role of the Hellenic diaspora in the Arab world has been a contributing factor to such friendly relations, and one may recall in particular the Suez crisis in 1956 when Egypt was attacked by the British and French, following the nationalisation of the Suez Canal Company by President Nasser. Greece was one of the first countries to support Egypt, and the numerous Greek pilots who worked for the former Canal company were instrumental in keeping the specialised services in working order. Perhaps the most important aspect of Graeco-Arab relations is the fact that they are not only governed by common state interests but are also based on a genuine sentiment of friendship.

Since the end of the Second World War, the Palestinian question has been the most difficult problem facing the area, and four wars between Israel and the Arabs did not solve the Middle East question, as it came to be known, leaving the Palestinian Arabs without a country of their own. However, the peace process initiated by Prime Minister Begin and President Sadat led to an agreement between Egypt and Jordan on the one hand and Israel on the other, and efforts are now concentrated on achieving a similar agreement between Israel and Syria. Within this climate the most striking progress has been the agreement between Israel and the PLO regarding the creation of autonomous entities in the Gaza Strip and around the town of Jericho, as the first step towards a comprehensive solution of the Palestinian problem. Greece has always been ready to help any initiatives leading to a peaceful solution of the

Palestinian problem, and, equally, the Arab countries have worked for a peaceful solution of a problem that is of paramount importance to Greece, namely the question of Cyprus.

Over the years, Greece has tried to help the promotion of peace through diplomatic means, and the Palestinian leader Yasser Arafat has acknowledged such help. Additionally, Greece has provided the Palestinians with financial aid. It is estimated that since 1992 such aid has reached around $21m, the bulk of which was a $15m low-interest, long-term loan in 1994 with a four-year period of grace and the remainder was in outright aid. The aid was used for medicines, pharmaceutical and hospital equipment, the setting up of a training centre for women and the establishment of a commercial printing enterprise. In January 1996 at a conference in Paris, Greece with other donor nations and organisations pledged to provide the Palestinian Authority with $1.365bn for new development projects. Greece has agreed to grant the Palestinian Authority $1m in economic aid, and Athens is examining the prospect of participating in the planned regional bank with a stake of 2 per cent and donating $500,000 to stock-breeding projects, to replace livestock destroyed by a foot-and-mouth epidemic. Further, the medical school of the University of Crete provides the PLO with various medical testing equipment as well as medicines, while Athens has undertaken the technical organisation of the Palestinian parliament and has increased the number of scholarships to Palestinians studying in Greece.

In addition, it is worth mentioning that Graeco-Arab cultural relations are blossoming, with the translation of the works of Greek authors into Arabic and of Arab writers into Greek. The great success that has marked the edition of the Arabic translation of the complete poems by Constantine. Kavafis, the Alexandrian Greek poet of the twentieth century, is just one of the many aspects of this successful development in cultural relations. This will be promoted further by the 'Foundation of Greek Civilisation' opening a branch office in Egypt and further planned offices in the capitals of other Arab countries.

There are many examples of the declarations made by various Arab countries, showing deep regard for Greece and genuine sentiments of friendship. Similarly, Greece has always shown understanding of views expressed by individual Arab countries, something which is unusual for other European states. It is precisely because of this difference of approach that EU member countries believe Greece to be the ideal bridge between Europe and the Middle East, able to play an important role as a link and a mediator in political and, particularly, economic matters. This role is fully appreciated by the Arab countries, which regard Greece as a friendly country that would never betray their trust. Greece's special position in the collective consciousness of the Arab world becomes more evident in documents issued by the Arab League. For example, in a recent speech Mr H. Khorshed, head of the Arab League's Athens office, expressed, inter alia, the following sentiment: 'The League of the Arab States is interested in tightening relations with the European Parliament and in general all parliaments in the world, but more particularly with the Greek Parliament.'[2] In the same speech he went on to refer to the efforts of the Arab-Greek Chamber of Commerce and Development as a factor in increasing commercial and economic activities between the two sides. He also announced that the League of Arab States, through the Council of Arab Ambassadors in Greece, aims at launching a 'Foundation of Greek-Arab Friendship', to act as a coordinator of all attempts to develop further relations between the Arab and Greek peoples.

Greece and Israel

Not surprisingly, these close and friendly Graeco-Arab relations put a strain on relations between Greece and Israel. Greece was the only Christian European country to vote against the partition of Palestine at the United Nations in November 1947, a vote which led to the establishment of the state of Israel.[3] Greece did so conscious of the inherent injustice of partition to the local Arab population and, perhaps more importantly, of the safety of the large Greek diaspora living at that time in the Arab world, of which probably 150,000 were in Egypt alone. And while political expediency may have been more important in 1947, in later years it was the former consideration that acquired more prominence, as a large part of the Greek diaspora had left the Arab countries.

However, despite the fact that Greece recognised Israel only in 1990, the official relations of the two countries were cordial and their missions to each other, while officially below full diplomatic status until 1990, enjoyed full diplomatic rights in practice. The reason for this cordiality was that, at the individual level, relations between Greek and Jew have always been warm and close, since the two peoples shared many common elements, cultural and religious among others, which united rather than separated them. Their common experiences and sufferings, as well as their deep mutual understanding and respect, as befits two of the oldest peoples in that region, made the Greeks probably the only Europeans not to harbour anti-Semitic sentiments. Over the centuries Greeks and Jews have coexisted in various environments and faced each other in the market-place as traders and commercial rivals, but such rivarly never degenerated into the anti-Semitism so prevalent in the rest of Europe.[4]

On the contrary, Jews enriched both the cultural and economic life of Greece and added particular vibrancy to Thessaloniki, the host of the largest Sephardic Jewish community in Greece for some 450 years, before 60,000 of them perished in the gas chambers of Auschwitz in 1943. In addition, Greek Jews, particularly Romaniot Jews, who had lived in small communities throughout Central Greece and on the islands for almost 2000 years, were almost wholly assimilated into Greek life and society, playing a full role in the national struggle. It should be noted that the first Greek to die defending the fatherland against the Italians in the Second World War was a Jewish second lieutenant. The rounding up and extermination of practically the entire Thessaloniki Jewish community, and the persecution of the other smaller Jewish communities elsewhere in Greece, reflected the fate of other sections of the Greek population which, in addition to 60,000 Jews, lost in excess of another 400,000 Christian Greeks during the Second World War and the German occupation of 1941–4. During those years many Jews were hidden by Greek families until they could escape to the areas of Free Greece in the mountains or flee to Palestine.[5]

More recently, Greece and Israel have signed a military cooperation agreement, which provides for joint exercises in the eastern Mediterranean, reciprocal training of officers and cooperation in the military industry sector. Certain common experiences and asymmetries seem to unite the two countries in relation to their neighbours: both are small countries with a limited territorial depth for defence in regions characterised by instability and uncertainty, and therefore need flexible and effective armed forces; they also have small economies requiring them to be highly competitive in international markets. Perhaps more importantly, Greece has sought in recent years, through ministerial visits to Egypt,

Israel and Syria, to promote bilateral defence relations and collective primary security arrangement in the wider region of the Middle East.

Greece and Turkey

Since 1974, Graeco-Turkish relations have gone from bad to worse and in January 1996 they reached their nadir, when Turkish troops landed on the uninhabited island of Imia, part of the Dodecanese archipelago, which was ceded by Italy to Greece through a treaty after the Second World War. This is, to say the least, an unhappy state of affairs between two nominal NATO allies.

Before 1974, Graeco-Turkish disputes were confined to the treatment of their respective minorities, an issue covered by the Treaty of Lausanne in 1923, which had settled relations between Greece and Turkey – following the catastrophic defeat of the Greek army in Anatolia in 1922 – and provided for the exchange of populations. That exchange was an early example of a reciprocal kind of ethnic cleansing and led to the abandonment and destruction of Greek settlements and communities in Asia Minor, which had lasted for over 3,000 years. Exempted from this exchange were around 180,000 ethnic Greeks who were allowed to remain in Constantinople as Turkish citizens, and around 100,000 ethnic Turks who remained in Western Thrace as Greek citizens. However, continuous persecution on by the Turkish authorities has reduced the Greeks of Constantinople to fewer than 4,000 today, whilst the Turkish minority in Western Thrace numbers around 120,000.

In 1974 Turkey, as a guarantor power of the Cyprus Republic, occupied 37 per cent of the northern part of Cyprus and continues to occupy it to the present day, claiming to provide protection to the Turkish minority of the island following a short-lived coup against the government of Cyprus by Greek Cypriot extremists, backed by the junta then ruling Greece. In addition, Turkey does not recognise the right of the Aegean islands to the continental shelf, as provided by the Convention of the Law of the Sea, and claims to have jurisdiction over practically half the Aegean Sea (incorporating many Greek islands). Also, it does not accept the International Civil Aviation rules regarding jurisdiction over airspace, thereby allowing its airforce to violate Greek airspace. More ominously, Turkey has recently raised issues of sovereignty over a number of Greek islands and, in particular, has adopted a bellicose stance against Greece, as expressed in a resolution adopted by the Turkish National Assembly on 8 June 1995, authorising the Turkish Government to use military force should Greece exercise its legal right to expand its territorial waters to 12 nautical miles, according to the UN Convention of the Law of the Sea. In short, Turkey attempts to intimidate Greece so that it will forfeit a right, acknowledged by all signatories of the Convention of the Law of the Sea, and does so at a time when Turkey has extended its own territorial waters to 12 nautical miles in the Black Sea and the Mediterranean.

Turkey's bellicose actions and expansionist policies may be dictated by fears of internal instability and even of the breaking-up of the country; fears raised by the separatist Kurdish movement and the Islamists movement. In short, Turkey may be responding to domestic problems by adopting an aggressive foreign policy towards her neighbours, principally Greece. The *Lebensraum* argument has surfaced many times in the form of 'Turkey has a large population of sixty to seventy million and needs space to expand'. This is an absurd argument in the 1990s. Moreover, where between one-fifth and one-quarter of Turkey's population is in open defiance of the state and a part of it in open rebellion, it is questionable that one can refer to Turkey as a homogeneous nation. Having committed genocide against the Armenians in 1916 and having expelled most of the Greeks in 1924, Turkey still has to deal with the 'mountain Turks' (the Kurds) to complete its policy of ethnic cleansing.

Turkey's policies may also be dictated by possible oil deposits in the Aegean Sea, and by making exorbitant claims, Turkey may hope that, in an eventual bilateral discussion, pressure could be applied to Greece to make concessions on grounds of equity. Such a possibility has prompted a number of Greeks to question the Greek government policy of making no claims against Turkey, especially when the islands of Imbros and Tenedos, ceded to Turkey with their exclusively Greek populations, have been subjected to discrimination, depopulation and human rights violations in ways reminiscent of the continuous harassment of the Orthodox Patriarchate of Constantinople.

For its part, Greece has reiterated that the guiding principle of its foreign policy is the establishment of good neighbourly relations with all countries of the region, based on respect of international law, national sovereignty and human rights, and on the non-interference in the domestic affairs of other states. As far as the Greek positions on the Graeco-Turkish conflict are concerned, they are crystallised into three principles: (a) respect for international law and international treaties; (b) avoidance of the use of violence or the threat of violence in bilateral relations; and (c) the acceptance of the International Court of Justice in The Hague as the appropriate forum for resolving existing differences. Turkey has refused to accept the Greek way of resolving differences, and in response Greece has frustrated Turkey's European aspirations.

Greece, the Balkans and the Black Sea countries

Despite the fact that for the last twenty years or so Greece had established good neighbourly relations with Bulgaria, Yugoslavia and Romania, the sudden collapse of communism in these countries and the breakup of Yugoslavia caught Greece unprepared as to the best way to respond. This was exacerbated by the fact that one of its new northern neighbours, the former Yugoslav Republic of Macedonia (FYROM), claimed through its constitution the Greek province of Macedonia and the right to speak for the 2.5 million inhabitants of this area. FYROM also incorporated into its flag the star of Vergina, the symbol of the kings of the ancient Greek kingdom of Macedon, which the Greek government saw as a claim to direct descent from them. The Greeks rejected this act, regarding the inhabitants of FYROM as Slavs – their ancestors therefore having arrived in that part of the world 800–900 years after the demise of the Kingdom of Macedon – and accused the republic of appropriating the name of Macedonia on the basis of a tenuous connection without any qualifying prefix. In addition, relations with Albania were non-existent despite the presence there of a large Greek ethnic minority, which was continually persecuted, thus providing grounds for tension and wild claims by some extreme nationalist elements in Greece. Matters were not helped by the fact that, technically, a state of war existed between the two countries dating back to 1940, when Greece was attacked by Italy through Albania. However, the fall of communism in Albania in the early 1990s led to the opening of the Graeco-Albanian border and an influx of around 200,000 Albanian immigrants (legal and illegal) into Greece. Despite the continued persecution of the Greek ethnic minority and a nasty incident, resulting in the death of two Albanian soldiers inside Albania by unidentified Greek nationalists, relations between the two countries have now been normalised, thus allowing business and economic contacts to flourish. As regards Greek disagreements with FYROM, the signing of an interim accord in September 1995 in New York, in which FYROM has undertaken to drop from its constitution any claims against Greece and also to remove the star of Vergina from its flag leaving the question of the name of the new state to be resolved later, has allowed a new era to be established in relations between Greece and FYROM. The accord has also created the climate for bilateral cooperation between the parties, both for their mutual benefit and for the sake of peace, cooperation, stability and prosperity in the Balkans.

The new climate between Greece, her Balkan neighbours and countries in post-Soviet Europe has been encouraged by economic and commercial interests. In the years since 1990 in excess of $500m has been invested by Greek firms in these countries, and a similar amount is planned to be invested until the year 2000. Greece has been until recently the recepient of foreign investment, with the exception of shipping and banking.[6] However, Greek outward foreign direct investment other than shipping and banking has now acquired a much greater momentum, involving many sectors of the economy such as energy, manufacturing, telecommunications, construction and various services. Such investment can be explained by a number of theoretical considerations, but as they have been discussed by the present author elsewhere,[7] they are not pursued here. The potential for investment and trade in the area is enormous. The Balkan countries have a market of 58 million people, Russia 150 million and the Black Sea basin 52 million. The challenge for Greece, which has the most developed economy in the region, is equally enormous.

Consequently, the Greek government has sought to assist these efforts by producing a coordinated programme of back-up, including bilateral trade agreements with other states in the area, increased product support through the Organisation for the Promotion of Exports and a doubling to 300bn drachmas of the level of political risk insurance guarantee that may be provided for exports and investments by the Exports Credits Guarantee Organisation. In addition, in a multilateral agreement known as the Black Sea Economic Cooperation Agreement it has been decided to set up the Bank of Commerce and Development of the Black Sea in Thessaloniki, primarily to finance trade. Member states have agreed to deposit share capital of $1.6bn with Greece, Turkey and

Russia each contributing 16.5 per cent, Bulgaria, Romania and Ukraine each 13.5 per cent and Georgia, Moldavia, Armenia, Azerbaijan and Albania 2 per cent each. In addition, a Balkan Commodities Exchange, complemented by a Balkan Commercial Centre, is to be set up in Thessaloniki, supported by the European Union's initiative Interreg. The Balkan Commercial Centre will be a permanent exhibition centre for the producers of the Balkan countries, whilst the Balkan Commodities Exchange will deal in transactions in raw materials and commodities, representing over 40 per cent of Balkan trade.

In a recent survey of Greek investments in post Soviet Europe, quoting data from the Ministry of National Economy, the number of investments in the various countries were as follows: Bulgaria 573, Albania 100, Romania 1,348, Former Yugoslavia 150, Poland 28, Hungary 48, Czech and Slovak Republics 19, Russia 42, Ukraine 24 and Azerbaijan 1.[8] The value of such investments is given in Table 2.

Since then, a number of other investment projects have began to materialise; for example, in banking, The Ionian Bank, the Bank of Attica, the National Bank, the Chios Bank and the Macedonia Thrace Bank are proceeding with 11 initiatives either opening their own branches or engaging in joint ventures in Albania, Bulgaria, Romania, Serbia and Russia. Similar activity is evident in other sectors.

Perhaps the most important investment proposal to emerge concerns the plan to build a 275 km oil pipeline of 107 cm diameter with an annual capacity of 30 million tonnes and the necessary facilities at either end for transporting crude oil from the Bulgarian port of Burgas in the Black Sea to the Greek port of Alexandroupolis in the Aegean, in order to alleviate congestion in the straits of Bosporus and the Dardanelles. The project document has been initialled by Greek, Bulgarian and Russian officials and its total cost is estimated at $660m. It would be built by Gazprom (the Russian oil and gas company) and a consortium of Greek interests involving the Latsis group (oil and banking), the Copelouzos group (construction) and Prometheus Gas (a joint venture between Gazprom and Copelouzos). The project will be financed by a combination of private capital from the main private principals, support from the European Union and borrowing from the European Investment Bank and commercial banks. It has also attracted the interest of the European Bank for Reconstruction and Development with a view to financing the Bulgarian part of the project.

TABLE 2
Value of indicative Greek investment projects in the Balkans and the former Soviet Bloc countries 1992–5

Company and field of activity	US$ million
Leventis/Hellenic Bottling (beverages)	178.8
Varust (oil/petrol stations in Russia)	90.8
Meton-Etep (food, cement, distribution, etc.)	52.0
Intracom (telecommunications, electronics, software)	25.1
Euromerchant Balkan Fund (banking)	25.0
Thrace Papermill (paper products)	23.2
Brewinvest (beverages)	21.7
Bulvar (consumer goods)	15.0
Commercial Bank (banking)	15.0
Delta Dairy (food)	15.0
Michaniki (construction)	14.0
Alpha Credit Group & Partners (banking)	10.0
Magrizos (textiles)	8.0
Gleoudis (tobacco processing)	4.8
Hellenic Fabrics (textiles)	2.0
K & N Efthymiadis (agro-chemicals)	1.0
DDD-Needham (services – advertising)	0.4
Interamerican (services – insurance)	0.2
TOTAL	**501.2**

Source: *Viomichaniki Epitheorisis*, no. 17 (October 1995).

In short, Greece has started, albeit somewhat belatedly, to tap the rich opportunities available in the large area of the Balkans and beyond, which is its natural hinterland, particularly of Northern Greece. It is an area the Greeks know well and, apart from any local sympathies, they can also tap into the services of ethnic Greeks living in the area, the descendants of political refugees who had left Greece at the end of the civil war. It is estimated that 50,000 university-educated Greeks speak Bulgarian, Romanian, Czech and Hungarian, while there are communities with historical Greek ties around the Black Sea basin. This human capital can prove to be invaluable to Greece, as recent export figures indicate. With the exception of Turkey, Greece enjoys good relations with the peoples of these areas and even with Turkey there are flourishing economic and commercial relations. If these can be exploited more fully and prove mutually beneficial, they may provide a firmer basis upon which to build trust among the various peoples and further reduce conflict. In the words of one of the Greek entrepreneurs, prominent in the push to open up these vast markets, 'We want our neighbours to be rich. People think less about hostilities when they have a nice house and garden to look after.'[9]

NOTES

1 P. Nathanail., 'Greek–Arab relations', *Bulletin Athens News Agency* (feature), no. 32 (26 May 1995).
2 Ibid.
3 Britain and Yugoslavia abstained, while all other European countries voted in favour of partition.
4 A.R. Burns, *The Modern Greeks* (Alexandria: Nelson, 1944), p. 17.
5 M. Mazower, *Inside Hitler's Greece: The Experience of Occupation 1941–44* (New Haven and London: Yale University Press, 1993), Chapter 19.
6 G.A. Petrochilos, *Foreign Direct Investment and the Development Process: The Case of Greece* (Aldershot: Avebury, 1989); G.A. Petrochilos, 'An analysis of foreign direct investment in Greece 1953–92' in C. Collis, and F. Peck (eds.), *Foreign Direct Investment and Regional Development* (London: Regional Studies Association, forthcoming).
7 Ibid.
8 R. McDonald, 'California here I come: a Survey of Greek investments in post-Soviet Europe', Special Survey, *Industrial Review* (*Viomichaniki Epitheorisis*), Athens, no. 17 (October 1995).
9 Ibid., p. 58.

Bibliography

Afrasiabi, K.L., *After Khomeini: New Directions in Iran's Foreign Policy* (Boulder, Colo.: Westview Press, 1994).

Akhavi, Shahrough, *Religion and Politics in Contemporary Iran* (Albany: State University of New York Press, 1980).

Algar, Hamid, *Religion and State in Iran 1785–1906* (Berkeley: University of California Press, 1969).

Ali, Lubna Abid, 'Foreign policy behaviour of a post-revolutionary state: a case study of Iran', Ph.D. Dissertation (Islamabad: Quaid-Azam University).

Amirahmadi, Hooshang, 'Iranian economic reconstruction plan and prospects for its success' in Hooshang Amirahmadi and Nader Entessar (eds.), *Reconstruction and Regional Diplomacy in the Persian Gulf*, (London and New York: Routledge, 1992).

—'The Islamic Republic and the question of Palestine', *Middle East Insight*, 10:4/5 (May/August 1994).

Amstutz, J. Bruce, *Afghanistan: The First Five Years of Soviet Occupation*, (Washington DC: National Defense University, 1986).

Arjomand, Said Amir, *The Turban for the Crown* (Oxford University Press, 1988).

—*The Shadow of God and the Hidden Imam* (Chicago University Press, 1984).

Barkashli, Faridum, 'Mulahizati darbareh-ye esteratejiha-ye mantaqah'i-ye Jumhuri-ye Eslami-ye Iran' [Some notes on the Islamic Republic of Iran's regional strategies] in Seyyed Rasul Musawi (ed.), *Manabe' va zarfiyatha-ye eqtesadi-e Asiya-ye Markazi va Qafqaz* (Tehran: AH 1374).

Bayat, Asef, 'The coming of a post-Islamic society', *Critique* (Fall, 1996).

Bazargan, Mehdi, 'Enghelab-e Iran dar dou harkat' [The Iranian revolution in two phases] (Tehran: Chap-e Cevom, 1983), pp. 110–11, quoted in R.K. Ramazani, 'Iran's foreign policy: contending orientations', *The Middle East Journal,* 43:2 (Spring 1989).

Beeman, W., 'Double demons: cultural impedance in US–Iranian understanding', *Iranian Journal of International Affairs* (Summer/Fall 1990).
Bill, James A., 'The United States and Iran: mutual mythologies', *Middle East Policy*, 11:3 (1993).
Black, Ian, 'Britain tries to halt US sanctions bill', *The Guardian*, quoted in *Reuter News Service*, 19 February 1996.
Blank, Stephen, 'Russia, the Gulf and Central Asia in a new Middle East', *Central Asian Survey*, 13:2 (1994).
Bonner, Arthur, *Among the Afghans* (Durham, NC: Duke University Press, 1987).
Boroujerdi, M., 'The encounter of post-revolutionary thought in Iran with Hegel, Heidegger, and Popper' in S. Mardin (ed.), *Cultural Transitions in the Middle East* (Leiden: E.J. Brill, 1994).
Browne, E. G., *A Literary History of Persia* (Cambridge University Press, 1928), vol. 4.
Calabbrese, John, *Revolutionary Horizons: Regional Foreign Policy in Post-Khomeini Iran* (London: Macmillan, 1994).
Chanda, Nayan, 'Red rockets glare: China's sale of missiles to Pakistan and alleged shipment of nuclear weapons to Iran', *Far Eastern Economic Review*, 156:9 (September 1993).
Chubin, Shahram and Sepehr Zabih, *The Foreign Relations of Iran* (Berkeley, Calif.: University of California Press, 1974).
Cordesman, Anthony H. *Iran and Iraq: The Threat from the Northern Gulf* (Boulder, Colo.: Westview Press, 1994).
Cordovez, Diego and Selig S. Harrison, *Out of Afghanistan* (Oxford University Press, 1995).
Dabbashi, Hamid, *Theology of Discontent: The Ideological Foundations of the Iranian Revolution* (Albany: State University of New York Press, 1993).
Dahl, Robert A., *Democracy and its Critics* (New Haven, Conn.: Yale University Press, 1989).
Daneshku, Scheherazade, 'Grappling with a sluggish economy', *The Middle East*, 198 (April 1991).
Dragadze, Tamara, 'Report on Chechnya', *Central Asian Survey*, 14:3 (1995).
Ehteshami, Anoushiravan (ed.), *From the Gulf to Central Asia: Players in the New Great Game* (Exeter University Press, 1994).

—*After Khomeini: The Iranian Second Republic* (London: Routledge, 1995).
—*The Politics of Economic Restructuring in Post-Khomeini Iran,* CMEIS Occasional Paper, no. 50 (University of Durham, July 1995).
—*The Changing Balance of Power in Asia* (Abu Dhabi: The Emirates Center for Strategic Studies and Research, 1998).
Ehteshami, Anoushiravan and Mansour Varasreh (ed.), *Iran and the International Community* (London: Routlege, 1991).
Ehteshami, Anoushiravan and R. Hinnebusch, *Syria and Iran: Middle Powers in a Penetrated System* (London: Routledge, 1997).
Enayat, Hamid, *Modern Islamic Political Thought* (London: Macmillan, 1982).
Esposito, John L. (ed.), *The Iranian Revolution: Its Global Aftermath* (Miami, Fla.: International University Press, 1990).
Ferdinand, Peter (ed.), *The New States of Central Asia and their Neighbours* (New York: Council on Foreign Relations Press, 1995).
Forgacs, D. (ed.), *A Gramsci Reader* (London: Lawrence & Wishart, 1988).
Fuller, Graham, E., *The Center of the Universe: The Geopolitics of Iran* (Boulder, Colo.: Westview Press, 1991).
Fullerton, John, 'A rift among rebels', *Far Eastern Economic Review,* 29 (October 1982).
Gammer, Moshe, 'The conqueror of Napoleon in the Caucasus', *Central Asian Survey,* 12:3 (1993).
Garnnet, Sherman W., 'Ukraine's decision to join the NPT', *Arms Control Today,* 25:1 (January–February 1995).
Ghaus, Abdul Samad, *The Fall of Afghanistan* (Washington DC: Pergamon Brassey's, 1988).
Gramsci, A. *Selection from Cultural Writings,* ed. D. Forgacs (London: Lawrence & Wishart, 1985).
Green, Jerold D., 'Ideology and pragmatism in Iranian foreign policy', *Journal of South Asian and Middle Eastern Studies,* xvii:1 (Fall 1993).
Haddad, L. 'Open door policy and the industrialisation of Iran', *Journal of Contemporary Asia,* 24:1 (1994).
Hafizullah, Emadi, *State, Revolution and Superpowers in Afghanistan* (New York: Praeger, 1990).
—'Exporting Iran's revolution: the radicalization of the Shi'a movement in Afghanistan, *Middle East Studies,* 31:1 (January 1995).

Halliday, Fred, *Islam and the Myth of Confrontation* (London: I. B. Tauris, 1996).
—'An elusive normalisation: Western Europe and the Iranian revolution', *The Middle East Journal*, 48:2 (Spring 1994).
—'Introduction' in Anoushiravan Ehteshami and Mansour Varasteh (eds.), *Iran and the International Community* (London: Routledge, 1997).
Hauner, Milan L., 'The disintegration of the Soviet Eurasian Empire' in Mohiaddin Mesbahi (ed.), *Central Asia and the Caucasus after the Soviet Union* (Gainesville, Fla.: University Press of Florida, 1994).
Hegel, G.W.F., 'The German Constitution' in *Hegel's Political Writings*, trans. T. M. Knox (Oxford University Press, 1964).
Hiro, Dilip, 'The Iranian connection', *The Middle East*, 207 (January 1992).
Hooglund, Eric, 'Iranian populism and political change in the Gulf', *Middle East Report* (January/February 1992).
Huban, Mark, 'Russia warns of Afghan intervention, *Financial Times*, 18 December 1996.
Hunter, Shireen T., *Iran After Khomeini* (Washington DC: Center for Strategic and International Studies, 1992).
—*Iran and the World: Continuity in a Revolutionary Decade* (Bloomington & Indianapolis, Ind.: Indiana University Press, 1990).
Huntington, Samuel P., 'Will more countries become democratic?', *Political Science Quarterly*, 99:2 (September 1984).
—'The clash of civilisations', *Foreign Affairs*, 72:3 (Summer 1993).
Hussain, Mushahid, 'Prospect for the peaceful settlement', *Seminar Report on Afghanistan* (Islamabad: Institute of Strategic Studies, December 1990).
Iran Times, 13 August 1993.
Jalali, Ali Ahmad, *Motali'aye tarikh-e Afghanistan az negah-e askari* (Kabul, 1967), vol. 2.
—'Fero-pashi sakhtar-e davlat der Afghanistan' [The breakup of the state structure in Afghanistan], *Mehragan* (Summer 1998).
Karshenas, Massoud and M. Hashem Pesaran, 'Economic reform and the reconstruction of the Iranian economy', *The Middle East Journal*, 49:1 (Winter 1995).
Kapur, Ashok, 'Relations with Pakistan and India' in Miron Rezun (ed.), *Iran at the Crossroads: Global Realities in a Turbulent Decade* (Boulder, Colo.: Westview Press, 1990).

Kaye, John William, *The History of War in Afghanistan* (London, Richard Bentley, 1851).

Keddie, Nikki R., *Iran: Religion, Politics and Society*, (London: Frank Cass, 1980).

Keddie, Nikki R. and Mark J. Gasiorowski (eds.), *Neither East nor West: Iran, the Soviet Union, and the United States* (New Haven, Conn.: Yale University Press, 1990).

—'Observations on the information world' in *Fears and Hopes*, trans A. Mafinezam (Binghamton University: Institute of Global Cultural Studies, 1997).

Khatami, M., 'On the virtues of the West', *Time*, 151:2 (19 January 1998).

—'Hope and challenge: the Iranian President speaks' in *Fears and Hopes*, trans. A. Mafinezam (Binghamton University: Institute of Global Cultural Studies, 1997).

Khattak, Khushal Khan, *Collected Works* (Peshawar, Pakistan: 1953).

Khorran, Ali, 'Afghanistan and the national security of the Islamic Republic of Iran', *Amu Darya*, 1:2 (Summer and Fall 1996).

Konarovsky, Mikhaili, 'Russia and the emerging geopolitical order in Central Asia' in Ali Banuazizi and Myron Weiner (eds.), *The New Geopolitics of Central Asia and its Borderlands* (London and New York: I. B. Tauris, 1994).

Kutschera, Chris, 'Doing it our way', *The Middle East*, 203 (September 1991).

Kuzio, Taras, 'The Chechnya crisis and the near abroad', *Central Asian Survey*, 14:4 (1995).

Lekhovski, Alexander, *Traggediya i doblest Afghana* [Afghan tragedy and valour] (Moscow, 1995).

Lerner, Daniel, *The Passing of Traditional Society: Modernising the Middle East* (New York: Free Press, 1958).

Lotfian, Sa'ideh, 'Kazakhstan's nuclear status and regional security', *Amu Darya*, 1:2 (1996).

Lubin, N., 'Islam and ethnic identity in Central Asia: a view from below' in Y. Ro'i (ed.), *Muslim Eurasia: Conflicting Legacies* (London: Frank Cass, 1995).

Magnus, Ralpy and Eden Naby, *Afghanistan: Mullah, Marx and Mujahid* (Boulder, Colo.: Westview Press, 1998).

Maleki, Abbas, 'Ravabet-e Iran va jomhuriha-ye Asiya-ye Markazi' [Iran's relations with the republics of Central Asia], address to China's

Institute of International Affairs in June 1992, *Motale'at-e Asiya-e va Qafaz (MAMQ)* (Central Asia and the Caucasus Review), 1:1 (1992).

—'Cooperation: a new component of the Iranian foreign policy', *The Iranian Journal of Foreign Affairs*, 5:1 (Spring 1993).

—'Into the year 2000: the vista of Irano-Russia relations', *Central Asia the Caucasus Review*, 4:12 (Winter 1995/96).

Malik, Hafeez, 'Pakistan and Central Asia hinterland option: the race for regional security and development', *Journal of South Asian and Middle Eastern Studies* (Fall 1993).

Mandelbaum, Michael (ed.),*Central Asia and The World* (New York: Council on Foreign Relations, 1994).

Mannheim, K., *Ideology and Utopia* (London: Routledge & Kegan Paul, 1960).

Matin-Asgari, A., 'Abdolkarim Sorush and the secularisation of Islamic thought in Iran', *Iranian Studies*, 30:1/2 (Winter/Spring 1997).

Matinuddin, Kamal, *The Taleban phenomenon: Afghanistan 1994–97* (Karachi: Oxford University Press, 1999).

Mazower, M., *Inside Hitler's Greece: The Experience of Occupation 1941–44* (New Haven, Conn.: Yale University Press, 1993).

McDonald, R., 'California here I come: a survey of Greek investments in post-Soviet Europe', Special Survey, *Industrial Review* [Viomichaniki Epitheorisis], no. 17 (October 1995).

Menashri, David, *Iran: A Decade of War and Revolution* (New York: Holmes and Meier, 1990).

Mesbahi, Mohiaddin, 'Iran's emerging partnership with Russia', *Middle East Insight,* 11:5 (July–August 1995).

Mesbahi, Peter (ed.), *The New States of Central Asia and their Neighbours* (New York: Council on Foreign Relations Press, 1995).

Mohammadi, Ali, 'Central Asia Uncertainties', *Third World Quarterly*, 15:4 (1994).

Mohyeddin, Hossein, 'Constitution of Islamic Republic of Iran' (translation), *Islamic Guidance* (1985).

Mojtahedzadeh, Piruz, 'Didgahha-ye Iran dar rabeteh ba darya-ye Khazar, Asiya-ye Markazi, Khalij-e Fars, wa Khavar-e Miyaneh [Iran's views on the Caspian Sea, Central Asia, the Persian Gulf, and the Middle East]', *Ettila'at-e Siasi-Eqtisadi*, 9:11/12 (1374/ 1993).

Moshiri, Mohammad (ed.), 'Rostam-ul-Hokama, *Rustam-a-Tawarikh* (Tehran: 1344/1965).
Mottahedeh, Roy, *The Mantle of the Prophet* (London: Chatto and Windus, 1986).
Mozaffari, Mehdi (ed.), *Security Politics in the Commonwealth of Independent States: The Southern Belt* (London: Macmillan, 1997).
Murphy, J. P. *Pragmatism* (Boulder, Colo.: Westview Press, 1990).
Nathanail P. 'Greek-Arab Relations', *Bulletin Athens News Agency* (feature), 32:26 (May 1995).
Noorbakhsh, Mehdi, 'The Middle East, Islam and the United States: the special case of Iran', *Middle East Policy*, 2:3 (1993).
Pahlavan, Tschanguiz, *Afghanistan: asr-e Mujahedin ve baramadan-e Taleban* [The era of Mujahedin and the rise of Taleban] (Tehran: 1999).
—'Afghanistan emtedad-e hayat-e farhangi mast' [Afghanistan is the extension of our cultural life] *Donya-ye Sokhan* (January 1992).
Parsons, Anthony, 'Iran and Western Europe', *The Middle East Journal*, 43:2 (Spring 1989).
Payind, Alam, 'Evolving alternative views on the future of Afghanistan', *Asian Survey*, 235:9 (September 1993).
Peterson, Scott, 'Iran split over how to punish Afghans', *Christian Science Monitor* (30 September 1998).
Petrochilos, G.A., *Foreign Direct Investment and the Development Process: The Case of Greece* (Aldershot: Avebury, 1989).
—'An Analysis of Foreign Direct Investment in Greece 1953–92' in Collis, C. and Peck, F. (eds.), *Foreign Direct Investment and Regional Development* (London: Regional Studies Association, 1998).
Pipes, Daniel, *In the Path of God: Sunnah, Islam and Political Power* (New York: Basic Books, 1983).
Rajaee, Farhang, 'Iranian ideology and worldview: the cultural export of revolution' in John L. Esposito (ed.), *The Iranian Revolution: Its Global Impact* (Miami, Fla.: Florida International University Press, 1990).
Ramazani, R.K., 'Iran's export of the revolution: politics, ends, and means' in John L. Esposito (ed.), *The Iranian Revolution: Its Global Impact* (Miami, Fla.: Florida International University Press, 1990).
—'Iran's foreign policy: both North and South', *The Middle East Journal*, 46:3 (Summer 1992).

Rashid, Ahmed, *The Resurgence of Central Asia: Islam or Nationalism* (London: Zed Books, 1994).

—'The new proxy war', *Far Eastern Economic Review* (1 February 1996).

Rathmell, Andrew, *The Changing Military Balance in the Gulf* (London: RUSI, 1996).

Rezun, Miron (ed.), *Iran at the Crossroads: Global Relations in a Turbulent Decade* (Boulder, Colo.: Westview Press, 1990).

Rishtiya, Sayid Qasim, 'The right way out of the current danger crisis in Afghanistan is to resort to the will of the general public in Afghanistan under UN observation', *The Writers Union of Free Afghanistan (WUFA)* (23 May 1993).

Roy, Olivier, *Islam and Resistance in Afghanistan* (Cambridge University Press, 1986).

—'L'Iran, l'Asie centrale et l'Afghanistan', *Geopolitique*, 64 (January 1999).

Roy, Sara M., 'Gaza: new dynamics of civic disintegration', *Journal of Palestine Studies*, 22 (Summer 1993).

Rubenstein, Richard E and Farle Crocker, 'Challenging Huntington', *Foreign Policy*, 96 (Fall 1994).

Ruggie, J.G. 'Continuity and transformation in the world polity: toward a neorealist synthesis' in R.O. Keohane (ed.), *Neorealism and Its Critics* (New York: Columbia University Press, 1986).

Sajjadpour, Seyyed Mohammad Kazem, 'Negaresh-ha-ye mowjud dar gharb darbarah-ye raftar-e Iran ba Jomhuri-ha-ye Shawravi-ye Sabeq' [The West's views on Iran's behaviour towards the republics of the former Soviet Union], *MAMQ*, (Autumn 1371/1992).

Sciolino, E., 'The cleric who charmed Iranians', *The New York Times*, 1 February 1998.

Shahabi, Sohrab, and Farhi, Farideh, 'Security considerations and Iranian foreign policy', *The Iranian Journal of International Affairs*, 7:1 (Spring 1995).

Shirazi, Shaikh Sa'di, *Gulistan* (Tehran: Forouqi, 1988).

Staar, Richard F., 'Russia and the Islamic Middle East', *Mediterranean Quarterly*, 8:2 (Spring 1997).

al-Suwaidi, Jamal S. (ed.), *Iran and the Gulf: A Search for Stability* (Abu Dhabi: The Emirates Center for Strategic Studies and Research, 1996).

Tarock, Adam, 'Iran's foreign policy since the Gulf War', *Australian Journal of International Affairs,* 48:2 (November 1994).
Thompson, J., *Ideology and Modern Culture: Critical Social Theory in the Era of Mass Communication* (Oxford: Polity Press, 1990).
Yusaf, Brigadier Mohammad and Major Mark Adkin, *The Bear Trap*, (Lahore: Jang Publishers, 1992).
Velayati, Ali Akbar, *Iran Daily*, 24 October 1996.
Waller, John H. *Beyond the Khyber Pass* (New York, 1990).
Weinbaum, Marvin G., *Pakistan and Afghanistan: Resistance and Reconstruction* (Boulder, Colo.: Westview Press, 1994).
Zahid, Mohammad, 'The Taleban and Afghanistan imbroglio', *The Writer's Union of Free Afghanistan (WUFA)* (December 1995).

Contributing Authors

Lubna Abid Ali is Associate Professor at the University of Quad Azam in Islamabad, Pakistan. She has written extensively on the relationship between Iran and Pakistan. Her publications include 'Kashmir uprising and human rights violations by India in occupied Kashmir', *South Asia Studies*, 8:2 (July 1991).

Alireza Ansari is Lecturer of Middle Eastern affairs at Durham University in England and has written various articles on ideology and politics during the Pahlavi period in Iran. Dr Ansari is also Associate Fellow at the Middle East Programme of Chatham House where he is pursuing a project relating to the prospects for political pluralism in the Islamic Republic of Iran.

Mohammad Farhad Atai is Associate Professor of International Relations at Imam Sadeq University in Tehran. He has written various articles on Iran, Turkey and Central Asia.

Anoushiravan Ehteshami is Professor of International Relations and Director of the Centre for Middle Eastern and Islamic Studies at the University of Durham. Among his many publications are *After Khomeini: The Iranian Second Republic* (London: Routledge, 1995) and *The Changing Balance of Power in Asia* (Abu Dhabi: The Emirates Center for Strategic Studies and Research, 1998). He is co-author of *Syria and Iran: Middle Powers in a Penetrated Regional System* (London: Routledge, 1997).

Fred Halliday is Professor of International Relations at the London School of Economics. His most recent publications include *Islam and the Myth of Confrontation* (London: I. B. Tauris, 1996); *Revolution and World Politics: The Rise and Decline of the Sixth Great Power* (London: Macmillan, 1997).

Ali A. Jalali is Chief of the Farsi Service of the Voice of America. He has written extensively on Afghan military history and Central Asia, and his most recent publications include 'Islam as a political force in Central Asia: the Iranian influence', *Central Asia Monitor*, 2 (1999); and 'Taleban: a model for islamicising Central Asia?', *The Cyber Caravan* (Johns Hopkins University) 1:4 (6 March 1999).

Ali Mohammadi is Reader in International Communication and Cultural Studies at Nottingham Trent University. His most recent book is *Globalization and International Communication* (London: Sage, 1997).

Alam Payind is Director of the Middle East Studies Center at the Ohio State University. He was formerly a professor at Kabul University. His publications include 'Evolving alternative views on the future of Afghanistan: an Afghan perspective', *Asian Survey*, 33 (1993).

George A. Petrochilos is Senior Lecturer at Coventry Business School, Coventry University. He has written numerious articles on various aspects of the Greek economy and the Balkan countries. His most recent publications include 'Theory, policy and practice of Greek outward foreign direct investment in D. Kantarelis (ed.), *Business and Economics for the 21st Century: An Anthology* (Worcester, Mass.: B&ES1, 1997).

Mohammad R. Saidabadi is Researcher in International Relations at the National University of Australia.

Gholam-Reza Sabri-Tabrizi is Fellow of Edinburgh University and Professor of Central Asian Studies at the University of Baku in Azerbaijan. He has written extensively on Iran, Azerbaijan and Central Asia. His recent publications include *The Literature of South Azerbaijan: Collected Articles* (Baku, 1998).

Index